## Also by Diane Johnson

# Terrorists and Novelists

*DIANE JOHNSON*

# Terrorists and Novelists

Alfred A. Knopf    New York    1982

Grateful acknowledgment is made to the following for permission to reprint from previously published material: *The
New York Times:* From *The New York Times Book Review,*
"African Calliope" ("The Traveling Self"), "The Letters
of Gustave Flaubert" ("Flaubert Dashes Off a Letter"),
"Jamesian Characters" ("Alice and Henry James"), "Possibly Parables–Great Days" ("Possibly Parables") © 1979,
1980 by The New York Times Company. Reprinted by
permission.

Some of the pieces in this collection have appeared previously in *The London Times, The New Statesman,* and the
*New York Review of Books.*

Library of Congress cataloging in Publication Data
Johnson, Diane. Terrorists and novelists.
I. Title
PS3560.03746T4    1982      813'.54      82-47818
ISBN 0-394-52161-7      AACR2

# Contents

## II. Fictions Stranger Than Fiction

## III. The Real World

Books Discussed

# Preface

WHAT FOLLOWS ARE pieces written since 1975 and first printed, with a few exceptions, in *The New York Review of Books* and *The New York Times Book Review* on topics suggested by the editors. Though I have often declined to review books for one reason or another, I've never volunteered myself as a reviewer for a particular book, preferring instead the surprise and stretch of an unexpected suggestion, the pleasure of looking into something I would not have thought of. But for this reason, the shape of the present collection, any unity it may have, is owing in part to others, to their idea of me, and to circumstances—for instance, that I live in California, or that I have an interest in nineteenth-century literature, or in novel-writing. If Oscar Wilde is right that criticism is the only form of autobiography, there is a sense, then, in which this volume is biography, made by others; and reading it over for revelations, I was a little surprised by certain things—for instance, a preoccupation with violent events. The consistency of other attitudes and prejudices is, I suppose, mine, like mistrust of the legal profession, whose morality, or lack of it, comes up again and again in the books under review. So do travel pieces about how it is not to live in New York—I've always wondered how it would be *to* live there.

I see how much I have learned from writing these pieces—often things I should have known already. The earliest one, Susan Brownmiller's book about rape, was probably suggested to me because of a rape that occurred in the ending of my novel *The Shadow Knows*. If I had read Ms. Brownmiller's work first, I would not have ended my novel just that way. After reviewing John McPhee's book about Alaska, I was invited to visit Alaska, where I had never been.

A number of the pieces reveal an interest of mine in the convergence, in the writing of our day, of objective reality and fiction, both in works of fiction and in the non-fictional genres—autobiography, biography, letters, and diaries, where strategies of self-dramatization require the truth-teller to hold some traffic with fiction. That is the focus of part I, according to the way I have arranged the essays. The pieces in part II are concerned with the connection of history to fiction—in the so-called true-life novel, such as Norman Mailer's work about Gary Gilmore, or in novels like Beryl Bainbridge's *Young Adolf*, where a historical character (Hitler) is followed through a course of non-historical events. I have always wondered why we are, as we seem to be, concerned about which things in a literary work are "true" and which are not; we test all writing, like alchemists, to understand the admixture. I myself have never been sure which, fact or fancy, is the silver and which is lead, but these essays ask the question.

A number of pieces touch on the differences between men and women writers, whether as narrators, autobiographers, writers trying to give account of ethnic experience, whatever. My impression is that women's writing is still greatly misunderstood, often, alas, by male book reviewers who have not learned to read books by women and imagine them all to be feminist polemics. Such half-readers have not learned to make a connection between the images, metaphors, and situations employed by women (house, garden, madness), and universal experience, although women, trained from childhood to read books by people of both sexes, know the metaphorical significance of the battlefield, the sailing ship, the voyage, and so on.

The third part concerns public issues that have attracted general interest and that, perhaps, characterize the second half of the seventies: post-Vietnam repercussions, as in C. D. B. Bryan's

*Friendly Fire*, the SLA kidnapping of Patty Hearst, the sad death of the People's Temple followers in Jonestown, and some others.

It seems fair to note that certain things in all the latter pieces, and in many of the others, were objected to in letters to the editors of *The New York Review of Books*, and usually I answered the objections. But we have not printed the letters or my replies here. For instance, Norman Mailer wrote in to correct the sum (which I had taken from a newspaper account) given, for their cooperation, to the widows of Gary Gilmore's victims, and I have changed the present text. The only place I sincerely admitted myself to be in error, however, was at the end of my review of Jane Kramer's book about Texas, where I failed (though myself raised, practically, on a farm) to understand the meaning, in connection with male farm animals, of the expression "to cut." I was corrected by a kindly Texan, whose observation, that I ought to stay off such subjects, may be right.

What interest the pieces in this book may have is really owing to the wonderfully helpful and supportive editors who proposed them, discussed and corrected them, and forbore to object to opinions they may not have shared: in particular, at *The New York Review of Books*, where most of these pieces appeared, Barbara Epstein and Robert Silvers; at *The New York Times*; Richard Locke and Harvey Shapiro; then at the *Washington Post*, Eve Auchincloss and William MacPherson; at the *New Statesman*, Julian Barnes; and at the *TLS*, in the last busy week that preceded a year of suspended publication, an immensely pleasant stranger whose name I cannot now ascertain. And, for this book, as well as for earlier novels, Robert Gottlieb and Martha Kaplan at Knopf have my grateful thanks.

# I

---

# Self-Deceptions

# Anti-Autobiography:
# Maxine Hong Kingston,
# Carobeth Laird, and
# N. Scott Momaday

AUTOBIOGRAPHY, BY FAR the more durable tradition, has never been honored for art the way fiction has, presumably because it lacks the requisite property of "invention." But it might be argued that to impose significant form on the chaotic materials of life lived, instead of fashioning them from the more restricted, more determined, more orthodox contents of the imagination, or from the more restrictive conventions of fictional genres, requires a superior faculty of invention, or at least the grace and clearheadedness of an inventor. The artist writing his memoir is in double jeopardy; first he must lead the risky life worth reading, must come through it and face in retrospect the awful disparity between what it meant and what he had intended. Then he must make a fiction of it, a work that has many or most of the formal properties of fiction.

Autobiography, that is, requires some strategy of self-dramatization. It normally contains, as in fiction, a crisis and denouement, and it appears, very generally, that the form of this crisis in autobiography by men has tended to be different from that of women, and that fully fictionalized dramatizations tend to be different still. Men—for instance, in the great nineteenth-century autobiographies (Mill, Carlyle, Newman, and countless others)—

recount disillusion and depression, followed by recovery and action. In fiction this is, curiously, often dramatized as crime, as in much of Dickens.

In writing, as in mourning, it sometimes appears that women have reserved or been assigned the duty of expressing human resentment, leaving men to fashion the consolations. Perhaps this is division of labor, rather than native querulousness; but it has meant that wisdom and "adjustment" are often qualities of the masculine tone, and women since Margery Kempe have tended to write in tones of protest and madness. The crisis is of silence or withdrawal, and is dramatized as "being silenced."

There are exceptions, of course, but three recent memoirs, by N. Scott Momaday (*The Names*), Maxine Hong Kingston (*The Woman Warrior*), and Carobeth Laird (*Encounter with an Angry God*), reflect these sexual distinctions and also suggest that the distinction between fiction and what is autobiographically true has become somewhat arbitrary; fiction and memoir have come to resemble each other more and more. Novelists make real historical figures speak to fictional characters. Memorialists dramatize the thoughts and speeches of their forefathers, as in a novel about them. The access of the autobiographer to dramatic techniques has allowed him to handle root meanings, the mysterious crises of spirit, even the intangibles of heritage, more essentially—that is, more truly—than he once could.

Ancestors in autobiographies seem really to belong there, unlike the fashionable gramps and grannies whose rather boring recurrence in contemporary fiction probably arises from the same nostalgic impulse. How much more immediate the sometimes baleful influence of real ancestors than the academic caperings of those prehistorical ancestors whose tribal arrangements and religious rituals we are asked so often lately to believe have determined our "reading readiness," our attitudes toward violence, motherhood, and so on.

Momaday is an American Indian man, and Kingston a Chinese-American woman. Both explore the way in which their ethnic traditions have made them as they are. The differences in tone between the two memoirs, the one nostalgic and approving, the other vital and angry, reflect, no doubt, cultural differences, but also perhaps sexual differences.

Momaday's Indian father was born in a tepee, and wanted to become a painter. His part-Indian mother, the daughter of a Kentucky sheriff, wanted to write. Both parents became teachers. Momaday tries to imagine the things they saw and felt. He can imagine what old Pohdlohk, his grandfather, must have seen as he visited the woman Keahdinekeah, and he can remember Keahdinekeah's memories. Through myth, imagination, affinity, and empathy come ancestral qualities—a love of the plains, of Indian ways, of animals and old stories—that Momaday understands as part of himself. He has wonderful photographs of old, wizened Indians sitting blanket-wrapped on chairs on the prairie, and of his parents—marvelously beautiful people who look rather like Theda Bara and Rudolph Valentino—somewhat self-consciously dressed in feathered headdresses for their wedding picture.

Except for his Indian background, Momaday's upbringing seems to have been a lot like that of other American kids, especially ones brought up in that period (he was born in 1934) in that region. His parents, educated middle-class people, made sure to send him off to a good prep school so he could go to a good college. Now he is a professor of English at Stanford. In spite of the recent vogue for emphasizing ethnic differences instead of identifying what is central or American and shared by many groups, from the tepee to Stanford is really the good old American story.

Momaday does not appear to feel, or does not discuss, any conflict of the Kiowa and the white traditions; he is their product, an artist, heir to the experiences of his ancestors and conscious of the benignity of their influence. As a child he was taken to see his great-grandmother Keahdinekeah: "Long afterwards I think: That was a wonderful and beautiful thing that happened in my life. There, on that warm, distant afternoon: an old woman and a child, holding hands across the generations. There is great good in such a remembrance; I cannot imagine that it might have been lost upon me." If he will discover disillusion and crisis, it lies beyond this book, which ends when he is about fourteen, just beginning his journey.

How manly is this reverent sense of the past bequeathing to the present the special intention that the present shall include oneself. But what of malevolent ancestors who harry the living and blight the life of the young American with their old ways of terror? Maxine Hong Kingston's memoir of a Chinese-American girlhood presents another side, perhaps the female side, of growing up in a tradition, perhaps any tradition. Women perform for any society the service of maladjustment that Kingston here brilliantly performs for the society of Chinese immigrants in California. She, like Momaday (and unlike most Chinese-Americans), fulfills an American pattern by moving away from an ethnic tradition the distance required to memorialize and cherish it; but she is unlike Momaday because her ancestors have hurt and haunted her.

The little girl grows up in Stockton's Chinatown surrounded by the ghostly and similar Americans and other foreigners, and by the many ghosts her family has brought with them from China. There is the ghost of an aunt who drowned herself in a well after the people of her village savaged her house, protesting her illegitimate pregnancy. Afterward the family killed her name, so little Maxine, who hears the story from her mother, Brave Orchid, does not know the name of that ghost. Then there is the sitting ghost who sat on Brave Orchid's stomach all one night; and the ghosts of all the murdered women and little female babies left out to die back in China.

In Maxine's imagination she is herself a ghost, a swordswoman, a female avenger of these cruel murders. She has been given hints of female power, and also explicit messages of female powerlessness, from her mother, who in China had been a doctor and now toiled in the family laundry, where they wore masks and burned candles to avoid "the germs that fumed out of the ghosts' clothes." "She said I would grow up a wife and a slave, but she taught me the story of the warrior woman, Fa Mu Lan. I would have to grow up a warrior woman."

The warrior woman of Maxine's imagination avenges with her sword the injustices that a real, little California girl can only throw tantrums about. When other Chinese said, "Feeding girls is feeding cowbirds," she would scream and cry. The others were puzzled.

"What's the matter with her?"

"I don't know. Bad, I guess. You know how girls are. 'There's no profit in raising girls. Better to raise geese than girls.' " In China, she has heard, girls were often sold by their families. The Chinese word for the female "I" is "slave."

"What do you want to be when you grow up, little girl?" "A lumberjack in Oregon"—that is, American and a man. She was glad to be a bad little girl: "Isn't a bad girl almost a boy?"

I read in an anthropology book that Chinese say, "Girls are necessary too"; I have never heard the Chinese I know make this concession. Perhaps it was a saying in another village. I refuse to shy my way anymore through our Chinatown, which tasks me with the old sayings and the stories.

Messages that for Western girls have been confusingly obscured by the Victorian pretense of woman worship are in the Chinese tradition elevated to epigram: "When fishing for treasures in the flood, be careful not to pull in girls."

Like many other women, Kingston does not wish to reject female nature so much as the female condition, and even then she would reserve the female biological destiny: "marriage and childbirth strengthen the swordswoman, who is not a maid like Joan of Arc." But she is not without a sense of its difficulty:

Do the women's work; then do more work, which will become ours too. No husband of mine will say, "I could have been a drummer, but I had to think about the wife and kids. You know how it is." Nobody supports me; . . . I am not loved enough to be supported. That I am not a burden has to compensate for the sad envy when I look at women

loved enough to be supported. Even now China wraps double binds around my feet.

But of course these are the bindings on every woman's feet. In the
vivid particularity of her experience, and with the resources of a
considerable art, Kingston reaches to the universal qualities of female condition and female anger that the bland generalities of
social science and the merely factual history cannot describe.
Women may reject the culture that rejects them, but such
brave and rare disassociations are not without serious cost. Kingston is dealing here with the fears and rebellions that recur in
much of women's writing, often displaced in other ways, and dramatized or actually experienced as suicide, catatonia, hysteria,
anorexia—maladies common to many female protagonists, both
fictional and actual, from Brontë heroines to Sylvia Plath. Kingston recounts such a gesture of protest in her own life, a period of
refusal to play culture's game.
In a strange scene, she tortures another little girl in the bathroom after school, a passive little Chinese girl who never speaks.
Maxine pulls her hair, twists her nose and ears, pinches her
cheeks, derides, berates her. The other child weeps but will not
speak even so, goading Maxine to greater desperation and fear:

You don't see I'm trying to help you out, do you? Do you
want to be like this, dumb (do you know what dumb
means?), your whole life? Don't you ever want to be a cheer-
leader? Or a pompon girl? What are you going to do for a
living? Yeah, you're going to have to work because you can't
be a housewife. Somebody has to marry you before you can
be a housewife. And you, you are a plant. Do you know
that? That's all you are if you don't talk. . . .

But the other child never speaks, and her silence is triumphant.
This scene has many fictional analogues, such as Susan Yanko-
witz's recent novel *Silent Witness*, where the woman protagonist is
a mute, accused of a crime, and is raped by the other women in

prison. In life, the protests she cannot make the other girl utter are Maxine's own, and consume her; she must spend "the next eighteen months sick in bed with a mysterious illness. There was no pain and no symptoms, though the middle line on my left palm broke in two." She herself recognizes the tradition of this illness, its relation to women in general: "I lived like the Victorian recluses I read about." One thinks of Catherine Earnshaw in *Wuthering Heights*, consuming herself in her willful decline until death. But Maxine thinks her malady is particularly Chinese, too. In all the Chinese households she knows, women fall into implacable protesting silences; every family has its "crazy woman," and she is afraid she is hers.

The Chinese-Americans are a notably unassimilated culture. It is not unusual in San Francisco to find fourth- or fifth-generation American-born Chinese who speak no English. Generations have not eased their mistrust of American culture, and they will not tell Americans certain things about their own. Once, Maxine's teachers, concerned because her school paintings are entirely covered in black paint, call her parents in, but there can be no communication, and not just because the parents speak no English. The parents would say nothing anyway, because in China, "the parents and teachers of criminals were executed." All the Chinese children in the class laugh at one of their number who does not know his father's name, pretending to think, as the teacher did, that he was stupid, but knowing, really, that a Chinese child does not know his father's name. They pitilessly abandon anyone who attracts the special attention of the ghosts. Their own parents have given them fake names to say.

There is much Americans would not know. There, in Stockton in the 1940s, the mother was cooking them raccoons, snakes, garden snails, turtles, hawks, city pigeons, wild ducks and geese, catfish, a skunk, flowers from the garden, weeds. Chinese people began coming to California before the Gold Rush, but still the names, the food, the shape of the parapets (defying the earthquake rules) remain Chinese.

But since the revolution in China, many of these people have been forced to relinquish a dream of someday returning there. Torn between the reality of the known America and the mysteries of the new China, many have made their peace with the idea of staying. To Kingston this was welcome because it would reduce the likelihood of being sold.

> While the adults wept over the letters about the neighbors gone berserk turning Communist . . . I was secretly glad. As long as the aunts kept disappearing and the uncles dying after unspeakable tortures, my parents would prolong their Gold Mountain [California] stay. We could start spending our fare money on a car and chairs, a stereo.

They do. With the loss of the old, the new becomes more possible. Her generation turns with less reluctance toward America, let the ancestors scold as they were accustomed to do. Third Grand-Uncle is in the habit of denouncing all the girls in the family:

> "Maggots! Where are my grandsons? . . . Eat, maggots. . . . Look at the maggots chew."
> "He does that at every meal," the girls [his granddaughters] told us in English.
> "Yeah," we said. "Our old man hates us too. What assholes."

There are no ghosts in Carobeth Laird's memoirs, and no ancestors. She is self-created, and, writing when nearly eighty, has the tone of an old intelligent woman for whom the terrors and impressions of youth have congealed into meanings and facts. Her anger, like the price of a car or the color of a dress, is just another fact, all arrayed together like treasures on a tea tray, for the reader to select among. She does not urge on us the impression that she was a remarkable woman, but that is the one we select; in her day she flouted nearly every conceivable convention, first by having an illegitimate child, then by abandoning the ordinary role of wife for a brief career as a talented anthropologist, and finally by marrying an Indian. The fact of her anger follows from the sum of many matter-of-record details. We see that the early twentieth century was a very different time for women warriors.

Born in 1896, she met the now famous anthropologist John Peabody Harrington when she was nineteen and enrolled in his summer-school class in linguistics. He was already in the grip of his obsessive passion to record all that could be known about American Indians and their languages, an obsession that ultimately produced literally tons of data, most of it still stored in Washington, D.C., warehouses and virtually unanalyzed. She was already the mother of an illegitimate child. He was attracted to her, perhaps because of her talent for linguistics; they were married and for several years lived a rough life in the field, collecting data. They had one child, who was raised, together with the first one, by Mrs. Laird's mother. Further pregnancies, which would have hindered her helpfulness to Harrington's work, were prevented by the adoption of a "perversion" (undisclosed) which she found distressing. In time she fell in love with an Indian informant, George Laird, and, after divorcing Harrington, married him and lived with him on a small farm until his death in 1940. She bore Laird four children.

Mrs. Laird's subject is, ostensibly, her life with Harrington, with a view to shedding some light on his curious personality, in response to recent interest in him and his work. She is not of an age or an inclination to talk of "role conflicts" and "female frustrations"; yet the things she leaves unsaid are almost as interesting as the things Kingston says, and they afford a significant historical comparison. She, like Kingston, responded to the sexual and cultural tensions of which she was a victim—to the double bindings on her feet—with a silent breakdown.

Her life with Harrington had been by certain contemporary standards ideal; she was valued for her intellectual accomplishments, freed from ordinary domestic cares that she might pursue them, guarded from pregnancy yet a mother, and a mother without the constant responsibility of child care; and she had, for the era, considerable personal freedom and professional responsibility. But she was not happy.

Instead she yearned for the traditional perquisites of female life—"nice" things, a home, proper entertainments, pretty clothes. She yearned for legitimacy. In Kingston's terms, that she was not a burden could not compensate her for the sad envy she felt when she thought of women loved enough to be supported. Probably, though she does not say so, her longing for a conventional female life was a reaction to the terrifyingly unprotected experience of being a teen-age unwed mother, the shocking consequence of her first attempts at self-assertion. (She told Harrington she was a widow.) Harrington treated her like a man. But that was a condition a woman of her generation could not easily accept, until she had made her peace with what society had directed her to believe was woman's destiny.

Now an old woman, she is alert but not self-aware. Her work, not her former, young self, interests her. Through her testimonials to the happiness of her years with Laird, it is up to us to catch a glimpse of the price she must have paid. Unlike Momaday, who in the masculine tradition receives his culture from his fathers with pride and gratitude, and Kingston, who must resist hers to triumph over it, Mrs. Laird, who wishes to play culture's game, becomes its victim. Married to George Laird, she is poor; they have to sell ten of their twenty acres for debt. Rapid pregnancies wear her out. A child is stillborn, her parents die. It is now, in these "happy" years, fulfilling her destiny, that she, too, falls silent, like the Chinese crazy women, like women in books. "I drifted further and further into a realm of dreams, then abruptly lost all but tenuous contact with everyday reality. The 'nervous breakdown' lasted five months. All the guilts and fears I had repressed since infancy came flooding into consciousness, assuming strange and terrible forms."

She saw Harrington in later years, after Laird's death. He had changed some, but "I had changed more drastically. I was overweight, had lost several teeth, and child-bearing, physical toil, poverty, illness, anxiety, and the ultimate grief had left their mark." Still later, when she was in her seventies, she was to take up again her Indian studies, write a book about the Chemehuevi Indians, write this memoir, publish papers in the *Journal of California Anthropology*, and is still at work. But most women, after such long silence, do not speak again.

# The I as Male:
# Charlotte Brontë

SINCE THEIR OWN DAY, which misprized Emily, the Brontës have been installed in the literary constellation in fixed relation: Emily with her colossal masterpiece, and with the moral advantages of a solitary nature and an early death, has been set far above not only the sad Anne and Branwell but also the more heroic Charlotte, whose unlucky combination of passion and candor exposed her to the strictures of her contemporaries—for being coarse and preoccupied with sex—and whose confessions of timidity and more prosaic needs for company and usefulness have qualified the regard of posterity.

A Victorian woman whose cheeks were said to owe more to art than to nature was not approved of, and the same seems to apply to the books of women, then and, it sometimes seems, now, too. Part of the respect in which Emily is held depends on an impression of her "natural" genius; but art, too easily associated with policy and craft, has not been held to be an entirely attractive accomplishment for a female, and so the undoubted artfulness of Charlotte Brontë's last two novels has been overlooked, or perhaps even held against her.

*Jane Eyre* is still acknowledged to be a good read, especially for adolescent girls—exactly the class of person it was kept from in its own day—but *Shirley* and *Villette* are seldom read by anybody but literary critics, the tradition being that they were a falling off, devoid of the naïve power, the thrilling excesses, the blood and artless self-revelation of her first published book, and disappointingly lacking in the rather stunning symbols suggesting female sexuality—madwomen and raging fires, bolts of lightning blasting phallic trees—whose meaning was sensed, delightedly if disapprovingly, by the Victorians and described at length by modern criticism.

But biographical and critical rescue has been coming Charlotte's way in platoons lately, with Helene Moglen's book (*Charlotte Brontë: The Self Conceived*) a quite helpful contribution, first as a kind of new broom to sweep away some encrusted biographical clichés, second because of its ambitious and for the most part plausible analysis of the development of Charlotte's personality in relation to her work, and finally by giving convincing readings of the widely neglected *Shirley* and *Villette*. Restored to respectability together with *Jane Eyre*, these and *The Professor* make the sum of four good books—about as many as most major Victorian novelists wrote.

Literary biography usually concerns itself with how an artist's life and personality influence his work, and usually fails to engage the problem of how the writer's work affects the growth of his personality. A new work may change an artist's life in some apparent way—may make him rich, or bitter, or exhausted—but by the time it comes into existence it has already altered his consciousness. This is a mysterious process, and to account for it convincingly has conspicuously defeated scholarship much of the time, with the circular relation of books and life, books and life spinning the dizzy critic into the dusty corner of new criticism on the one side or into the grimy one of psychoanalytic reduction on the other. Professor Moglen grabs hold of Charlotte, books, life, inner life, and all, and holds on with a certain creditable, dogged tact. The result is perhaps cursory, but is often suggestive and corrective, a helpful adjunct to what remains the most magnificent Brontë biography, Mrs. Gaskell's life of Charlotte.

Despite the things she chose not to say, Mrs. Gaskell, in her intuition of her friend, and her avoidance of certain revisionist pieties that have since crept in, still brings the reader closer to a sense of Charlotte Brontë than anyone else has. But the twentieth century does undoubtedly have a few things to add. As happens so often, it is not the major events and scandals, which scholars tend to scrutinize, but the small details that are got wrong, and that, accumulated, can obscure the writer's personality and thereby perhaps his work, too. In particular, the strangeness and painfulness of the Brontës' lives have stupefied, perhaps embarrassed, biographers into a kind of unthinking reliance on literary conventions which never did have anything to do with the facts of human feeling—or of human biology. Here, for instance, is Winifred Gérin on the death of Emily, from the received biography of Charlotte (*Charlotte Brontë: The Evolution of Genius*):

> So far as material causes are reckoned, Emily died of galloping consumption. Never known to ail before, once the illness was declared she was dead in three months.
>
> For those who feel there is an enigma to be explained there remains *Wuthering Heights*; and if anyone doubts how Emily felt about the liberation of death, the longing of the imprisoned spirit to cast its chains, and of the lonely soul for reunion with the universal fount from which it came, they had better re-read the death of Heathcliff.

Against this kind of sentimentality, any attempt at common sense is welcome.

About Charlotte, then, Moglen points out that as a child of six when her mother died, so far from not remembering or minding, as is usually held, she would indeed have minded keenly, might have felt responsible, and in any case must have suffered from intense guilt throughout her life at being the only survivor among so many talented and deserving dead. Moglen traces Charlotte's lifelong feelings of unworthiness and anxiety to this source.

She also addresses herself to Charlotte's sexuality, particularly to the tradition of her "innocent" love for the Belgian schoolmaster Heger. She avoids the vulgar idea of innocence as describing love where the people do not actually make love, which has persisted strangely, even though modern people are not themselves so innocent as to believe that the physical agonies recounted in such detail in *Villette* were anything but strongly sexual.

It seems clear that Charlotte (and Emily) Brontë, so far from being innocent, had access to their erotic feelings, and an understanding of the ways in which will and power are related to eroticism, to a degree unusual in Victorian women. The conditions peculiar to Haworth Parsonage—the relative freedom from the conventions of female regime, the absence of a mother, and the masculine nature of their education by their father—explain in part how they were spared an ordinary repressive feminine upbringing.

But Charlotte's self-knowledge may also have arisen out of the exceedingly free imaginative world which the Brontë children lived in, and from which only she was able partly to emerge. Until the end of their lives the others were involved in writing and enacting an elaborate psychodrama, begun in early childhood. The unself-conscious and uncensored preoccupation of Charlotte's juvenilia with seduction, adultery, passion, and power well illustrates how the basic forces of the Brontës' personalities were dramatized in these early stories and plays. Because these were the very forces that Victorian women were encouraged to repress, for Charlotte the mature artistic struggle was to fit her stories to censorious reality, just as the task of her life was to accommodate Victorian social expectations to a nature that had been nurtured, in a forcing house of imagination and feeling, to a condition of acute self-awareness.

The Brontë juvenilia bears further, closer study. Moglen, like other critics, passes over it rather quickly. She seems to assume that it was unremarkable for artists to spend decades at playing. But here the protracted and intense nature of their imaginary lives complicated the attempts by the players to escape into the unhappier real world. The numerous and extraordinary artifacts of the imagination of the child-artists might provide an almost unique opportunity to come closer to understanding the developing egos, the psychosexual forces, and the expressive choices of people who would later find expression in art. Much that is really not known about artists, especially about women artists, might emerge from analysis of this strange canon to shed light on the vexed questions of feminist criticism and female sexual psychology.

These are questions Moglen does not enter into. The jacket description, "the evolution of her feminism from Byronic romanticism," lends a misleading modishness to what is really a conservative view of the development of female personality (Freud, Deutsch, Horney), which here, as so often, does not seem quite to fit the case. The imaginations of the Brontës, like those of many other children, had indeed been fired by various romantic heroes like Byron, fleshly symbols of will with whom they identified. Moglen assumes that this posed a psychic problem for Charlotte, that her fictional identification had to be mostly with her women characters: "Because she was female, her identification with their beloved, Byronic Zamorna was equivocal. She could not, after all, *be* the fantasized hero. She was, in fact, 'the other' [the not-I]." Forlorn and alienated being if that were so. But it isn't. Which is the I and which the not-I is only a problem of definition for the psychologist, not for the self. Of course Charlotte could be, and it seems likely that she was, the hero, the I, and the male as much as the female of her fictions (as Emily was Heathcliff).

Contrary to Moglen, Charlotte's personality seems to have been strong and integrated, not in conflict with itself but with society. That society was the threatening thing to her explains the shift of her interest, in *Shirley,* to the political and social powerlessness of women, and in her masterpiece *Villette* to a deeply considered psychological presentation of the emotional effects of this powerlessness. The fiery imagery that rages through the mythic world of *Jane Eyre* is replaced by the chill at the heart of Lucy Snowe as the artist herself confronts what it means to live in the real world.

"Feminism," with its current connotation of sisterly solidarity, does not seem quite the word for someone who so clearly hated finding herself to be a woman, her spirit stuck in a rather arbitrary (it must have seemed) incarnation, like a statue or a diving suit, speechless, movements hampered, the form completely controlling people's response to her. When Charlotte Brontë became famous and went to London and was stared at like some kind of feral child, she found out that what she knew she knew, about human love and human will, was constantly in conflict with what the world professed to know, and that even women she respected, like Mrs. Gaskell and Harriet Martineau, were involved in a strange collaboration to misrepresent female nature.

Indeed, in all her writing, Charlotte Brontë, who was no more charitable than Jane Austen in her treatment of fools of either sex, reserved particular scorn for women. She understood how society had made them what they were ("envious, backbiting, wretched"), but she seemed to despise them, perhaps because she, more than most people, knew them to be capable of manliness. George Eliot is often like this, too. Liberated women artists at that time were almost obliged to identify at some level with their heroes rather than their heroines, however disappointing that may seem today. Charlotte also hated children.

Moglen attributes Charlotte's personal insecurities, the passivity and plainness of her heroines, and their yearning to "look up" to men, to female masochism (in the adaptive, rather than instinctual, sense); but it seems more likely that it is the measure not of psychic diffidence but of artistic daring to risk heroines so deviant as to be plain, the way Jane Austen risked bossy Emma and mousy Fanny. Besides, Charlotte herself was poor, plain, and little, and had a few things to say about it. She might be forgiven for wishing herself to be pretty, if only because beauty seemed to her the only proper embodiment of the human spirit, and, in practical terms, to confer a measure of temporal power denied to the plain. What Charlotte longed for was power in the world to match the power of her spirit. That she denied beauty to her heroines is part of her genius and her strategy; she does give them power.

Finding herself a woman, she turns in *Shirley* to an analysis of power and sexual politics, describing, as Moglen says, "the connections which could be drawn between women and the poor and socially dispossessed, between women and unemployed laborers, between women and children." Read in this way, the book, which has been thought to lack unity, achieves a terrible coherence.

It is somewhat surprising to find in the author of *Jane Eyre*, with its elaborate emotional symbols, a woman who was also a social analyst of such wit and subtlety. One is unprepared for the authority of the narrative voice, the cynicism and penetration. The heroines, in common with other Brontë heroines, are outspoken and firm. Caroline Helstone says, talking of spinsters, apparently a hush-hush topic:

> I feel there is something wrong somewhere. I believe single women should have more to do—better chances of interesting and profitable occupation than they possess now. And when I speak thus, I have no impression that I displease God by my words; that I am either impious or impatient, irreligious or sacrilegious. My consolation is, indeed, that God hears many a groan, and compassionates much grief which man stops his ears against, or frowns on with impotent contempt. I say *impotent*, for I observe that such grievances as society cannot readily cure, it usually forbids utterance, on pain of its scorn; this scorn being only a sort of tinselled cloak to its deformed weakness. [*Shirley*]

And so on, in a very long declamation, surely one of the most advanced of the period. Impotence is of course the operative word.

But *Shirley* transcends the merely polemical, projecting, often wittily, on a social canvas what is internalized in the wonderful *Villette*. *Villette* combines artistic authority, shrewd social observation (based on Charlotte's Belgian experience), and the painful power of self-knowledge and self-revelation that had so startled in *Jane Eyre* and was now much matured and warier. As Brontë herself becomes better adapted to mid-Victorian social norms, so, too, her fiction moves closer to the realistic mode in which Gothic symbols find domestic embodiments. In *Villette*, Lucy Snowe becomes, as David Daiches said, the first antiheroine, demanding the equal right of imperfection in the face of the Victorian ideal, eschewing the various female adaptive stratagems of Ginevra, Paulina, and Madame Beck, and finding a love that is spared the perils of consummation by the fortuitous drowning of the lover after a three-year absence ("Reader, they were the three happiest years of my life"). At the end, Lucy has masculine independence, she has work, and she has self-regard; it is an ending to be compared to the ending of *Jane Eyre*, where the resolution of a conventional marriage is qualified, as has often been remarked, by the symbolic castration of Rochester and the enhanced power of Jane.

Many recent critics have seen Lucy as an "unreliable narrator," unreliable because she reports her own neurotic and hysterical states of mind, her "hunger, rebellion, and rage," as Matthew Arnold objected. This view, I think, contradicts the entire direction of Brontë's art and points indirectly to a problem confronting all women writers of fiction.

An unreliable narrator is one who reports on his own or Mr. Jones's meanness, say, while the author makes sure we see his generosity. But between Lucy's reports of her own mental and emotional condition and her judgments of others, and our own perceptions, no such discrepancy exists. On the whole she seems to understand herself rather well, considering that she is not a post-Freudian psychologist. It is true that she does not interpret her responses, merely reports them, but perhaps for the sound literary reason that too much interpretation would be boring. It is her candor that is disconcerting, not any disorder of her mind, though to be sure hers is an intensely personal and eccentric voice—a modern "I" narrator in that respect.

That Lucy has been taken as somehow unfit to describe herself or others truthfully is related to a problem shared by many female narrators, whose claims to be authoritative ("reliable") presiding intelligences in novels often go unheard amid a chorus of other female narrators, variously deranged by the female condition, whose laments bring down suspicions of madness or at least unreliability on all. No doubt the fiction of lamentation is very extensive, and *Villette* shares some of its qualities; the fiction of growing up, with which *Villette* has more in common, is unusual for women to write, as if there were no type of female maturity or wisdom and therefore no endings, so to speak, for such works, except resignation, a conspicuously different quality from the graceful mood of understanding that informs the masculine voice at the end of a *Bildungsroman*.

Perhaps there are no endings for women's novels, but it seems that there could be. The trouble is that many women writers, like their readers, did not believe female narrators, especially ones with sexual potential, capable of reporting reliably on society, politics, others, themselves. A female child or an elderly woman might, under special circumstances, qualify. But even Nelly Dean's veracity, in *Wuthering Heights*, has been questioned, by someone who figured out the chronology, because she was young enough to have been in love with Heathcliff herself, or because of some social disorientation arising from her condition as a servant. Women are suspect as interpretive consciousnesses because of their historical and biological dilemmas. The merest quaver of fallibility reverberates in a woman's novel as a *cri de coeur*.

But Lucy Snowe is just as reliable as Pip—and a lot more perceptive. The right to be honest, and to be taken as she was, the unidealized self, poor, plain, and little, subject to headaches and faints, was an artistic struggle with the world Brontë seemed for a long time to have lost. The ability to write so truly about a woman so far from ideal was no doubt born of her interior struggle, but it is her artistic triumph.

Moglen points out that solving the problem of Lucy Snowe's destiny in her book must have contributed to Brontë's ability (after numerous proposals by various suitors had been rejected over the years) finally to marry in real life. In life, however, the assaults on her self, by the husband and to a far greater degree by pregnancy, seem to have caused her death from psychosomatic complications of pregnancy, surely one of the few known Victorian deaths from a condition of the spirit, notwithstanding the fondness in Victorian fiction for this form of ending. How sad that she didn't just stick to writing; but of course no artist could.

# The I as Female:
# Elizabeth Hardwick

IN AN ESSAY on fiction and moral philosophy, Iris Murdoch has remarked that both virtue and freedom are concerned with "really apprehending that other people exist," and that this is also the essence of art. The artist "*is* the good man; the lover who, nothing himself, lets other things be through him"; and she adds that this is probably what "negative capability" means.

These remarks are apposite to Elizabeth Hardwick's virtuous and liberated novel (*Sleepless Nights*), or work, to beg the question of its genre. One feels its beauty and goodness; it is not so certainly a novel, or, more important, it seems that the ways in which, although it is fiction, it is not a novel, are themselves meaningful and perhaps admonitory. The charity and empathy with which the author experiences others in the world might not extend to the shrill "I"s of much contemporary fiction. Could Henry James have imagined a self-center? This is a work of negative capability.

The narrator is a woman, Elizabeth, thinking back on her past, of her childhood home in Kentucky, of time spent in Boston, New York, Amsterdam, Maine. She remembers people she has known, is mystified and moved by their courage and separateness, and brings them to life for us in vignettes connected by the thread of her own life and thoughts. She remembers rooms, houses, associations prompted by a hairpin, a lipstick stain on white paint. The memories that frame her contemplation of the lives of others eventually also define her own, of which she at first says, without apology, that it "certainly hasn't the drama of: I saw the old, white-bearded frigate master on the dock and signed up for the journey. But after all, 'I' am a woman."

This is not mere dinner-table diffidence, the hostesslike stance of the well brought up ("tell me about yourself"), but the essence of the sensibility that informs the work and the nature of its virtuousness, born, perhaps, of the need to confirm, as one might worry an aching tooth, "the tendency of lives to obey the laws of gravity and to sink downward, falling as gently and slowly as a kite, or violently breaking, smashing."

Hers is a pessimism with a long tradition, "the fierce pessimism of experience and the root empiricism of every troubled loser." It is the abiding preoccupation of our oldest literature and the burden even of the great nineteenth-century novels most expressly contrived to conceal or deny it with conventions involving progress or retribution. For all its modern inconclusiveness, it is to nineteenth-century European literature that one feels the affinity of this work. Causality, that essential ingredient of things we call novels, has been left out, but a dignified conception of personality has been left in. *Sleepless Nights* might be a notebook called "Ideas" for Chekhov or Zola to work from; if it were longer, because of the nature of history, it would become as dramatic as Proust. All the characters would meet up; Alex, the bachelor intellectual, would rescue Miss Lavore from her rooming house. As it is, we use other names for works of this kind—memoir, meditation with *exempla*, spiritual exercises with a common theme: "despite the kindness of damp afternoons, the solace of opening the door and finding everyone there . . . the cemetery waits to be desecrated."

This book rejects crisis, denouement, and also confession. Some may find the narrator's reticence disappointing. The rewards offered for personality are always, it seems, larger than those offered for thought, though why this should be is unclear. Nor is it clear why the spectacle of another contemplating his Self should fascinate, or why selflessness has lost its moral charm. When Matthew Arnold said of Charlotte Brontë that her mind was filled with "hunger, rebellion, and rage," he meant to reproach her. Now it would be considered a compliment.

"After all, 'I' am a woman" is not said with a sense of injury, although it is said with the knowledge that womanhood presents special difficulties. Here, as in many of her essays, Hardwick claims for a woman the rank of person, differently preoccupied but as worthy as men to attract the notice of fortune, to be in the game and to be dealt a hand, good or bad. This is not to be a victim but a gambler. There are few female gamblers in modern fiction—there are more victims—and consciousness, and the power of reflection, are more usually the properties of male protagonists and gamblers. Not of victims—not, say, of Tess of the D'Urbervilles. (If the women in this book have harder fates, if the men in it feel sorrier for themselves than she feels for them, it is not because she lacks sympathy; this is just something women notice about men.) Of women—of her mother, for instance, the narrator concludes that she should not "make too much of my mother's dreadful labors, labors laid to rest long ago." In the long run she gives every human being a lot of credit.

That is, she forbears to feel that people get what they deserve. Character is not necessarily destiny. She is sympathetic to "the balm of the vices," has a "prying sympathy for the victims of sloth and recurrent mistakes," and keeps in mind that "what began as a green start may turn overnight into a desert filled with alarm." Eventually this particular tone of awareness and acceptance makes the narrator the main character, the person of Character, an unusual heroine in the era of the injured tone.

So we become involved with "Elizabeth," as we do with the main protagonist of any fiction; yet we have a sense of her unwillingness that we should. She wants neither to complain nor to dominate. Her observations and emotions nonetheless become the account of her own passage. The "I" has watched and inquired (in "asking a thousand questions of many heavy souls, I did not learn much"), has learned much, and is now wise, resigned, a lover—

an excellent spiritual condition which in her reticence she cannot
call attention to, or, absorbed in art, is perhaps unaware of.

For the narrator-artist, the thing is to describe and reflect, to
carry us on the flow of each interesting episode, each paragraph,
each interesting *word*. She exercises care. She has a tremendous
power of summary and analysis which she alternately indulges and
corrects, mindful that our sense that other people are heroes to
lead the lives they do is to some extent patronizing, in need of
correction. Her summarizing self is witty, shrewd, incisive: Alex
"was very handsome and a little depressed by nature, but anxious
to please and in this pleasantness somewhat impersonal. For that
reason he was doomed to more fornication than he wished." "His
handsomeness created anxiety in me; his snobbery was detailed
and full of quirks, like that of people living in provincial capitals,
or foreigners living in Florence or Cairo."

The corrective is pity, charity, and love: "Her large, muscled
arms hold me for a moment in a pounding embrace. The smell
of the laundry is, truly, like a bitter, sacred incense. Her cropped
hair is damp. Her legs are swollen, the large, aching ankles seem
to groan as she pulls her weight along. She stands there, the great
teeth throbbing in her round, gleaming face. Oh, Ida."

"The bag ladies . . . have mercy on them, somebody." Of
course if this book contented itself with instancing the pathetic,
which is always apparent to everyone, it would not be so impressive. It is harder to venture into people's happiness. Of the clean-
ing woman, Josette, and her timid husband, Michael, "many,
many beautiful memories they had of the way the water and lights
hooked up, the wandering people with their news of other parks,
good sites and bad, the comradeship, the radio, the cans of beans
for the miraculous little stove, the cans of beer from the perfect
cooler." Or Miss Lavore, who "had a life":

Nearly every night of the week she went to Arthur Murray's
dancing classes. A framed, autographed portrait of Murray
and his wife hung over her bed. It would be florid to say it
hung there like a religious icon, but certainly the two secular

persons filled Miss Lavore's heart with gratitude. It could be said they had changed her life.

In this Hardwick runs the greatest risks, but faces down the danger that haunts the writer of fiction: How do *you* know? Do you presume? How do you know Miss Lavore dreams of being "Lavore and ———, famous European dancing team"? Perhaps her dreams are simpler, or grander, than this. The specter of condescension is routed by the sincerity of the narrator's love—in turn somewhat belied by the astonishing, inventive language. Brilliance always calls suspicions down on itself. Easy to imagine the narrator sharing in the sadness of Michael's decline, harder to imagine that she can imagine the pleasures of a trailer park.

Yet finally she can, and more than that. As James remarked of Balzac, she does not love these characters because she knows them so much as she knows them because she loves them. And here, finally, is why this, although not a novel, is a work of fiction, or a "new novel," but not history, not autobiography. It makes the invisible visible, it goes beyond the evidence, to borrow E. M. Forster's phrase: "each of us knows from his own experience that there is something beyond the evidence." Hardwick's power of embodying it is singular.

For the artist, the material and the state of grace are the same thing. Her attention is on others and on the *manner* of speaking of them, the brilliance of her language almost a liability, like one more vanity the virtuous artist must mortify. Ultimately the language is the triumph here. "Tell me, is it true that a bad artist suffers as greatly as a good one?" she asks, but she finds with ease, it seems, the startling adjective, the amazing simile: a city has "contaminated skies like a suffocating cloak of mangy fur." Of possessions she writes, "of course these things are not *mine*. I think they are usually spoken of as *ours*, that tea bag of a word which steeps in the conditional." She is at once a Symbolist and a master of the ordinary discursive properties of language. It is a style that is literary, learned, manly—how many women have such courage of their aphorisms?—and womanly, bounded by images of windows, mantelpieces, the behavior of people indoors.

Prose fiction cannot show us ourselves; it can show us others, better than poetry or pictures or essays can. If it is true, as seems likely despite much contemporary talk to the contrary, that we know ourselves through the recognition of the otherness of others, with whom we share the condition of humans, then prose fiction can do the best that can be done for us to console and affirm. That is why, in spite of its traditional skepticism, this book brings happiness.

# The Traveling Self:
# Edward Hoagland

IN TRAVEL BOOKS, the traveler himself is apt to interest the reader more than he perhaps intended to. We remember Marco Polo, not his journey. This is also the effect of a collection of essays, where the author, speaking personally in articles published separately over many years, produces a kind of cumulative autobiography. Inevitably the first and most engaging effect of Edward Hoagland's two new books is to draw our interest to the writer himself. Despite his rooted WASP belief that "personality is quarrelsomeness," his personality, or, rather, his character, emerges and we're glad. Our estimation of it becomes essential to our appreciation of his work. One thing his admirers like most about his writing is his quite distinctive combination of subjectivity and authority.

Any essayist, setting out in a frail apparatus of noticings and jottings, is a brave person. Maybe this is why there are so few good ones at work today—Hoagland mentions John McPhee, Peter Matthiessen, Edward Abbey, with whom he shares an interest in the world of nature; and he might have mentioned a few who write about current affairs or the arts, such as Joan Didion, Gore Vidal, and Hunter Thompson; but all together there are very few in this special category of reflection. Stand-up musings are tricky, because the closer they come to the bone, the more they are imperiled by silliness, sentimentality, or egotism, shoals that Hoagland, in the richness of his various talents, manages to avoid.

Maybe the reason novels exist is to disguise human musings. The novelist, afraid his ideas may be foolish, slyly puts them into the mouth of some other fool and reserves the right to disavow them. Yet most of us are fond of philosophizing and homely wisdom, and the part we like best in novels is where the character reflects upon his situation. It is then that our pencil is drawn to the margin to affirm his moralizing: How true! In the essays collected in *The Edward Hoagland Reader* (published earlier in a variety of magazines), he pulls off the considerable feat of being interesting without being in disguise.

There are essayists who, like anxious hosts, amuse you with confessions, as if they fear that only a bit of scandal will make you string along. Hoagland tries the riskier business of presenting thoughts. Reading his essays together, you learn a lot about him—he is from an old family, originally Dutch, his father was a lawyer, he went to Saint Bernard's School and Harvard, he stutters and has been married twice, and has written three novels, two travel books, and many essays and reviews. All this does not add up to "fame trained up as carefully as a tomato plant" (as he remarks of Norman Mailer's). He has instead something of the elusive authority of a respected headmaster, whose idiosyncrasies are known but whose opinions are sound. The special tone of his work, whether it is a description of a carnival or a city walk, is personal and magisterial, and persuades us to take his view of things.

With what does he concern himself? The world of nature—salmon spawning, bears—but also people and, most successfully, the frail, big subjects: a run of bad luck, or pain. "Dogs and the Tug of Life." "Other Lives." "The Courage of Turtles." With sly discursiveness he tells us how things tasted, looked, and felt, and what the people said. He has a strong sense of what the life of others is like—it is perhaps this that gives him a certain air of diffidence or, as he appears (without foundation) to fear, a "lack of panache." Among the chaotic sights and smells of Africa, it is individuals who catch his ear: " 'These are my golden years, wasted!' a haggard boy named Issayas would say at the Metropole, plucking angrily at his porter's tunic." He sees the drama of Issayas's life to Issayas.

The broad political issues, accordingly, do not seem to interest him so much as the particulars of ethnicity, including his own. "I wore a crumpled green wool hat to indicate that I was an American who summered in Vermont. I had my countrymen's air of trust, optimism or goodwill as a sort of national emblem." An Armenian friend has a "belief in the infinity of possibilities—the plausibility of holocaust and genocide as well as nights under the full moon." Norwegians, unlike the British, are not afraid to be gloomy in Africa. "The British think they will be finished if they ever get gloomy," he reports being told.

In a well-known essay entitled "On Not Being a Jew," originally published in *Commentary*, he describes the beginning of his writing career in the 1950s, a time when a young writer had three literary establishments to deal with—the Southern, *The New Yorker*, and the Jewish. It was the time of the "historic coming of age of American Jewish writing," when as a WASP he was "told in print and occasionally in person that I and my heritage lacked vitality, that except perhaps for a residual arrogance the vitality had long ago been squeezed dry—if in fact it had ever existed in thin blood like mine. I was a museum piece, like some State of Mainer, because I could field no ancestor who had hawked copper pots in a Polish shtetl." To reassure himself, he goes and looks up old photographs of his great-grandfathers in Kansas, and is relieved to find "their faces as unsteady and mad as John Brown's," and to recognize an "equivalent rashness" in himself.

Being rash, then, he has led an interesting life as naturalist, lionkeeper, wanderer, and city-dweller. But the best moments of his collection concern not actions or escapades but general matters of enduring interest—the death of a father, childbirth, the relation of man and animals, qualities of the human heart. These are subjects about which wisdom is of better use than wit, and rarer—wisdom and a lively sense of the role of the imagination in getting through life. "To hunker naked on a riverbank in the heart of Africa was quite dramatic, if you thought about it—drama, like sex, being primarily in the mind." He is vivid and observant, responsive to how things grow and to the habits of lions, but above all to the private dramas of other people.

It is this responsiveness that makes him a wonderful travel writer, sharing qualities with other good travel writers, and with other good travelers—they keep a low profile, have resources and strong digestions. Like the great Victorian travelers—who, elaborately attired and umbrella'd, making ponderous progress up African rivers and mountains, behaved politely when chieftains tried to buy their wives, ate strange parts of strange animals—Hoagland has an aplomb of which the modern conveniences of travel have mostly deprived the rest of us. Ours has shrunk like a vestigial organ, but not Hoagland's. So with backpack and notebook he betakes himself to the Sudan. And when his digestion does let him down he is apologetic: "It is only as the weak sister in camp that I mention my problems at meals." He is among a group of nomads, and besides stomach problems, he and his companion were "at some disadvantage in the group of men we always ate with because we could not finger hot food as well" as the tough-fingered Arabs.

Describing Africa presents a particular challenge. In *African Calliope* Hoagland meets a man who puts it neatly: "You can explain all you like, really, dine out on all the things we've seen here very thoroughly. But they're not going to believe you. It's such a jump. It's just too different." And the nature of the difference is more elusive than the differences that preoccupied wanderers of old, who could recount wonders of utter strangeness.

The travel writer now has to explain a world that has for the most part met and been influenced by the West. While Hoagland hunkers naked by the river, an African strolls by in a sports coat and paisley vest donated by some American church group. Now it is not odd customs but matters of accommodation that are salient. A little mission hospital copes futilely with Green Monkey Disease, tribesmen use World War II telegraph wires to snare animals, a man tries to cross the desert on a bicycle. The subject is not so much other cultures as the implications of our own. An African tells Hoagland that his education by priests had not been altogether a blessing, for "we are educated but we have to return home, and then we marry an African girl who has not been to town" and they are not suited.

Hoagland travels to the Sudan, a country near Ethiopia, Uganda, and Zaire peopled by black Africans, Moslem Arabs, Copts, and others, who fight and have long been fighting with one another, with Europeans, and most illustriously with the British forces commanded by General Gordon at Khartoum. Now mostly neglected by Arab and black African states alike, the Sudan has fallen a decade behind such nations as Tanzania, Zambia, and Nigeria, and still suffers the effects of a long civil war, referred to vaguely as The Troubles. As in other parts of Africa, food production has declined since independence.

Hoagland stays four months in tribal villages, nomad camps, and in the hot, dispirited towns. He darts over the border into Eritrea, the former Italian colony, and meets, everywhere, handfuls of Western isolates—veterinarians, teachers, missionaries, strays—and is attuned to "the cry of a homeless adventurer, with his shabby intestinal ailments and threadbare bank account, meeting the condescension of homebodies who believe he is roaming the world only because he is maladjusted or professionally second-rate."

Hoagland's only fault as a reporter, if he has one, is his discursiveness. It is a virtue in his essays and occasional pieces, but in a travel book some might prefer the facts up front: geography, political history, an explanation of the author's presence. Instead he parcels out these disorienting bits from time to time, as if, trudging across the Sudan, he occasionally feels the need to lighten the load of his pack by shedding a piece of notebook paper.

His essays meander like streams, and it is part of a desired effect, but here the meandering alters the chronology and confuses the geography. The logic of this organization strains against the logic of journeys, which the reader is deeply familiar with: journeys must begin somewhere, go from here to there, and then end.

While with him on the journey, however, one is merely caught up in his meticulous and wonderful descriptions of things: "the thorn trees bore sweet tiny fruit that the kids knocked down with sticks, and, as firewood, snaked out sparks like fireworks." A man with a headache "carried himself like a bottle of liquid that was tipping." His style is imaginative and bold: "When made to kneel, their camels showed their teeth in snide, snobbish mouths, expostulating through slitted nostrils with snarls, whines and whuffles although later they slept as meekly as turtles, with their necks stretched out." He notices the smallest things: "The officers laid their hands on their hearts between handshakes. One wore a bandolier studded with rifle bullets; the other wore shotgun shells."

His conclusions about Africa are few and modest; he is more interested in the particular than in the large view. He had gone there because "the myth of blackness, darkness . . . might be a sounding board." But "far from learning something new about the black-white torque that is such a misery in America, here I was freer of it." The villainy of nationalism is implied in his intuitive brotherhood with all factions, tribes, colors, enemies, and aliens he meets up with.

Without his quality of empathy, people should probably be forbidden to travel. They should be made to stay home and improve themselves with books like this. In his essay "The Problem of the Golden Rule," Hoagland recounts how when he was a child he stumbled onto something: "My astonishment evolved as I realized that people often would not do the smallest thing to convenience another person or make him feel easier for the moment. Of course I'd known that *kids* wouldn't, but I had thought that was because they were kids. It was my first comprehension of the deadness of life."

Altogether, in his essays, in his fiction, and in his travel books, it is against the deadness of life that Edward Hoagland writes, or at least that is the effect of his writing. Beneath the wise and faintly elegiac tone of regret for this deadness there always lies a confidence about life that is reassuring.

# Hollywood Make-Believe:
# Brooke Hayward

HOLLYWOOD MEMOIRS ARE the moral fables of our time, the modern form of the traditional *exemplum*, combining glamour and drama with the reminder that too much of the good things of this world brings ruin. Yet because the luxury, fame, and freedom of Hollywood life are the epitome of the American dream, we take a personal interest in these stories, scrutinizing them with special care for tragic flaws, searching for ways one might enjoy the privilege and yet avoid the fall that seems inevitably to lie in wait for Stars.

Brooke Hayward's memoir (*Haywire*) of her family—mother Margaret Sullavan, father the producer Leland Hayward, children Bill, Bridget, and herself—is a provocative contribution to the literature of the beautiful and damned. The Haywards seemed to have everything. Not only were they famous and rich, they were also intelligent, well educated, tasteful, not alcoholic or dope addicted, had values, avoided ostentation (Nash Ramblers), sent the kids to plain public schools. They were not bewildered overnight stars from the sticks, were not preyed upon by the kinds of external forces that appear to have helped destroy Monroe or Garland. They had, or feigned, a "family life," approximating the approved norm (discipline, affection, and concern).

Yet mother and father had, between them, nine marriages. Both parents and two of the children would spend time in mental institutions or "private hospitals," two would die, perhaps as suicides. The family was pursued, it seems inexorably, by the rather conventional tragedies of Hollywood life despite taking great care to avoid the conventional errors. Brooke, surviving, asks what went wrong.

But it is not a question she can answer. Her intelligent and wistful account, remarkable for its lack of anger and the absence of overshrunk hindsights, can only challenge, in a fascinating way, the clichés of explanation with which she might have rounded off her story, though she is, apparently, too honest or too reticent to do so.

Hayward and Sullavan were married for ten years. Each had been married before—she to Henry Fonda and William Wyler. This marriage was a success. They had a normal, quiet life; their friends were other people with values, like the Fondas. The children were rigorously sheltered from awareness of their parents' fame. Then, abruptly, the divorce. Sullavan went back to acting and married a man named Wagg. Hayward married twice more— the last time to a woman who had once been married to Randolph Churchill and had "lived a life of some considerable comfort, given her friendships with some of the world's wealthiest and most powerful men, including Averell Harriman (currently her husband), Gianni Agnelli, the Baron de Rothschild and Ali Khan. ('It cost ten thousand dollars a year just to keep her apartment in fresh flowers,' marveled Father.)"

After their parents were divorced, troubles engulfed the children—health and school problems, estrangements. Bill was hospitalized in Menninger's, then joined the paratroopers; Bridget went into a mental institution too, with a problem belatedly diagnosed as epilepsy. She was found dead in her New York apartment at the age of twenty-one, six months after Margaret Sullavan had died similarly, perhaps of an overdose. (Leland Hayward died in 1971 of natural causes.)

From all this we may perhaps receive intimations that these were not the just plain folks that they tried to behave as and convince their children they were. But would their children have

wanted them to be just plain folks? Were not they, too, impli-
cated in the perquisites of a Hayward identity? Brooke writes with
too much honesty and candor to protest otherwise. She simply
presents the things she remembers—the addresses, the pattern of
the curtains, what they got spanked for, the famous friends. The
things she cannot herself remember, she asks others about—
Jimmy Stewart, Henry Fonda, Diana Vreeland, and numerous
others give accounts. But when it comes to judging, even to spec-
ulating on, the inner lives of her complicated parents, she is
rather becomingly reticent.

Many things speak for themselves. There is a fine moment
when, as adolescents, Brooke and Bridget find that their mother,
who had resolutely disclaimed any interest whatever in her career,
had in fact preserved whole scrapbooks containing "every photograph—whether personal or publicity—that had ever been taken
of her. And not only photographs, but magazine covers, press
releases; every review, interview, or article that had ever been
written about her; every note, letter, telegram from anyone who
had ever mattered to her; every single memento that pertained
both to her personal and her professional lives since the days when
she was a child in Norfolk, Virginia." The reader can make of
this what he will; Brooke only repeats what Margaret Sullavan
herself told her children: "Honestly, I don't think I've ever known
one—not one!—star who was successfully able to combine career
and family life. The children usually grow up to be delinquents.
That's why . . . I didn't want to delude myself that I could do it
either . . . and I so much wanted to have the fun of being just a
mother and nobody else. Believe me, I've never for one day regretted forgoing my career. . . ."

Did Brooke believe her? Do we? Does anybody still believe in
the outworn myths of explanation which indict working mothers
and broken homes, and which if taken seriously would predict
for half of America the tragedies in store for this family? Whatever went wrong, it was something else. The tantalizing thing
about this memoir is that nothing at all emerges from between the
lines; the secret moral is disconcertingly absent; no clues reveal to

the smug reader any underlying pathology that is inapparent to Brooke. Just as she regarded and loved, and does not judge, her family, she compels our acceptance, certainly our pity.

Mere riches, mere fame, do not seem like potent villains in the face of the determination of these charming people to do everything as well as they could. (Though they seem to have got some bad advice, especially from the expensive psychiatrists.) The poignancy of this and other such tales lies really in their mockery of all human aspiration. If it is not possible to have beauty and intelligence and worldly things and love—all the things that people try for—then perhaps the lesson is the traditional one, that rewards, if any, must be hoped for in a Better World, or at least that you'd better keep a low profile in this one, and hope to escape the glaring ray of cosmic malice that sweeps over the scene in search of the visible target.

# Experience as Melodrama: George Sand

V. S. PRITCHETT, reviewing new editions of four of George Sand's novels, observed that the revival of interest in her work is owing at least in part to "opportunism of the women's liberation kind." This "disconcerting sybil," in his wonderful phrase, is, no question about it, a rich topic for hungry feminist scholars and alert publishers. Sand herself remarked of her complete works, "They are endless," and of her rather good novel *Consuelo* (published by Da Capo Press) and its sequel she could say, only half joking, "Are they mine? I don't recall a single word of them."

If anything the Sand revival has gathered momentum, still owing to opportunism of the women's liberation kind, but also to the coincidence of these concerns with growing general interest in romantic literature, and, in addition, to the availability in recent years of reliable texts in French of her letters and other autobiographical writings—the monumental edition of *Oeuvres autobiographiques*, prepared by the great French textual scholar Georges Lubin, and the Lubin edition of her correspondence.

It is likely that the autobiography and letters will do more than her novels to enhance her stature in the modern view. Her work is suprisingly readable, full of plots, retaining for all its melodrama a reassuring core of eighteenth-century worldliness: "All this is fine, my dear," says the worldly husband in *Valentine* to his much younger wife when she confides that she is attracted to someone else,

> "but it is supremely ridiculous. You are very young. Please accept some friendly advice: a woman should never use her husband as her confessor; it demands more virtue of him than his situation allows. . . . It seems to me that I have done enough for you by closing my eyes. You force me to open them, and thus I have to go away, because the situation between us would no longer be bearable and we could no longer look at each other without laughing."

Her pastoral novels have always been admired; her more sensational novels, like *Consuelo* or *Mauprat*, are better than just entertaining. But her life, with its prodigies of accomplishment and perhaps the most distinguished array of lovers ever assembled, was, like the lives of other great romantic writers of her generation, more interesting yet. And she is at her most interesting when she writes about herself, although her tone is modest, equable, honest, and informed—quite unlike the self-dramatizing reputation she has acquired—and although she leaves out all the scandalous bits.

Two recent works are of autobiography: *My Life* is a condensed translation of her twenty-volume *Histoire de ma vie*, prepared by Dan Hofstadter, and Joseph Barry's compendium *George Sand in Her Own Words* is a selection from the autobiography, from her travel writings, journals, and letters, and from several of the novels. The idea is to present her character, emotions, and opinions, together with a sample of her literary style, and although such hodgepodges are rarely successful, this one largely succeeds; one could even wish both these works were fuller. Next comes an edition of Sand's letters to and from Flaubert (translated by A. L. McKenzie), and finally yet another biography (*The Double Life of George Sand, Woman and Writer* by Renee Winegarten) of this much-scrutinized woman, of whom at least nine biographies, either new ones or reprints, have been issued in English in the last three years alone.

The lives of artists, like those of religious figures, retain at any period a singular power of example, Why? Perhaps because life itself, for the writer, is a sort of busman's holiday. As with the saint, it is his professional duty to examine matters of behavior and the heart, and we await his expert conclusions. How closely the world watched writers as different as Byron, Charlotte Brontë, Thomas Carlyle, George Sand. Today the writer who would lead an exemplary life is obliged to practice asceticism. Flesh is no longer equal to the efforts required to shock us today the way Byron or Sand shocked their contemporaries. Sand was fortunate in her times and, unlike Byron, in her constitution.

Sand herself did not believe that people should watch or be affected by the lives of artists, only by their works: the artist "does neither good nor ill when turning to the right or to the left. His end justifies all." Yet it is the testimony of this excellent woman's life, much more than of her (highly virtuous) works, that we are apt to value.

What Flaubert, like many other artists, thought of Experience is implied by his industry. He stuck to his desk. A "sense of the grotesque has restrained me from an inclination to a disorderly life. I maintain that cynicism borders on chastity," he wrote to Sand, who was always too sincere to be chaste. She in her long life had taken wide risks ("everyone is free to embark either on a great ship in full sail, or on a fisherman's vessel"). But she also put in a lot of time at her desk—she went further both in life and in art than she needed to, and is seen to have collected a reward. Life provides too few of these inspiring examples of people collecting their rewards—mountain climbers, Eagle Scouts, valedictorians—of effort and courage paying off, for us to take them lightly. George Sand's reward was being George Sand, a soul in health. The conclusion of her latest biographer, that she was "in some ways a tragic figure," raises some questions about us, about these days, and about the real meaning of that glib description.

George Sand wrote her autobiography in 1854–55, when she was fifty, with twenty-two years more of productive life ahead, her most famous novels and most notorious liaisons behind her, and at a time of relative calm after decades of domestic tumult. Adultery and tumult are matters, in general, that she does not discuss, doubtless to the disappointment of her contemporaries, who were accustomed to "confessions" in the style of Rousseau and who were familiar, through gossip and scandal, with the outlines of her affairs.

Instead she writes about the development of her character, her literary interests, and her intellectual concerns, with particular emphasis on the origins of these in her early childhood and family relationships. Her purpose in writing, apart from money, was closer to that of Mill or Carlyle, or authors of other nineteenth-century autobiographies, whose formal continuity is provided not by events but by a spiritual or mental theme, in the service of which "facts" can be bent a little. Here, nearly a third of the original work was taken up with family history, including the correspondence of her father with his mother, causing a contemporary to observe that she should have called it "The History of My Life Before I Was Born." It is interesting to note that Sand doctored this correspondence, with the abandon of a novelist, to make it more interesting and affectionate than it really was. All in all, her awareness of the influence of early life (and allowing for the fact that these are selections) produces a work quite modern in effect, and so little emphasis on accomplishments is disarming.

Autobiographies have always been a rich source of error for biographers, no doubt because, as Dr. Johnson observed, although an author has the "first qualification of an historian, the knowledge of the truth . . . it may plausibly be objected that his temptations to disguise it are equal to his opportunities of knowing it." Modern readers are more familiar than Dr. Johnson with the idea that the autobiographer may also be unwilling or unable to perceive certain truths or patterns in his own life, something biographers are often insufficiently aware of; and sometimes the meaning of autobiographical memories emerges from patterns common to the genre itself. Sand's infant memory of "a blurred train of hours spent sleepless on my little bed and filled with gazing on some curtain fold or flowers in the wallpaper" might suggest to a biographer of Ruskin, for instance, the possibility that the hard view posterity has taken of his ordinarily indulgent parents, which originates in part from his mentioning that they gave him no toys but a bunch of keys and no pastimes but to trace the design in the carpet, has prevailed because the elderly autobiographer was remembering a time in his infancy, before he could walk or talk.

The translator of Sand's autobiography, Dan Hofstadter, remarks in his preface that what she writes is "experience transformed by self-advocacy into melodrama," an opinion belied by the work itself, but nonetheless the view that has prevailed, mostly because, as Curtis Cate deplored in his 1975 biography, she has too long been depicted as "a voracious nymphomaniac, moving insatiably from the exhausted body of one genius to the next in vain search of inexhaustible virility." No doubt she was supremely energetic, and remarkable for fitting in so much real life between the hours spent in composition of her tremendous *oeuvre* (tremendous, though in the same scale as her contemporaries Dumas, Balzac, Scott, Sue).

The impression conveyed by her autobiography, however, is one of wisdom, modesty, and calm, perhaps slightly tinged in places with satisfaction:

> I had a sound constitution, and as a child seemed likely to become beautiful, a promise I did not keep. This was perhaps my fault, since at the age when beauty blossoms I was already spending my nights reading and writing.
>
> On the whole, with decent hair, eyes, teeth, and no deformities, I was neither ugly nor beautiful in my youth—a serious advantage, I think, since ugliness prejudices people one way and beauty another. . . . It is best to have a face which neither dazzles nor frightens, and with mine I get on well with friends of both sexes.

Renee Winegarten observes in her biography of Sand that it was Sand's particular vanity to see herself as "a frank, sober, straightforward person of simple tastes, one who easily forgave injuries and who was really the victim of other people's passions"; and perhaps every autobiographer does indulge some vanity or other. Rousseau was vain of his wickedness and Mill of his reason. But on the whole it is easy to take Sand at her own valuation. She is not a writer with a variety of fictional poses at her command—her heroes and heroines all sound remarkably alike. And the first person is a difficult voice for dissimulation, let alone through twenty volumes.

Joseph Barry's collection seeks to present Sand's character as it emerges not only from the autobiography but also in selections from journals, letters, articles, and in novels, especially the novels that were most widely viewed as autobiographical, particularly *Indiana*, her first novel, a tale of an unhappily married young wife, like Sand herself at the time. There are also bits of the controversial *Lélia*, which scandalized and titillated its audience with its hints of lesbian love and complaints about rude sexual behavior in men ("When he had dozed off, satisfied and sated, I would lie motionless and dismayed at his side. Thus I passed many hours watching him sleep"). Barry's volume also includes a useful chronology of Sand's life, a list of principal works, a bibliography of secondary sources in both English and French, and of editions of her works in English. All this makes it a most useful introductory collection. It is too bad it does not appear in hardcover.

The late Ellen Moers, in an excellent introduction to these selections, remarks on the process of "denigration familiar to experts in women's history," by which "the name of George Sand came to mean to most people not an author at all but a target for labels: transvestite, man-eater, lesbian, nymphomaniac." She points out that in Sand's own day she was seen as a great, though controversial, woman, and a great writer. A fresh view of her work may restore her to the reputation of her own time; literary reputations always sink and rise this way. But it seems that the sinking of Sand's was also strongly owing to her sexual behavior, born of the anxiety society apparently feels at women who embellish, in any fashion, traditional female roles. Literary history, for its part, tends to be uncomfortable with books by women that attempt to describe, however mildly and literally, the actual conditions of female life: even the most judicious descriptions are usually taken for dangerous symptoms of rabid feminism. Poor Sand is also in our day attacked as being no feminist, because she disapproved of the vote for women, and of free love, and she enjoyed making jam and doll clothes for her grandchildren.

Certainly she was in advance of her day in advocating divorce and sexual and legal equality for women, and in wanting a decent education for them. The specifics of her views today seem unimportant, but the criteria by which she has been judged in biographies over the years, even by her most sympathetic biographers, remain interesting. Some recent critical comment will serve to illustrate the general tone of disapproval, sometimes strong, sometimes only faint, as here in *The New York Times* review, by Patricia Meyer Spacks, of Barry's book: "The compilation provides relatively little evidence of Sand's art, but a vivid impression of personality: a woman intense in political and personal passion, opinionated, self-absorbed, ever projecting herself on the external world"—the kind of personality, in short, that is often congratulated in men and practically required in writers. On the other hand, André Maurois and Curtis Cate, in their biographies, both admire her capacity for "feminine" self-sacrifice.

Sand was aware that her society believed, as society may still really believe, that female character is most becomingly produced in reaction to an array of customary choices (marriage, maternity) rather than by projection. In fact the singular and most admirable thing about Sand was that she seems to have considered herself a free and responsible moral agent, accountable, and capable of theorizing, like a man. If she did slightly despise other women it was because they did not act freely in the world but only in response to it.

Society encourages artificial sexual differences; in fact "there is only one sex." This feeling allows her to be unself-conscious in her enjoyment of "female pursuits," and yet an artist, and the confidante and intellectual adviser of many men, including Gustave Flaubert, seventeen years her junior. They were drawn into close friendship by the patterns of their respective lives—Sand, always generous to genius, was also an old hand at younger men. Flaubert, who had so few human contacts, and had lost his beloved mother during the course of his friendship with Sand, found in her much maternal consolation and support. Their affection seems to have transcended their differences, in age, in political persuasion, in temperament, and in ideas of art, where each embodies the perspectives of his different generation. Sand remained a romantic idealist, and Flaubert was afflicted with the "modern ennui."

Their wonderful letters range from art and politics to cold remedies, family gossip, and advice. Sand thinks Flaubert should get married, and that he needs more exercise. There are some famous exchanges on democracy and on literary realism, two topics where they diverged utterly. After the Franco-Prussian War, both were in political despair, but disagreed about the future, and their disagreement is the model of nineteenth-century ambivalence about democracy, which wasn't working out very well. To Flaubert, the revolution had been "an abortion, a failure," proceeding from the Middle Ages and from Christianity—deplorable epoch, deplorable creed. "The crowd, the common herd will always be hateful." "The idea of equality . . . is opposed to that of justice. . . . People are now not even indignant against murders." His rather Saint-Simonian remedies are criticism, science, and an end to metaphysics. He also would do away with universal suffrage and compulsory education.

Sand's reply, which grew immensely long and was published in *Le Temps*, implores people not to abandon good will, love of and faith in humanity. Her views are those of the generation of Shelley; Flaubert's like those of many intellectuals of his age, in England as well as in France, and on art as well as on liberty. He deplores romantic sentimentality, and holds it responsible for political ills. She deplores the absence of ideology in his work: "You especially, lack a definite and extended view of life. Art is not merely painting. . . . Art is not merely criticism and satire. . . . I think that your school is not concerned with the substance, and that it dwells too much on the surface. By virtue of seeking the form, it makes the substance too cheap."

Flaubert protests that he is "constantly doing all that I can to enlarge my brain, and I work in the sincerity of my heart. . . . I do not enjoy making 'desolation,' believe me, but I cannot change my eyes! As for my 'lack of conviction,' alas! I choke with convictions. But according to the ideal of art that I have, I think that the artist should not manifest anything of his own feelings, and that the artist should not appear any more in his work than God in nature."

"That desire to depict things as they are, the adventures of life as they present themselves to the eye, is not well thought out, in my opinion," Sand replies. "Depict inert things as a realist, as a poet, it's all the same to me, but, when one touches on the emotions of the human heart, it is another thing." This is the debate in current fiction even now.

They did not resolve their differences, of course, nor did they resent them. When Sand died, six months after this exchange, Flaubert wrote to her son Maurice that it had seemed to him, at the funeral, that he was burying his mother a second time. "Poor, dear, great woman! What genius and what heart! But she lacked nothing, it is not she whom we should pity."

Men liked George Sand better than women did; similarly, she may have been more fortunate in her male than in her female biographers. Renee Winegarten, although able to interpret some of Sand's sexual activities and ambivalence toward female duties with a woman's understanding, has nonetheless something of the tone of a plain woman who doesn't like to think of others being fooled by the ruses of a pretty one: "When she created women who were lonely, a prey to nerves, hysteria and mysterious illnesses; who saw themselves as their husbands saw them (that is, as irresponsible children or virtual idiots) . . . she had not far to look. She had only to examine her own heart, for she herself was one of them." "(If she knew about feminine ruse, it was because she shared it while despising it.)"

Winegarten's is a kind of wound-and-bow view in which Sand tries to compensate for the early loss of her father, and childhood feelings of being unloved, by strenuous efforts to win love and admiration as an adult. Naturally. It seems rather odd for the author of a biography with, ostensibly, a special interest in Sand as someone who seriously contended "on behalf of all women, with the central experiences and issues of womanhood: with daughterhood, with motherhood, and finally, with the desperate need for selfhood," to conclude that for all her success Sand "ultimately remains, through some deep inner flaw, a tragic figure." And she incurs this patronizing judgment, moreover, in part because "she never found an equal partner in life (as distinct from a friend) to accept her on equal terms."

No doubt a view can be defended that all human beings are tragic. By Winegarten's definition, certainly, more are tragic than not (tragic George Washington, tragic Mrs. Gaskell). And are those tragic who enjoy being the superior of their partner in life, as Victorian husbands were admonished to be?

And by what qualities, indeed, do we define a life as successful or tragic? One criterion might be the owner's contentment with it. George Sand did not feel herself to be a tragic figure. Instead, is she not better thought of as the very pattern of a successful and lucky human being—generous, kindly, rich in possessions, experience, friendship, independent, accomplished, a woman who lived to be famous and old and whose children survived her, and whose personal qualities of wisdom, humor, tolerance, and compassion were acknowledged by all. It's as if we have got so used to looking at lives for their secret disappointments and neuroses, to debunk or to empathize, that we have got out of the habit of remembering that some lives can be really marvelous and inspiring.

Perhaps some of Winegarten's points would be clearer if the book were more clearly written; it has the quality of a bad translation from some other language: of Sand's grandmother, "after a lucky escape from consummating her first marriage to a diseased debauchee by his timely demise, she had married Maurice's father, the experienced, cultivated, elderly tax collector of the Châteauroux district and hence a man of considerable means, whom she called 'my papa' and who died in 1786." Or, "thanks to George's interest in natural history, the destructive ideas of Charles Darwin concerning spontaneous creation, the animal origins of mankind, and the survival of the fittest were already being discussed at Nohant in the autumn of 1853, even before the publication of his major work." This is surely impossible, for Darwin's ideas were not generally known even in England then, though the notion of evolution had been around a long time. Nor, I think, did Darwin address himself to spontaneous creation. One is sure, however, that the talk at Nohant was very good indeed.

# Flaubert Dashes Off a Letter

"LAST WEEK I spent *five days writing one page.*" What lazy novelist has not felt reproached by the example of the industrious and self-sacrificing Flaubert, toiling over his phrases, eschewing the world, for the sake of his art exacting from himself prodigies of effort, patience, and perfect taste. We know of these prodigies mostly from often quoted passages from his letters: "What trouble my Bovary is giving me! . . . This inn scene will perhaps take me three months, I can't tell. There are moments when I want to weep, I feel so powerless. But I'll die rather than botch it."

An edition of his correspondence has been selected, edited, and translated by Francis Steegmuller, the admired biographer and translator of *Madame Bovary*, an earlier, briefer volume of the letters, and other works from the French. The Flaubert who emerges in this, the first of two volumes, is reassuringly not quite the long-sufferer we may have thought he was—he was even odder, and much more a creature of his time and place, than his timeless *Madame Bovary* has allowed him to seem. The letters cover the period from 1830, when he was nine, to 1857, after the publication and prosecution (for "outrage of public morals and religion") of *Madame Bovary*, and include, most notably, some precocious, prescient letters to a boyhood friend, letters to a friend of his young manhood to whom he confides sexual details of an eighteen-month trip to the Middle East (and other letters about it to his mother), and letters to Louise Colet, who was for some years his mistress and the only woman with whom he would have an extended affair. Mr. Steegmuller's selection, based on the French Pléiade edition being prepared by Jean Bruneau, is accompanied by valuable biographical material and extensive notes.

Flaubert was the son of a provincial doctor of Rouen, brother of another doctor, and himself destined for the law, perhaps because, as Jean-Paul Sartre has suggested, his sensitive and bookish nature had made his robust father think him unfit for medicine. He was kept from finishing his law studies, which he hated, by the onset of rather propitious epileptic fits. He had in fact always wanted to be an author. At nine he was writing his friend Ernest Chevalier, "if you'd like us to work together at writing, I'll write comedies and you can write your dreams, and since there's a lady who comes to see Papa and always says stupid things I'll write them, too." In this he more or less perfectly foresaw his own artistic direction, except that he would write the dreams, too. And Ernest would become the respectable lawyer.

The epilepsy came on when Flaubert was twenty-four. He lived to the age of fifty-eight. "My illness has brought one benefit, in that I am allowed to spend my time as I like, a great thing in life." And that, on the evidence of these letters, is exactly what he did, settling down to a sedentary bachelor existence with his mother, who lived until 1872. Apart from some travel and social visiting, and an occasional turn in Paris, he spent his life writing—with excruciating deliberation, to be sure, but also with love and satisfaction. The context of his cries of protest—"if you knew how I was torturing myself you'd be sorry for me"—makes them appear a little more strategic than may have been thought. To be sure, they contain recognizable articulations of any artist's suffering: "Now, I will confess to you it seems to me I have nothing that everyone else doesn't have, or that hasn't been said equally well, or that can't be said better." But it also seems that he may have exaggerated, no doubt unconsciously, to protect himself from the demands of others, most conspicuously Louise Colet, who lived in Paris and was always teasing him to visit, but perhaps from his poor old mother as well, who may have wished for a more sociable domestic companion than this strange son who spent long hours shut away in his study shouting his phrases aloud.

One interruption in his solitary life of reading and writing was to influence his future choice of Oriental subjects. In December 1849 he set out with a friend, Maxime DuCamp, for a journey of a year and a half to Egypt, Palestine, Turkey, Greece, and Italy, ostensibly charged with a trivial government mission but actually poeticizing, romanticizing, photographing, working their way through brothels and Turkish baths with truly astonishing energy and, if Flaubert's letters to Louis Bouilhet do not exaggerate, picking up a truly astonishing amount of venereal disease. In their determination to experience all types of exotic vice they were the most conscientious of travelers, alert to the cross-cultural implications of everything:

> In Beirut I picked up (I first noticed them at Rhodes, land of the dragon) VII chancres, which eventually merged into two, then one. . . . Finally it cured itself. In two or three days the scar will be closed. I'm being desperately careful about it. I suspect a Maronite woman of making me this gift, or perhaps it was a little Turkish lady. The Turk or the Christian? Which? Problème! Food for thought! That's an aspect of the "Eastern Question" the *Revue des Deux Mondes* doesn't dream of.

This and other, more elaborately described, anecdotes give one of the most vivid pictures, by any literary man, of what young men of the nineteenth century expected to do on their Eastern grand tours. (Young Englishmen seemed to expect they had to travel no farther than France to do such things; but English travel accounts of this period are notably more modest, and Dickens's little references to "oystering and roistering" seem reticence itself.) On the subject of venereal disease, Mr. Steegmuller thoughtfully acknowledges one's curiosity by providing an appendix, "Flaubert on Syphilis," which confirms one's impression that "more or less everybody" was afflicted with this epidemic disease, of which many famous French writers—Mr. Steegmuller mentions Maupassant, Jules de Goncourt, and Baudelaire—would die in their forties; and it does make you wonder about those bouts of blindness and ataxia which afflicted many famous English writers, too, at the ends of their lives.

Although Flaubert's celebrated pronouncement, *"Madame Bovary, c'est moi,"* has usually been understood to express a literary principle about an author's identification with his characters, it is clear from his letters that Flaubert was also expressing his preoccupation, if not identification, with fallen women. "I like prostitution," he wrote Louise Colet. "My heart has never failed to pound at the sight of one of those provocatively dressed women walking in the rain under the gas lamps, just as the sight of monks in their robes and knotted girdles touches some ascetic, hidden corner of my soul." That he suffered to an unusual (or, rather, usual) extent from the malady Freud was to describe as the primary degradation in the erotic life of nineteenth-century men may account as much as artistic self-preservation does for his failure to marry, or even, apparently, to feel any sexual desire for women in the same station of life as his sister or mother.

His one long romance, with Louise Colet, came to an end because, among other reasons, she insisted on meeting his mother, something he evidently could not bring himself to permit: "It is because I am persuaded that if she were to see you she would behave coldly toward you, less than politely, as you put it, that I prefer you not to see one another. Besides, I dislike this confusion, this bringing together of two very dissimilar kinds of affection."

Colet was a beautiful, rather tiresome woman, a minor poet and friend of other literary and artistic figures living in the semi-respectable demimonde of Paris. She was married, with a daughter by a well-known lover, and had received a little unwelcome notoriety by trying to stab a gossip columnist with a kitchen knife. Her connection with Flaubert was first in 1846–48 and later, after she was widowed, from 1851 to 1855. The affair was broken

off because of her importunities about meeting his mother, perhaps because of a general cooling of affection, and when Flaubert's
friends warned him that she was hoping for marriage. The last
letter, provoked by circumstances not known, is notably cruel: "Madame: I was told that you took the trouble to come here to see me
three times last evening. I was not in. And, fearing lest persistence
expose you to humiliation, I am bound by the rules of politeness
to warn you that *I shall never be in*."

Luckily for literature, theirs had been a mostly epistolary affair
anyway, as Flaubert usually resisted efforts to get him to Paris.
The first letters are endearing in their passion and spontaneity,
and the later letters abound in thoughtful expressions of his views
on art ("What a man Balzac would have been had he known how
to write!") and on his own work habits ("This evening I was writing
a summer scene, with midges, sun on the grass, etc. The greater
the contrast between what I am writing and my actual surround-
ings, the better I see my subject") and in many of his famous
literary dicta—the best known of which ("an author in his book
must be like God in the universe, present everywhere and visible
nowhere") he saved and repeated to another lady, to whom he
was writing in 1857, after the publication of *Madame Bovary* and its
unsuccessful prosecution by the French Government had made
him famous.

The correspondence printed here is not complete: for instance,
the first twelve letters from Flaubert to Louise Colet have been
translated "almost" in their entirety; the last twelve, which
"abound in outrages," have been omitted, and many are left out
in between. This is a matter of editorial decision and could be
defended on the ground that people with a scholarly interest will
want to read the letters in French anyway, but it doesn't stop you
from wishing that they were all printed here, and in their entirety.
The usefulness of editions of "selected" letters is always somewhat
qualified; and the wisdom of elisions in any printed letters is open
to question. Omissions, especially those which seem to wish to
preserve the reader's good opinion of Flaubert, instead animate
his apprehensions. At the least, one wishes for a fuller discussion

of the translator's rationale in determining what to cut out. Shocking passages? Boring ones? Quotidian gossip? At least there is nothing boring or mundane left in these letters, which are interesting in every phrase even though they have a notably difficult subject—Flaubert himself.

Because of *Madame Bovary* he has been perceived as a great realist, and critics have expended much ingenuity reconciling this view with the undoubted romantic tendencies he exhibited in *The Temptation of Saint Anthony* and *Salammbô*. The impression of Flaubert that emerges from his letters and from the biographical material is decidedly that of a romantic, which is indeed how Flaubert described himself and was seen by later romantics such as Baudelaire, Wilde, and Pater. His love of Byron and of Oriental tales arises from the earlier period, his political conservatism and aestheticism from the later one, but his character was unusually consistent. As early as eighteen, he had expressed the wish simply to "tell the truth: but that truth will be horrible, cruel, naked," a clear intimation of the connection of the daily subjects that concern him in *Madame Bovary* to that most romantic of emotions, disgust.

When, once, in the stage of wanting to create "great sumptuous things—battles, sieges, descriptions of the fabulous, ancient Orient," he gathered his friends together to read aloud to them from an early version of *The Temptation of Saint Anthony*, the truthful Louis Bouilhet reportedly advised him to "throw it into the fire and never speak of it again," advice that some readers since have wished he had followed, and advice that doubtless had a salutary effect on his choice of his next subject, provincial adultery. How lucky that his friends did not put his letters into the fire—the fate of many such frank nineteenth-century letters. In his novels, Flaubert scrupulously followed the example of God. Only in his letters, these brilliant notes from underground, can one hear his unfailingly interesting human voice.

# Colette in Pieces

IN 1923, COLETTE's second husband, Henry de Jouvenel, left her for another woman. She writes to a friend, Mme Georges Wague, to whom the same thing has recently happened:

> But, my child, haven't you heard the gossip? We're in the same boat. If it is true that happiness is only relative, then think of yourself as happy, in comparison to me. . . . You don't have a child, which is a pity—or work to absorb you. But come and see me, not at *Le Matin*, though, and not before next week. Telephone me Tuesday or Wednesday morning. And, *above all*, arrange to move, to get out of the house where you've been tormented. Find another nest. I know that's hard, but find one all the same, and at once. I am sure I am giving you good advice. . . .
>
> As for me, I've been alone for a month. He left without a word while I was on a lecture tour. I am divorcing.

This gives an impression of a high-spirited and independent woman encouraging similar proud high spirits in her friend. But the translator, Robert Phelps, has omitted a few sentences, from this letter as from almost all the other letters in this collection. The first paragraph above goes on: "When he misses you, even if only for an instant in the course of a month, you score a point. Otherwise everything is against you." (*"Quand tu lui auras man-*

*qué, fut-ce un moment dans l'espace d'un mois, tu auras marqué un point. Hors cela, tout est contre toi.")* What seems to be a counsel of pride is instead a counsel of policy, a very different matter.

Robert Phelps explains in his preface (to *Letters from Colette*) that he has followed his "own taste, trimming freely and trying simply to show Colette in her daily zest. . . . Letters and memoirs to come will certainly deepen the image this book makes, but it is unlikely that they will radically alter it." His taste leads him to emphasize a zestful, simple Colette and to ignore the more prudent, calculating, and interesting woman who emerges from the complete texts of her letters. It is of course the defect of all collections of trimmings that the idea of the editor about the writer controls our understanding of his subject, the more particularly in cases of translated letters, which have the usual problems of translations in addition, among them that we are far less likely to go ourselves to the originals to see what is missing. Mr. Phelps, the editor and translator of *Earthly Paradise*, a compendium of Colette's autobiographical writings, and of *Les Belles Saisons*, a picture book, has had considerable influence on our view of Colette.

Phelps's note specifies his view of Colette, "a sort of twentieth-century earth goddess who lived most of her life in Paris, watching the world around her so attentively that she was able to describe how a single rose petal sounds when it falls." For him she is a "robust country girl" much as in her letters, which he sees as "spontaneous, abundant, dashed-off, like nothing so much as an armful of field flowers, fresh, fragrant, still sparkling with dew, which Ceres, let's say, brought in from her morning walk . . . , everywhere impulsive and intimate"—and "self-revealing," adds the jacket, though letters less self-revealing scarcely exist. Moreover, it is exactly the self-revelation that Phelps has cut out—for instance, all references to her unhappiness over the infidelity of M. de Jouvenel in the situation above. Whereas men like experience in women, they tenderheartedly hate them to have troubles.

Love of nature, on the other hand, is a truly unexceptionable sentiment, and Colette's is agreeable, doubtless sincere, and produces a lot of animated description: "In one evening, between six and ten o'clock we planted oleanders, geraniums, pelargoniums in jars, and it looked ravishing. What fun it is to go broke!" (The English-speaking reader especially appreciates translations here, where reading in French would mean looking up a lot of names of plants you don't really need to remember.) In the fifty years of letters represented (1902–52), we have truly impressive evidence of Colette's great vitality (learning to ski at fifty-two), hardiness (lots of cold sea bathing), appetite (wonderful descriptions of food cooked and consumed), and astonishing courage, for instance when breaking a leg:

> a true fracture of the fibula bone, on the slant, below the calf. And if you could see the Saint-Tropez hospital where they brought me to set the break! Happily, I was back home a few hours later—but I wasn't able to have my lunch until five o'clock, and I have no taste for five o'clock meals! I was still howling, but with hunger. Luckily there were some green beans with garlic, and marvelous local veal. It must have looked very funny to see me devouring my food in bed while Maurice looked on with stricken eyes and a clenched stomach. . . .

To some readers, however, this gusto so admired by Phelps may seem less welcome than the knowledge that the poor woman, like a normal person, included in this same letter some natural complaints omitted by Phelps: *"je m'ennuie dans la plâtre et en outre j'ai mal,"* *"mais je suis vexée, et ça me fait mal,"* etc. In touching up the portrait of an earth goddess, Phelps renders her as wearing as the gods of mythology, fuller of appetite than sense.

We are given a number of these word pictures, as they used to be called, but without the grace notes of salutations and conclusions or routine remarks on the weather or on business matters (though considerable evidence of Colette's financial prudence remains). Unimportant and dull sentences are left out. What remains sparkles, all right:

> If only you could see the monkeys running free in Chiffa! And antelopes in the hotel garden, with their black velvet eyes and long, almost curly eyelashes! And the mother monkeys with two little breasts, just like women! And the shrimps we eat, as large as sausages! And the sun, and a flower that looks like a cockatoo!

Sometimes he tones down the sparkle: *"j'avance peu, j'avance mal—j'avance"* (in writing a novel) becomes "my progress is slight and difficult, but it is progress." Mainly, though, one feels the need of the dull little businesslike sentences to make the fine writing palatable, the way Jane Austen felt the need of some dull chapters in *Pride and Prejudice*, some solemn nonsense to set off the sprightliness. But more to the point, it is in the little exclamations and reports that the real character of this amazing woman begins to be accessible.

Since her death, in 1954, Colette's literary reputation has followed the usual curve, at its apogee during her last years, by which time she had received the medal of the Legion of Honor, been elected to the Académie Goncourt, and much else. A dozen years after her death, the august Henri Peyre would pronounce "our own conviction that she was always grossly overrated and that she may well, more than any other cause, be responsible for the sad plight of feminine writing in France up to the fourth decade of the present century." Her heroines were "creatures who were all slightly venal, never forged bonds of comradeship with men, never discussed politics, ideas, ethics, aesthetics with them, never tried to found a loving relationship based on candidness and on loyalty, and accepted deceit as the condiment to their love life." The heroes were "brainless gigolos," and her world "one of boudoirs and of bedrooms with no genuine joy and no tenderness ever emanating from those unconvincing love gymnastics."[*]

Today we again admire her candor and penetration—the superb style has never been questioned—and assume her to have been an astute observer of her society. But because the "slightly corrupt sensibilities" M. Peyre believes Colette to have always had so poorly befit Mr. Phelps's earth goddess, one cannot help wondering what the connection is, and whether the censure by Peyre and the omissions by Phelps have anything in common beyond that these are both men wishing, as usual, to think of women as either better or worse than they are. Has Phelps removed the very things that make Peyre so uncomfortable?

For instance, the bit of worldly advice to Mme Wague, telling her how to score a point, may be for him a bit too much like Ceres telling Proserpine what to wear, the better to seduce Pluto. Colette's advice, like all advice, is concerned with love, money, or health, and while advice always originates in either morality or calculation, Colette's arises from calculation, or practicality, or whatever one will call that faculty which, when presented in men as business acumen or military genius, is always admired, and is never admired in a woman. To be sure, Colette gave advice to her men friends, too, for she was sympathetic to and understanding of their temporal ambitions and their erotic natures. She is unsurprised by them. Her attitude is never flirtatious, is instead that of someone disqualified by age, braininess, or even fatness from wanting anything from them, something she herself remarks upon in *The Pure and the Impure*: "I never had to go out of my way to be let in on masculine secrets. The average man overflows with confidential talk when he is with a woman whose frigidity or sophistication sets his mind at rest."

In her fiction, as well as in the letters, Colette's preoccupation with advice is striking—it is her great subject. She is interested above all in the protégé(e) and in the emotional plight of the protector, and in the communication of experience, especially of

*French Novelists of Today* (Oxford University Press, 1967), pp. 276–77.

love and its economics. As she moved in her own life from beloved child to protégée to protectrice, so are the characters in her
books arranged. Each person is in some sense the creation of
someone else in a natural hierarchy. She seems not to have
minded, really, being locked in the room by the awful Willy, so
much as she minded his infidelities. Locked in the room, she
learned the rudiments of self-creation.

Her view of men in her fiction is a little harsher than the sympathetic tone of her letters to male friends, which may explain
Phelps's affection and Peyre's anxiety. Men do not ever seem to
admire fiction by women in which the heroines are encouraged to
be unconventional, and we do understand the fate of fictional
characters, however autonomous they may seem in the course of
the story, to represent the views of the author. *"Je déteste Louisa
Alcott,"* cried Simone de Beauvoir, reading that Jo has married a
dull professor. Women readers, on the other hand, do like to read
stories in which the women succeed in being unconventional.
People of both sexes have always admired *Madame Bovary, Anna
Karenina,* or *Middlemarch,* say, but for women these are cau-
tionary tales of the kind men feel women need.

On the other hand, Colette's women often get revenge—the
fate of Chéri, the uppity independence of the Vagabonde. Colette's view of the relations of the sexes fundamentally in opposition
was founded upon observation and experience. At the outset of her
affairs with both Jouvenel and Maurice Goudeket, her third husband, she had to deal with jealous rivals who threatened scenes,
scandal, and even murder. She sees the real conflict of interests
of men and women—alien creatures involved like spiders in some
painful but inevitable biological conjunction which would lead to
the extinction of one or the other; but like a biologist or a UN
observer she can keep a certain sympathy for both sides; she's a
man's woman and a woman's woman both, and feels herself to
have "a genuine mental hermaphroditism." When she took up
with Goudeket, she found that they were "two tranquil comrades
who looked like friends. Oh the luxury of also being friends! It's
hardly believable!" Her wonderment seems very genuine.

It is rare in these selections, although we learn much of what Colette is doing, that we get much idea of what she is feeling or thinking. This is partly for reasons suggested, but partly because Colette seems to have had rigorous standards of self-presentation, at least to the people represented in this collection, intimates but not her nearest confidantes. She fears, or professes to fear, wearying them with the most taciturn of confidences ("*je m'excuse de ne parler que de moi*"). The letters are more often couched in terms of their recipients: "I'm sending you a copy of my first column in *Figaro*, but there's only one reason I am eager for you to read it: your name embellishes the last line. I embrace you with all my heart." One reason for the immediacy of these and all literary letters is of course the locution "you"; it is ourselves she embraces and admonishes with her abundant imperatives.

This may add to an impression, perhaps rather unfair, of formidable self-possession which belies Phelps's conviction of her spontaneity. Perhaps we are so conditioned by a literature of self-examination and complaint that a selfless, gregarious interest in others can seem to be self-interested posing. For Colette, if hardly selfless, was really gregarious, interested in others more than in herself—a product of an era and a society more interested in the social manifestations of self than in its penetralia. Colette does not dismiss the psyche but, rather, takes it for a starting point, and her own psyche she seems to take for granted, peevish and greedy to the normal degree, and forgiven. Her self-acceptance explains why she wrote lots of letters and not diaries; she is the opposite of, say, Anaïs Nin. It is possible that in letters to people more intimate—to her husbands, or daughter, or her early lesbian lover, Missy—one might glimpse a more vulnerable self. But these are not yet available.

The friends to whom she writes here are, in particular, the other great woman writer of her day, Anna de Noailles, Hélène Picard and Marguerite Moreno, Leo and Ma-Misz Marchand, Francis Carco the novelist; and there are a smattering of notes to Proust, Ravel. Unfortunately, the letters are so abbreviated that one loses the biographical thread that can unite a collection of letters with an inferred action—in the case of Colette an unusually eventful action. Instead husbands seem mysteriously to appear. Her dear Hélène Picard and Ma-Misz Marchand, the recipients of dozens of letters, drop from the pages almost without explanation, certainly none from the editor; and her accounts to others of their deaths are so heavily edited as to seem almost offhand. More numerous biographical notes would have helped, but there is a chronology given. There is no index.

Whether because it didn't fit within the chronological scheme of the book, which begins at 1902, or because Phelps believes Colette to have been a writer "without any pretension and theory," "nor can any comparable writer be said to have flourished so independently of the tastes and ideologies of the time" (the times of which M. Peyre finds her so deplorably representative), he does not include an 1895 letter to Proust, who had evidently written to Willy an appreciative note about his (that is, presumably, Colette's) work. She replies gratefully to Proust that he is *"le seul, je crois (pourtant je crois que Fénéon* [an art critic admiring of Mallarmé and Rimbaud] *avait fait la même remarque), qui avez si nettement vu que, pour lui, le mot n'est pas une représentation mais une chose vivante, et beaucoup moins un signe mnémonique qu'une traduction picturale."* ("The only person, I think, though I think Fénéon made the same remark, who has so clearly seen that for him the word is not a representation but a living thing, and much less a mnemonic sign than a pictorial translation.")

This suggests that Colette was very much as one would expect, a writer of her own day, influenced by the visual aesthetics of Wilde, Gautier, Proust, the senior writers of her youth. Her rapturous passages of natural description owe as much to art as to nature—remind, even, of the descriptions in Huysmans of art objects or perfumes: "one must live here to appreciate the four colors of figs: the green with yellow pulp; the white with red pulp; the black with red pulp; and the violet, or rather the mauve, with pink pulp." Colette's nature writing is a little *à rebours*, an attraction to style like her attraction to those turn-of-the-century lesbians, triumphantly stylish, whose wonderful evening costumes and dramatic decor she would so meticulously describe. Phelps has included a lot of her very interesting references to her way of working, slow and painstaking. She would often fall ill during the last stages of a work. Whether or not her letters were dashed off, they share all the qualities of *fin-de-siècle* aestheticism, applied instead to the natural world.

In what exactly does the interest of literary letters lie; why should we care about the lives of writers at all? But we do, cajoled, perhaps, by the "you" into the writer's confidence, or wishing to see how the writer practices what he preaches, or to enjoy the discrepancy between the mess he makes of things and the tidy determinism of his endings; or to understand the sly metamorphosis of the real unfaithful husband into the jilted lover of a book. Not just literary historians but every reader tests a book against the real—the real life of the author and his own real life; and the real lives of authors, like those of saints and politicians, and of everyone who sets up as moralist or whose work is ultimately didactic, do have a strange exemplary power. Or maybe all lives do.

Letters further our acquaintance. But trimmed and altered letters can no more do this than notes smuggled out from a jail. We don't know whether we can trust the intermediary or not. All is qualified and compromised. Given the realities of publishing and reading, we cannot have and probably wouldn't want the complete correspondence of every great writer. Of some we do. The letters of Henry James and of Virginia Woolf are two recent examples of wonderful and well-published letters which merit the many volumes they take up. One can also defend certain principles of selecting shorter volumes, of the letters of a writer to one person, for example, or letters written at one interesting period of life.

It's harder to defend making selections from letters, that is, tampering with the texts of individual letters. It's a bit like copying out a passage of somebody else's work in your own hand before submitting it to handwriting analysis. A truly self-effacing, tactful, perfectly invisible editor does not exist. The recent selection of

Flaubert's letters, ably translated by Francis Steegmuller,* is really spoiled because short passages of love talk and quotidian gossip are omitted. It's not so much that you value what Steegmuller has left out as that you are bound to wonder about it, and never feel able to think of Flaubert without worrying about those little dots. Yet a little more space would have allowed the letters to be presented entire.

Of mere snippets there is little to say. If they were maxims, like La Rochefoucauld's (or Kahlil Gibran's), that some reader or other might want to refer to, to regulate his conduct by, that would be one thing, and another if there were photographs to illustrate the bits of natural description ("Cats and dogs swoon in the sun, and yesterday evening Maurice found a tiny lizard, surely a fairy prince, long as your little finger, onyx-red in color, with black eyes. What is this miracle?"), the whole to lie upon the coffee table. As it is one is merely unsatisfied. Colette herself would never have served such skimpy fare.

*The Letters of Gustave Flaubert: 1830–1857, selected, edited, and translated by Francis Steegmuller (Harvard University Press, 1980).

# Alice and Henry James

THE FIFTH CHILD of Mary and Henry James, Sr., was, at last, a girl, Alice. To the rich gifts of fortune, affection, position, and intelligence that were hers by birth was added, as in a fairy tale, a mysterious bane, so that while still in her teens she began to suffer mysterious ailments for which no cause could be found. She spent her life as an invalid, but as her body grew ever weaker and more tormented, her considerable mental powers increased. Biographers of her brothers William, the great psychologist, and Henry, the great novelist, taking note of the acerbic and recumbent figure of Alice on her sofa, have sensed her importance without understanding her case—have found her, in fact, something of an embarrassment, a reproach to the excellent family of notable people.

Two new works look for the first time at Alice herself: a full-length study of her life by Jean Strouse (*Alice James*) and a selection of her letters with a long introduction by Ruth Bernard Yeazell (*The Death and Letters of Alice James*). Both of these interesting books raise the questions that Alice's life has always posed: Was she, the only girl in this talented, eccentric family, affected more seriously than her four brothers by the emotional problems that to some extent also affected them and many people like them in the post–Civil War period? Or were her illnesses the reflex of the family genius? Was she the family victim, the designated sufferer, sheltered and idealized by her brothers but also delegated to stay at home with the aging parents? Did she take upon herself the path of madness so that the "great wits" of the others would be free of it, or did the brilliance of her brothers cast her into the shade—or was the shade, where a woman was expected to stay, too gloomy for her? Were the intellectual demands of being a James simply too difficult? Or was she simply the victim of nineteenth-century medical mistakes?

Certainly being born female had a lot to do with it. The attitudes of the family, so unconventional on most subjects, were perfectly conventional concerning the innocence, purity, and goodness of females, even though this conflicted with other family attitudes about the special intellectual capabilities of the Jameses, in a rarefied Boston set of Brahmin friends with names like Emerson, Holmes, and Lowell. Alice James considered herself brilliant and bad ("I was born bad and I never have recovered"), but she had no way to express either quality. And so she got terrible headaches and strange paralyses.

In her judicious and beautifully written biography Jean Strouse asks, first, whether Alice—indolent, complaining, coddled, and wretched—warrants a biography at all. Her life was a failure by most standards, and it was not really representative of other women's lives because it partook so much of the special James world. "Still, the general outlines of her life parallel those of a great many other women of her period and social class [and] can be seen as a collective response to the changing shape of late nineteenth-century American life" or, as Freud's work suggested, of Western European culture generally. So a life of Alice James, a "sentient, articulate person whose particular history makes vivid the ideas, personalities, and social conditions of her time," is more than a biography, a complicated work of social history. Alice James lived at a time when widespread consciousness of women's problems first assumed its modern aspect.

Miss Strouse renders these complexities with great skill and, like Mrs. Yeazell in her introduction to Alice James's letters, avoids the temptation to make of the talented and wasted Alice either a heroine or a victim. For one thing, she was too exasperating to be either, and her case was too puzzling. It is clear that what she called her "disgusting sex" prevented the fulfillment of her undoubted intellectual gifts (she herself seems to have felt this most keenly). Her privileged life as a James—a sinister alchemy of enlightenment and solicitude—may have left her more powerless than a life of hardship would have. But it is too simple to say that a normal sexual life, marriage and children, or a career would have cured her. "Pray don't think of me simply as a creature who might have been something else had neurotic science been born," she cautioned her brothers, yet Miss Strouse, quite properly, treats this possibility with attention, and it is a possibility with implications for modern medical practice.

Alice first experienced some sort of unspecified breakdown in 1868, when she was nineteen. Her rich and worried parents made sure that she underwent or was subjected to the most advanced medical treatment of her day—nearly every substance, theory, and regimen that the puzzled medical establishment, confronted with a burgeoning number of cases like hers, could devise. Hysteria in women and the newly named "neurasthenia" in both sexes had risen dramatically after the Civil War, and so had advances in understanding of the nervous system, which led physicians to perceive a connection between ailments formerly thought to be either mental or physical. But it was believed then (as now) that women were more "nervous" than men, and this belief was sustained by the apparent connection between advances in women's education and the general improvement of their condition in other areas, and their increasing "nervousness."

Female illness was thought to be a product of the overstimulation of their more frail and excitable nervous systems. The coincidence of increasing nervous ailments among upper-class women reinforced traditional assumptions about female nature, and led to the conclusion that too much idleness and education diminished the capacity for childbearing and housework, thus denying these sufferers true happiness through service and self-sacrifice. (One shrewd physician of the day, however, noted the higher incidence of functional complaints among women upon whom had devolved the duty of caring for aged parents or nephews and nieces.)

In any case, these new psychosomatic invalids were somehow responding to changes in the forms of society, but nobody knew how, and it seemed (certainly in Alice James's case) they were opting out of the roles of motherhood and wifehood that society had designated for them. We are still, of course, embattled by the conflict between our notions of "human" nature and the need of society for a servant class. Reading of Alice James's case, one is struck by how very little the modern understanding of neurotic illness has improved its treatment.

Today most of the tons of tranquilizers prescribed in America are consumed by women. During her lifetime, Alice James received courses of galvanic shock therapy, laudanum, bromides, marijuana, rest cures, exercise cures, vapor baths, massages, and much else, for complaints that included headache, fainting, paralysis, "fits," and much else. All the James brothers at times suffered from neurotic ailments, crises of anxiety, forms of breakdown, and various functional ailments. They gave one another advice, suggested mild remedies (iodine poultices), and would seek changes of scene, visit home, or travel. With this they were more or less expected to get through difficulties that were thought to be products more of the human condition than of personal weakness, and get through their difficulties they more or less did.

The stiff upper lip required of men, and its relative efficacy compared with the infantilizing forms of treatment bestowed upon Alice, is striking. As years passed she grew more exacting and more prostrate, the manifestations of her mysterious complaints more peremptory and various, her principal victim above all herself. Her brothers improved.

Ruth Bernard Yeazell's discriminating selection of Alice James's often witty and sad letters were chosen for their "inherent appeal and for their representativeness, to help the reader sense the range of her concerns and the shape of her 'mortal career.' " They show her Jamesian mental energy, force of character, and verbal abil-

ity. As with other invalids, her subject often tends to be herself
and details of her complaints, but she possessed the family art,
the family instinct of social tact, too, and slyly conceals with wit
or makes diverting what might in a less articulate woman seem a
monotonous recitation, year in and year out, of faintings and
weakness, new doctors, new drugs. A nurse "towed my heart back
to its moorings by digitalis and poured a sufficient amount of Bro-
mide upon my gunpowdery nerves." A galvanic treatment has "the
starching properties of the longest Puritan dissent, and I wish very
much that you might try it some of these days." After some time
in a New York sanitarium, she began "to sympathize with the
lady who died and found Heaven delightfull [sic] 'only it was not
Boston.' " She was also a good, if somewhat malicious, gossip,
social critic, and political observer.

Her brothers, while protecting themselves from her with an air
of distant solicitude or by actual distance, nonetheless behaved
with entire sympathetic patience and affection throughout her life.
During her last years—from 1884 to her death at the age of forty-
three in 1892—she joined Henry in London, living not with him
but with a faithful friend, Katharine Loring, a well-educated Boston
lady, in a relationship common enough in their day and to their
social class to have a name, "Boston marriage." Katharine and
Alice received two visits a day from Henry, who had always identified with his sister, and Alice adored him as their parents had
done.

Reading the third volume of Leon Edel's distinguished edition
of Henry James's correspondence, which covers the years
1883–95, one can only concur with his family that he was an
angel. He had the same luminous inscrutability, and, despite the
extensive documentation his life and work have received, his
nature remains mysterious.

His understanding of others, however, was perfect, and in particular he understood and sympathized with Alice. The letters of
this period, especially to William and to his friend Grace Norton,
however, have a kind of realistic detachment about her impending
death that characterizes Alice herself. "Alice's condition presents

no essentially new feature—only a pretty steady and I fear pretty painful development of the old. The great circumstance is that, as you probably will already know, she has seen W. W. Baldwin . . . almost the only doctor that she has ever *liked* to see"; Baldwin had pronounced her to have cancer of the breast.

Henry gives William a minute account of her final illness. A few years earlier he had written of the death of their brother Willkie that it was a "liberation—which is a blessing unspeakable." Alice's final moments, he writes, were "the most appealing and pitiful thing I every saw. . . . I rejoice, unspeakably in the rest and liberation that have come to her."

Alice James wanted to die. In her biography, Miss Strouse weaves a complicated tapestry of many threads—education, medicine, the dynamics of the James family, post–Civil War society, Boston. In her long introduction to Alice's letters, Mrs. Yeazell, working with one thread, the theme of death, illumines in detail a preoccupation with death that seems, from a perspective more strictly psychological, to have controlled Alice's life. This difference in biographical perspective, in no way contradicting Miss Strouse's view, further illumines the extent to which Alice's own fascination with death or oblivion was shared by the other Jameses.

During her lifetime she considered suicide, the recourse of at least two of her friends, the Hooper sisters, one the wife of Henry Adams. When Alice knew she was dying of breast cancer, she remarked that it was rather a relief to have at least an actual, identifiable ill, "lifting us out of the formless vague and setting us within the very heart of the sustaining concrete." Mrs. Yeazell points out that Alice's "juxtaposition of a fatal tumor with the language of aspiration and fulfillment is not wholly ironic."

Her brothers seem to have agreed with her. William wrote to her "when that which is *you* passes out of the body, I am sure that there will be an explosion of liberated force and life till then eclipsed and kept down. I can hardly imagine *your* transition without a great oscillation of both 'worlds' as they regain their new equilibrium after the change! . . . It may seem odd for me to talk in this cool way about your end; but, my dear little sister, if one has things present to one's mind . . . why not speak them out." Alice replies that dying is "the most supremely interesting moment in life."

Henry's word for her death—"appealing"—suggests how difficult it is today to understand the particular Jamesian as well as the general Victorian view of death. (This difficulty is strongly felt, for example, by those readers who like me have trouble with *The Wings of the Dove*.) The Jameses were not religious in the usual sense and differed about the afterlife. William was interested in spiritualism, Henry uninterested, and Robertson hopeful: "Of course you and I do not know where she has gone." But all shared with Alice the Victorian view of death as a release, as a positive accomplishment, "supremely interesting."

Her brothers, like her biographer, worried over the significance of her life. "Dear Alice's life didn't seem beautiful, but I doubt not it was interiorly beautiful," her brother Robertson wrote to his wife. Of her diary, published by Katharine Loring after her death, Henry commented that "it also puts before me what I was tremendously conscious of in her lifetime—that . . . her tragic health was in a manner the only solution for her of the practical problem of life." In a manner, perhaps. It is tragic that she did not belong to another age. She would be pleased with this posthumous discovery, no doubt, but it seems, to use a Jamesian word, "unspeakably" sad that her own age did not know her.

# Not Right for Our Rose:
# The Diaries of Rose La Touche

STUDENTS OF THE nineteenth century tell stories of bonfires or of dusty attics, horror stories by which such things as Byron's journal or Turner's erotic drawings are lost forever, or, less often, tales of lucky preservation. *John Ruskin and Rose La Touche: Her Unpublished Diaries of 1861 and 1867* is an attic story and a bonfire story both.

It is a question whether the sexual peculiarity (from the modern point of view) of Victorians or just their enormous literary and epistolary output is more to be blamed for the bonfires conducted by their relations and literary executors, but it is safe to say that where there was a bonfire, anything that seemed sexually odd got burned. Luckily, Victorian heirs sometimes had different ideas from ours about oddness, and things were overlooked, for instance by the Gladstones. The passion of John Ruskin, nearly forty, for Rose La Touche, who was ten when they met, was embarrassing to his executors, who tried to erase her from the record of his life, but a number of traces of her have remained, in the letters and memoirs of their contemporaries, who unlike us had not, as Quentin Bell puts it, the "nasty twentieth-century habit of overturning screens."

To us, Victorian pedophilia remains the least sympathetic of quirks, and we tend most to mind the self-deception with which they adored the beauty and "purity" of little girls (sometimes boys), seeming genuinely unconscious of the prurience so perfectly illustrated in Victorian photographs, by Lewis Carroll and other pedophiles, of nice little girls, brought thither presumably by their mothers, posed in off-shoulder dresses, or showing fat little thighs, pouting seductively.

Conventional explanations, certainly borne out by the facts of Ruskin's or Carroll's life, include fear of adult sexuality, the need to separate "pure" from sexual love by focusing upon such sacred objects as mothers or innocent girls, and, in the case of Ruskin, madness. This battery of excuses is sufficient to enable modern biographers to discuss what his first biographers—who combined a Victorian inclination to protect his good name with a modern uneasiness about the nature of his real feeling for Rosie—do their best to cover up.

Much Ruskin material was destroyed after his death, much more has disappeared, but by good luck these small fragments of Rose's diaries were transcribed. Van Akin Burd's admirable presentation of them combines narrative fascination with a considerable contribution to Ruskin biographical scholarship, and introduces two new characters—first, Rose herself, heretofore so shadowy, seen and not heard. Now she speaks for herself, if not on the subject of Ruskin, at least on subjects that interested her more. Hers is a frail, affecting document in the large literature of miserable Victorian childhood, testifying in particular to the misery of evangelical religion in the lives of sensitive children.

The other interesting character is Helen Gill Viljoen, a leading Ruskin scholar who until her death, in 1974, was at work on what was to have been the major Ruskin biography, of which the prelude only *(Ruskin's Scottish Heritage)* was published. It was Viljoen who discovered and copied the diaries, and left them, with other papers, with the present editor, Van Akin Burd, himself a notable Ruskin editor and scholar. Whether from some testamentary obligation or merely from the gracious good sense that characterizes his entire discussion of Ruskin and La Touche, Professor Burd tells us something of the history of Viljoen's connection with

the Ruskin estate, and of her character and career. The format
of scholarly editions seldom allows for much discussion of the
editorial and historical problems encountered in their production,
let alone the character of the scholar, but since these are germane
to the provenance of the diaries, his narrative seems justified as
well as interesting.

The outlines of the story of Ruskin and Rose La Touche have
long been known. The La Touches were an upper-class Anglo-
Irish family whose father was a convert to evangelical religion and
whose mother was concerned with culture, which led her to the
acquaintance of Ruskin. Ruskin interested himself in Rose's
growth and development for a number of years, proposed marriage
when Rose was eighteen and he was forty-six, and was to receive
her answer ("no") when she was twenty-one. The marriage was
naturally opposed by her parents, who were concerned both by
the difference in age and by Ruskin's marital history.

Ruskin's first marriage, never consummated, was annulled after six years on the grounds of his incurable impotence, a charge
he did not deny at the time. Rose's mother applied for advice to
the first Mrs. Ruskin, now married to the painter Millais. Effie
Millais replied that Ruskin was "quite unnatural," and that he
was probably not free to remarry, an opinion with which Mrs. La
Touche's solicitors agreed. If Ruskin were not impotent, the validity of the annulment might be called into question, and conse-
quently the legitimacy of any subsequent marriages and children.

The anxiety and defensiveness felt by posterity about the sexual
failures of public men are themselves very odd. One thinks of the
furious attacks upon Froude which followed his revelations about
Carlyle. In the case of Ruskin, the annulment of his marriage has
engaged combatants into this century, defenders of Ruskin on the
one hand, concerned to prove that he could have if he'd wanted
to, and the descendants of Effie Millais on the other, concerned
to uphold her actions in leaving Ruskin, suing for a decree of
nullity and, eventually, replying as candidly as she did to the La
Touches, candor which the Ruskinian party has ascribed to mal-

ice and blamed for ruining Ruskin's chance of happiness. (Though it is hard to see what else she could have said.)

In any case, the question of marriage to Rose was then dropped, taken up, dropped again, and so on, during these vicissitudes, Rose herself sickened and died, at the age of twenty-seven, of one of those vague Victorian maladies, a nervous affliction which biographers have loved to hint may have been owing to the strain of it all, but which sounds from her own description organic enough, and terrible. This was not the end of Ruskin's life of affections—he would find another young girl, Kate Olander, to whom he proposed when he was nearly seventy—but it was a sad episode in a life filled with sad episodes.

A clear picture of the La Touches has been missing from Ruskin biography; they have seen sketched in as mysterious and unsympathetic, perhaps only because of their rather unfortunate names, "Rose La Touche" so perfect for a blooming nymphet, and "Mrs. La Touche" so like the villainess of a novel by Henry James. Quentin Bell has summed up the prevailing view of Rose as "sickly, distrustful, irresolute," and "religious to the point of insanity," while Mrs. La Touche has been presented as being in love with Ruskin herself, a nice Jamesian complication.

Ruskin died in 1900. His last home, Brantwood, in the Lake District, continued in the possession of Joan and Arthur Severn, cousins who had looked after him in his last years, but by 1929 they had died, and the house, still stuffed with manuscripts and papers, was unlived in and had fallen into disrepair. Helen Gill Viljoen, a young American scholar, obtained an introduction to a Severn daughter who gave her the run of the place and encouraged her to make copies of material that was soon to be sold, in particular Ruskin's diaries; while occupied at this, Viljoen writes, "tucked away behind a lot of books on a top shelf I unearthed . . . certainly the missing diaries, and a bound volume of family papers . . . letters written by Ruskin to people concerned with Rose La Touche," and, she would say later, "an autobiography of the immeasurably pathetic Rose." These papers had, remarkably, escaped the "holocaust" advised by Ruskin's executors, mainly Charles Eliot Norton of Harvard, who, apprehensive of "vultures" of gossip "hovering over what they have long marked for their prey," were concerned to destroy any trace of Rose, whose memory Ruskin had so elaborately preserved.

What escaped the first bonfires was put up for sale, and what was not sold, in a general auction of Ruskin's effects and manuscripts at Brantwood, was "piled in the garden and burned," including, presumably, Rose's diaries. Van Akin Burd's clear and delicate account of bonfires, cross-purposes, scholarly intrigue, misjudgment, and vanity, and his greatly enlarged and detailed account of the La Touches, are as absorbing as *The Aspern Papers*.

Burd's introduction is 142 pages long, while the diaries occupy only thirty-nine pages. The first excerpt, written when Rose was thirteen, is of the regular thirteen-year-old kind:

> The Louvre I thought most be-e-eautiful. Mr. Ruskin told us to look at the Titians. Well it's no use trying to describe what they were and what I thought of them. I won't attempt it.—I liked the statues just as well as the pictures. I can't say much more than that the Venus Victrie is so perfectly lovely though her arms are broken off.

Her later diary, an attempt at autobiography begun in an introspective mood at the time of her nineteenth birthday, is more remarkable, both for its affecting account of her physical sufferings during an early attack of the illness from which she would die, and for its clear description of the torments of conscience for a literal-minded and strictly brought-up child in an evangelical household:

> People should have been very careful, I think, about saying things were right if they knew what an impression it made upon me. Long before that I remember Mama or a nurse saying that one ought to sit or lie straight and for nights I used to torture myself in bed trying to lie on my back with my legs quite straight.

She also describes her experience of that peculiarly Victorian and, it would seem, unnecessary torment, Doubt. As a child of fourteen she was thrown into a long crisis of panic at overhearing discussions of the Higher Criticism, "more pains taken by them how all might be false, than how the whole thing I lived by might be true," and at night

> I could not say my prayers, for the doubts and arguments I had listened to quietly in the daytime would come thronging into my head till they were but cries of despair. . . . In the morning things began again and even lessons were a relief . . . but when I came to read the Bible (a habit formed from my Father's teaching, as regular as breakfast) all the night doubts arrived. . . . If the manuscripts were false, if they were not what they professed to be, what was the use of Faith—one could not believe a false thing. . . .

Ruskin's own judgment of Rose as a diligent girl of ordinary abilities reminds one of his view of Effie, a view largely accepted by biographers, as trivial and not very bright; neither is given much credit, but it is because Ruskin needs to see them as childlike and simple, and he sees them from his fiercely egocentric point of view. Of Rose he wrote approvingly that in her letters "there is not a sentence in which the child is thinking of herself. She knows exactly what *I* am thinking, and thinks only of that, without a shadow of vanity, or of impulsive egoism." The vanity and egoism of such praise could have been uttered by The Egoist, Willoughby Patterne, himself. Just as the amusing and acute letters of Effie Ruskin from Venice suggest her considerable wit and power, so does the bitter perspicacity of Rose's self-analysis suggest a more interesting mind than it was given to Ruskin to understand.

# More Letters From Ruskin

LIKE MANY GREAT WRITERS, Ruskin was not a great letter-writer, but because, like other Victorians, his correspondence was enormous, the wonder is that he could be interesting at all, let alone so often Ruskinian—admonitory, descriptive, confiding, or playful, in that tone of "avuncular playfulness" that has been described as the besetting fault of his style. This collection (*Reflections of a Friendship*), carefully edited and annotated by Virginia Surtees, consists of letters written by Ruskin to Pauline and Walter Trevelyan between 1848 and 1866 (the year of her death), some letters by Lady Trevelyan to the Ruskins, and some by Effie and John James Ruskin to her.

Several of these are of particular interest, especially those of Effie, who was a wonderful, swift, vivid letter-writer to "Dearest Pauline" during the fateful Scottish painting party which was to deepen her acquaintance with Millais—who was with the Ruskins to paint John's portrait—and strengthen her intention of leaving Ruskin. (Matters not mentioned, however, in the letters. After the separation, Dearest Pauline would drop Effie for the more famous Ruskin.) Lady Trevelyan's letters describing the work of Rossetti and his friends on the Oxford Union are thought to be the only existing description of that project; and in an appendix is Ruskin's letter to Henry Acland explaining his version of his marital trials, a letter that he asks Acland to forward to Sir Walter

Trevelyan ("It would save me the trouble & pain of writing another letter like this . . .").

Of the various moods of his letters, Ruskin is probably best at admonition, as he must himself have realized when he came to adopt an epistolary framework for *Fors Clavigera*. When Lady Trevelyan expresses the common Victorian relish for the Crimean War ("It's such a wonderful thing and will do everybody such a quantity of good and shake up the lazy luxurious youth of England out of conventionalism & affection to manhood and nobleness"), Ruskin rebukes her, saying that it is "intense folly—jobbery—wrongheaded wretchedness of insuperable—impenetrable Donkeyism—Moleism—Gooseism—Slothism—and if there be any animal that has no eyes—nor feet—nor brain—nor ears—that animalism." Most of the communications, however, are milder and more utilitarian than this, directed toward the complicated logistics of social acquaintance—explaining by what conveyance bits of tile or rock will be transported, announcing that a drawing has been finished or sent, accounts of safe arrivals, prospective partings, and, in this case, quite a lot to do with the ordering and receiving of lace caps and collars from Lady Trevelyan, who was the benefactress of a cottage lacemaking industry.

One difficulty for Ruskin biographers is the absence of a collected edition of Ruskin's letters. Published separately in the last two decades alone are Ruskin's letters to Froude, Sydney Carlyle Cockerell, William Ward, Swinburne, Fanny Talbot, Bernard Quaritch, Charles Eliot Norton, Lord and Lady Mount-Temple, the children of Winnington Hall, Mary and Helen Gladstone—to name but a few. Where comparison of them is possible, Ruskin is often revealed to be different things to different people at the same time. Here, for instance, we find him writing sprightly, rather cheerful letters to Pauline Trevelyan, barely mentioning "Rosie," at the same time that he writes distracted, anxious confessions of misery to Lady Mount-Temple about her. A collected letters (though probably too large to be feasible) would illumine the always interesting question of Ruskin's state of mind; but each new evidence of it, like this welcome volume, adds something to our picture of this puzzling man.

Recently a number of helpful general works on Ruskin have appeared, in the spirit of encouraging a wider reading of his work and providing a better understanding of his theoretical and critical positions: among these are books by Robert Hewison, John Unrau, Arnold Whittick, Jay Fellows, and a reissue of Quentin Bell's brief study of Ruskin. Patrick Conner's *Savage Ruskin* is directed particularly at Ruskin as critic, attempting to suggest answers to such questions as "What did Ruskin admire, what did he hate, and why? How did his taste differ from the tastes of fellow-critics? What made his writing so much more persuasive than theirs?" Large questions, of course, and if they are not answered completely, they are addressed. Mr. Conner feels that Ruskin's ultimate social criticism was owing, perhaps, not so much to a sudden blinding light of social sympathy as to his confidence in analysis—"his belief that each society could be analysed into detailed collective character-traits, which by its own momentum led him to explore the fundamentals of his own society." Conner interestingly derives many of the characteristics of Ruskin's analysis from traits manifested in the early *Poetry of Architecture*, and discusses the critical influences on Ruskin's thought. This brief, learned book also includes the general facts of Ruskin's biography, as it relates to his thinking, and is therefore useful as an introductory study.

# *II*

---

# Fictions Stranger
# Than Fiction

# Death for Sale:
# Norman Mailer on Gary Gilmore

LATELY WE HAVE BEEN SEEING more "true life" novels, as Norman Mailer has termed his *(The Executioner's Song)* about Gary Gilmore, the Utah killer who insisted upon being executed. Perhaps it's not so much because truth is stranger than fiction as because our interest in subjectivity has reached a point where no one but old nannies observes a distinction. Or maybe it's just a spinoff from the mini-cassette. All novels are based on life, of course, and if they aren't we don't like them, but some are based on history as well, and then it seems easier for some reason to accept ancient history, and speeches from the mouth of Napoleon, than that of real people who are still alive. Different conventions seem to apply, nagging questions of veracity intrude. However powerful one finds this book, there are reservations one may feel about the genre and about its social implications—if only what to make of the literary ambulance-chasing that the true-life novel encourages.

Perhaps the contradictions embodied in the idea of true-life fiction reflect Mailer's ambivalence about whether to take a journalistic or a novelistic direction with this fascinating material, involving as it does both dramatic elements of love and death and matters of worldly significance. Gilmore's assertion of his right to have the death sentence carried out and the legal bases of efforts to save him; the evident failure of the penal system to do anything for or with him in his nineteen years of prison, or to protect his victims from him either; the role of Mormonism and Utah history in the story—these and many other matters would repay the attention of a journalist of Mailer's penetration and energy. On the other hand, Gilmore's story partakes something (too little, it turns out) of popular literary traditions about tragic lovers and defiant condemned men ("My name is Samuel Hall / And I hate you one and all / Damn your eyes"), cowboys, *On the Road* types, *Tobacco Road* types, which would attract any novelist, especially one with Mailer's romantic turn of mind.

One can hardly bear to think of the real facts of Gary Gilmore's life—such a sad, dismal misery to himself and others, such a waste of a smart and funny and somehow doomed man. His mother, Bessie, looking at him as a little boy, feared he would grow up to be executed—surely not the usual form of maternal premonition. He was put in prison over half his life, beginning in junior high school. To be sure, he had a personality disorder, but also life in prison didn't teach him to live in the real world. Let loose, he tried hard to be a real person, even walked to work in the snow, but his hats were funny, he pilfered in the supermarket, he just couldn't get things together. Could anything have helped Gilmore or saved his victims? Obviously not prison psychiatry, which had turned him into a drug-dependent mess at the time of his last parole. (And the judgment of other doctors later of the sanity of someone so obviously crazy points up yet again, if more examples were needed, how these definitions and these doctors just aren't working out.)

Then there's the bleak and pitiful life of Nicole Baker, Gary's friend. Married first at fourteen, she was nineteen years old when they met, had been divorced twice, had two kids, had been in and out of mental hospitals since the age of thirteen. Since she was five, when she was made to "rub peepees" by "Uncle Lee," poor Nicole had been trying to give everyone everything he wanted—"Nicole was really hung up on the guy even when he began to hint to her that she would be befriending him if she would fuck his friends, you know." She had just passed her time putting out and getting knocked around and doing as she was told.

She would stick out her ankle for a tattoo ("Gary") when told, would try suicide when told, talk to the cops about Gary when they asked—infinitely compliant, she would eventually comply with Lawrence Schiller and Mailer and their tape recorders, whence this book.

Gilmore's history, Nicole's history are horrifying, sad, moving, and skillfully told in part I, book one ("Western Voices") in short, forceful paragraphs with extra spaces between, allowing quick shifts among a welter of interesting characters beginning with Gary's nice cousin Brenda awaiting the new parolee in Provo, Utah, where his people came from. We meet Uncle Vern, Aunt Ida, victims, cousins, cops, cons and guards, and notably the Baker family. Mostly these are trustful, hapless, well-meaning people whom Mailer wisely neither judges nor sympathizes with. He thereby avoids patronizing them on the one hand and on the other avoids associating them too obviously with his own known preoccupations with violence, execution, female masochism, and other tough stuff. Technically he keeps out of the book altogether; there is no evident point of view and no comment, only a matter-of-fact tone perfect for the baroque tale it will unfold, and even enough to conceal that here is, of course, a work of selection and interpretation, which sees Gilmore as something of a hero from a rough hick culture we are meant to think of as somehow the West, or maybe America after Genet.

The book is written in an apparently simple style—pure tape recorder, it seems at first—and given the fact that no one can make up things better than the things people actually say, this mode of quiet attention seems right. But maybe it's all made up and Mailer infinitely artful; the text is mined with Mailerisms when you look closely, as when Brenda sees Gary walk in wearing a big white hat that "wouldn't even have been happy on a black pimp," or when Nicole gets attention from the fellow inmates of her mental institution by saying "humph" "like she was smelling the finest and most peculiar shit," to take at random two figures you doubt often occur to Mormon housewives in Provo, Utah. The language mainly fits, convinces, but the voice of Mailer himself, once heard, lingers with strange insistence over the voices of the others, except perhaps that of Gilmore himself.

Then you begin to hear the great parodist in Mailer straining to get out, especially when he's representing the thoughts of Lawrence Schiller, his colleague and the central consciousness for much of the book. Schiller is given a number of callous, greedy, self-important, and dishonest thoughts and reactions, presented in a mock Hemingwayese perfectly catching his moral pretentiousness and inherently despicable pursuit—"Schiller's reaction to [Gary's] second suicide attempt was that Gary had to be a very impatient man. Didn't want to die because of reincarnation, just out of spite. Had attempted to kill himself to show the world Gary Gilmore was in control. So Schiller lost respect."

Other bits that might seem tongue-in-cheek on their own seem successfully bleak in context. "Debbie didn't know about matters outside the house. She knew a lot about plastic pants and disposable diapers and just about anything to do with children in the day-care center. She was terrific with kids and would rather mop her kitchen floor than read." Nicole "only went with him for a few months before they got married. Two weeks later, she left him. They just couldn't get along. It was depressing. She felt so bad she soon picked up with another fellow she met in church."

Sometimes the style sinks to pure research assistant, and little paragraphs that were meant to resonate with significance simply look embarrassed hanging there in the wide white space, and sometimes one misses the witty, trenchant Mailer of other books, and Mailer the wonderful describer. But there are flashes of this Mailer—"Gary sat there like he was grinding bones in his mind." On the whole the writing is fastidious and, given the lurid material, tasteful. It's just that you keep wondering which are the true parts.

In part I, we are moved and affected as at the beginning of a familiar play, because we know how it will end. Our response is one not of suspense but of pity as the characters, ignorant of their fates, perform their fateful actions. Mailer draws the large cast inexorably along by brilliantly managing the sequence of events.

Gilmore has killed once and is on his way to Ben's motel—how we long for Debbie to send Ben to the store or something, yet she cannot because she did not, and history is history.

It is finally the fact that all this really happened that moves us most. Thinking about Debbie and Ben is like looking at the photograph of the starving child in the CARE poster. Because that is so serious it demands explanation and reflection that are not forthcoming. Not even a writer of Mailer's skill can make us suspend our realization of history, can stop us from remembering the world and not this shadow of it. Since this is so, to make fictions of them exploits and trivializes these people at the same time that it may seek to ennoble or project them; in the service of a private (but popular!) mythology it takes over their words and thoughts while they are still around to speak for themselves, leaves them, as it were, without words, and diminishes their humanity.

Unfortunately, there's a Nicole in everybody's sixth-grade class, lots of Bessie Gilmores with sons in prison. Their lives are too painful to be borne, and the courage with which they bear them is deserving of celebration. And of course accounts of gang-bangs and mothers' tears are more reliably salable than delicate dramas of principle and legal maneuver that accompanied this first execution in the United States in more than a decade. In getting up the sex and violence, Mailer has only had time to sketch some of the most interesting aspects of Gilmore's case. There were questions of whether taxpayers' money could be spent at that time on executions, of whether judicial reviews were adequate, whether the state could abet suicide, and other issues raised by the ACLU and NAACP attorneys for members of Gilmore's family; there was the adversary relation of the Supreme Court and the state of Utah, the Utah Coalition Against the Death Penalty, student and Protestant and Mormon leaders, the eleventh-hour appeal—all these so harrowing even in outline that one would have liked to know more.

Mailer's misunderstanding or underestimation of Mormonism is also disappointing; for instance, he makes a lot of Gilmore's ideas about life after death, without realizing the extent to which these are orthodox Mormon beliefs. On the evidence he has presented, but not, it seems, attended to, the real Provo community is surely odder and more interesting than the macho frontier he has invented. Nicole and Brenda were married at fourteen and sixteen not because they were poverty-culture Lolitas but because of strong Mormon sanctions. Gilmore, the "eternal recidivist," was, after his last parole, in 1976, welcomed home into a coherent and very well-meaning community whose innocent ideas about love curing criminal tendencies seem to be shared by all its members. Cousin Brenda gets Gary sprung, Uncle Vern will keep him in line, all kinds of folks—mostly small businessmen—make sure he has a job and money, and lecture him sententiously but sincerely about hard work and earning your keep. When Gary gets into a fight with Pete, Pete only says, "Gary needs help." Beneath the presentation of dope, sex, and violence one can discern a cohesive if naïve group of people, whose rectitude (Cousin Brenda and others will also aid in Gary's capture) and sweetness make them no match for the ugly media types we meet in part I, book two, "Eastern Voices."

Part I, book one is a horror story where everyone behaves well; now enter hordes of people sensing a buck to be made out of Gilmore's refusal to appeal his death sentence, and big money if he gets executed. Into the lives of the sad, consternated people of Provo come reporters, TV people, film people, media lawyers, contracts, names they've heard of (David Susskind, Louis Nizer), names they haven't ("as you will see, I am Lawrence Schiller from ABC television. This is not the time and place, but when the occasion is right, I would appreciate it if you would open my envelope and read it"). Schiller was Mailer's colleague on *Marilyn*, and a veteran of other stories—Jack Ruby, Marina Oswald, Susan Atkins—and becomes the protagonist of part I, book two.

And once you are in the mind of Schiller, it becomes obvious why Mailer has kept himself out of the narrative. This account of the exploitation of the poor convict and his relatives is so appalling that the author of the end product—the book you are reading— must seem to be innocent of it, must seem not to be writing it at all, let alone making a huge sum out of it. It is the "carrion bird" Schiller who must seem the bad guy, and Mailer does such a job on him that you would suppose they are now estranged, though if Mailer's portrait is anywhere near true, Schiller may be too insensitive morally to recognize how loathsome he's been made to seem. The lies, tricks, and deals are all recounted. The sharpies even con the prison-wise Gilmore, with their sympathetic support for his death wish, and promises that they'll split with his loved ones their profits from his death. "Who's going to play me in the movie?" he wonders, only half ironically.

A few decent Utahans try to control all this—the director of Corrections says, "No movie producer is going to make one dime out of Gilmore. It's not fair"—but the media have smarter lawyers who get injunctions allowing interviews. Schiller even gets some court testimony sealed so that his rivals cannot overhear Gilmore's story. Indeed, if it weren't for Gilmore's evident death wish one might feel that Schiller and his own lawyers were responsible for his death by playing to his infantile us-against-them reactions to authority. " 'You have a right for it to be over,' said Schiller, 'an inalienable right.' " Altogether, the instances of Schiller's cupidity, callousness, and greed are so unbelievable that one asks oneself whether Mailer feels himself to be tarred with the same brush.

Mailer's creation of a character, Gary Gilmore, is splendid, but in the long run it seems not Gilmore and Mailer but Schiller and Mailer who are congruent sensibilities, projecting onto poor, crazy Gary a code of Hollywood heroism Gary couldn't care less about. Schiller is petrified of Gary's rage when he thinks that "*The National Enquirer* had impugned Gilmore's honor in death," and when Gilmore, only worried about getting a phone call through to his girl friend, doesn't react, Schiller wonders "whether he was qualified, at bottom, to know Gary Gilmore."

The doomed-lovers angle is a projection, too. Schiller has worried that Gary might be executed before he has wheedled his whole story out, but when he gets hold of Gary's letters (against Gary's wishes) he "began to feel a little security." Even if Gary got executed next week, "those letters still offered the love story. He not only had the man's reason for dying but Romeo and Juliet, and life after death. It might even be enough for a screenwriter." Hence Mailer's portentousness in book one: Brenda "was in all wrong sorts the rest of the day. Kept thinking of the tattoo on Nicole's ankle. Every time she did, her uneasiness returned," etc. Gary and Nicole were not Romeo and Juliet, of course, just recent acquaintances—Nicole too dim and suggestible, Gary too deranged. It's just wishful thinking from Mailer and Schiller, or mere venality. And to suggest disappointed love as an explanation for a Gary Gilmore is a somewhat irresponsible oversimplification.

Anyhow, Gary is executed. (Schiller attends but refuses to take extra money for an exclusive on it. "I owe that to whatever I am.") Now the book, which has taken from Gilmore a scary vitality which is so often also Mailer's, seems to have a big hole in it. We have liked the revolting Gilmore. Then new horror, as the reader realizes how this book has really come about. With Gary dead, Schiller gets Nicole out of the mental hospital where she and her mother had committed her, and takes them and Nicole's kids to Malibu, buys them a lot of food, lets them rest up a week or so, and then begins interviewing Nicole, for which she'll be paid, but to which, Mailer says, she anyway has a commitment "as deep as the beating of her heart," an opinion somewhat belied by bits of the interviews transcribed here:

> NICOLE: Larry, I'm trying. I can't say it, all right? I'm really
> trying. I can't. Forget it.
> SCHILLER: I'm not going to forget it. I'm not going to forget
> it.
> NICOLE: Okay. Another time.
> SCHILLER: I need to know this time. Not another time.

And so on. Of course Schiller resolutely gets what he wants from this poor dumb girl, just as every other guy always has. "With Nicole he got along. He didn't have to use tricks that often and it moved him profoundly." "Given the intimacy of the experience Nicole Baker was willing to communicate to Schiller, and then to me," Mailer writes, "I had enough narrative wealth from the start to feel encouraged to try for more." All Nicole's, all Gary's sad little secrets—"he had half a hard-on," or about his false teeth. Of course, maybe it was a comfort to her, or to lonely Mrs. Gilmore in her trailer, or to the others, to tell their stories. Gary left his mother two thousand dollars, and as far as one could tell, the Bakers would get twenty-five thousand dollars, out of which they'd have to pay lawyers and other expenses. When last heard of, Nicole was drifting in Oregon. You don't hear whether the widows of Gilmore's victims got anything from anywhere. You're supposed to rise above wondering what Nicole's children will make of this book someday.

Of course it's an extra-literary point, but the folks back home have a saying—"it just doesn't seem right"—to express moral unease in situations where the letter of the law is probably on the side of the "wrong." I think it was when it was announced that Son of Sam would write his memoirs that this collective sentiment surfaced somewhere in the form of a bill to make sure that the profits from crimes go to the victims. Maybe that's going a little too far, but it would be nice to have appendices of disclosure, the kind of accountings that are asked of university stock portfolios to find out whether they do business with South Africa. There isn't really any difference, and people might wish to go without true-life novels the way they went without grapes, if they disapprove of the distribution of the profits.

The author of a true-life novel tries to have it both ways—to improve the dull, invent the spicy parts, leave out the inconvenient things, and not be held accountable for veracity or completeness. Yet he hopes for significance, too. Playing neither by the rules of fiction nor by the rules of fact, he is in danger of sinking into facile sensationalism. The handling of Gilmore's letters is an example here of the inconsistency. Sagaciously edited by a fine writer, they are pretty impressive. Mailer has abridged them "because it seemed fair to show him at his best, not his average." "One wanted to demonstrate the impact of his mind on Nicole, and that was best done by allowing his brain to have its impact on us." Yet Nicole presumably read the letters entire. Mailer finds the real Gary Gilmore a good enough writer only at times, but he gets the advantage of Gilmore's real-life death.

No one has mythologized Son of Sam, so fat and creepy. You wonder whether if Gary Gilmore had looked less like a cowboy, this book would have been written. It does have sweep and charity and power; but in the long run it is a kind of socialist-realist ballet, where the redneck killers are recognizable by their bandannas, the nymphos by the "couple of bruises on those juicy thighs," a cast Mailer has assembled before. He seems to have grafted an Eastern urban dream of the Wild West, complete with sixpacks, CBs, and pickup trucks, onto a conventional paradigm about poverty and child abuse eventuating in anomie and murder. This doesn't seem to be quite the truth of Utah or Nicole or Gilmore—and Mailer has given us so much of a powerful and absorbing story, one can only wish to know how it really was.

# Young Adolf Goes to
# Beryl Bainbridge's England

BERYL BAINBRIDGE'S NOVELS are published in the United States but not much known here, which is something to be regretted. Like a family of gifted eccentrics, they are diverse, yet there are strong similarities, as there always must be in the work of an original and accomplished writer—perhaps it is the essence of accomplishment. In any case, Bainbridge's novels seem unlike those of other people, unless perhaps they resemble, in their economy and formal elegance, the novels of Henry Green. They are her own; the plots, each with its lurking catastrophe, are similar, the characters, each so memorable in his way, are similar, too. Four simple distinctions are preserved: they are divided into males and females, and into a type that is large, fleshy, and pale—those are the people with power and energy—and other, often more sympathetic, people who are small, thin, odd, and astounded, like Binny in *Injury Time* or like young Adolf. As in life, things divide men from women. They do not look at the world the same way. The men are imprisoned in conventions, slaves to little rituals to preserve self-respect or comfort. Their lustful impulses are often checked by bourgeois compunctions. The women, more passive, are oddly freer; social reforms just go on over their heads. They long to pass for normal but never to be normal, for they consider that they are normal. All of Bainbridge's books have a way of being about the assumptions of society about normality and people trying to fit in and have what they want, too.

For an American reader discovering Beryl Bainbridge, only one complaint mars universal admiration: the complaint concerns the passivity of the characters toward their environment and their fate. Masters of expedience, resilient despite their resignation, practiced at making do, at sly deceptions on the givens of their situations, they are capable of *tour de force* contrivance for the sake of comfort, respectability, or survival. In *The Bottle Factory Outing*, middle-class Brenda, finding she must sleep in a double bed with big, naked, energetic Freda, fashions a bolster and a row of books between them. Unwilling to lend it, Binny throws the vacuum cleaner out of the window. Perhaps Americans are surprised that the characters do not exert themselves more mightily than this against outrages of poverty and inconvenience; although exigency is certainly a fact of American life, it has little place in American fiction. We can represent ethnic, but not class, differences, because we have pretended class differences don't exist. Except for some Depression literature about cutting out shoe soles from cereal boxes, our stories are all about escape and change. In an American story, if you start out poor, you are bound to end up rich and/or disillusioned.

Bainbridge's creatures are not disenchanted. Their illusions are so trivial that circumstances do not conspire to remove them. On the big subjects—who they are and what will happen to them— they have no illusions at all. They never escape. "I knew it would be me," says Binny as the desperadoes carry her off. Bainbridge is wonderful on sex; for each character she seems to have located the exact conjunction of desire and social prudence that controls his sexual behavior. She knows the point at which people will say, "To hell with it," in any crisis. Her characters don't have illusions, they have bruises—always bruises of the spirit, often literal bruises, and sometimes lacerations. In *Young Adolf*, the brother Alois bruises his wife, Bridget, because she is slow, doesn't notice things. Not catching on is how you get bruised. Freda's bruised corpse is packed off in a keg. Adolf combs his hair over one eye to hide a cut.

Novelists, like after-dinner speakers, are often haunted by a sense that they are repeating themselves, that they have failed to put in a new disguise the same small incidents, the plaintive, insistent figure that recurs in their imaginations. Have I told that one before? *Young Adolf* gathers up with astonishing success some of these figures from Bainbridge's other books. An attentive reader might have seen him coming, might have glimpsed his face elsewhere, sensed his attraction for the novelist who had yet to unravel his place in her imaginary scheme. The girl Rita in *The Dressmaker* might speak for Bainbridge herself as she "stood in the doorway of the philately shop, sheltered from the rain, absorbed in a page of German stamps imprinted with Hitler's head. But for him, she thought, she would never have met Ira, never been happy. Uncle Jack said he was a maniac, a monster of the world. She thought he looked rather neat and gentlemanly with his smart black tie and his hair slicked down over one eye." In *A Quiet Life*, the girl Madge says she was chased by a German prisoner: "He looked like Adolf Hitler. . . . He had a little moustache. . . . He chased me . . . he didn't catch me."

In this new book, set in 1912, young Adolf, aged twenty-three, comes to Liverpool to visit his half-brother Alois, and Alois's Irish wife, Bridget. Alois works as a waiter and razor-blade salesman. They live in the house of Mr. Meyer, who works as a violinist at the hotel. They are all poor. Adolf is an inconvenience for the others: he is difficult, depressed, lies days at a time on a sofa, is reluctant to work, has not found himself. Things happen. Little by little, young Adolf acquires, if not the attitudes, at least the style that will later characterize him; he is given a brown shirt to wear, plans to grow a mustache, combs his hair over his eye. When a woman tells his fortune, and he draws a card that stands for Alexander the Great, he as well as everyone else imagines the fortuneteller is making fun of him. He steals a library book. He tells lies. Don't get him started on the subject of racial purity. Yet there is something likable about his continued hope for his own small life in the face of a world that despises him, there is something dignified in his self-regard, something commonplace enough in his powerlessness and capacity for self-deception.

In England, catastrophe attends him; he is confused, wretched, isolated, absurd. In the end they buy his return ticket. Alois suggests he go to Linz, Mr. Meyer suggests Munich because "he had some contacts in the city that could prove useful to Adolf—certain political organizations, certain persons of note and influence." Adolf goes away resolving that never "under torture or interrogation" will he mention that he has been "to this accursed city, visited this lunatic island."

"It is a pity he will never amount to anything," Meyer remarks as they put Adolf on the train. The irony here is obvious, as obvious as in Adolf's last words to them: "You will get what is coming to you," or "get what is owed you"—they cannot agree on the meaning. Mr. Meyer is right about the character in the book, and right in moral terms: it is history that provides the irony, on account of events beyond, after, outside the work of fiction.

History is a queer disrupter of fiction. People always seem to enjoy a dash of verisimilitude, the real name of a real newspaper or town, or a reference to a street they know. But the introduction and distortion of true events are often greeted with wild, rather mysterious approval: for instance, that which has greeted (in America, at least) the novels of Doctorow, with their "real" characters, Houdini, Julius and Ethel Rosenberg, and so on. Perhaps historical characters are preferred to real ones because they make the reader himself feel less frivolous. Soon you will read the seven volumes of the history of World War II; meantime, here's this interesting book about Hitler's early life. I wonder how much of it, the reader asks himself, is true.

But you could argue that fictions fitted into gaps between historical events take a larger liberty with truth than fictions made up only from the sense of reality (no real names), or than does a certain kind of historical novel, set very far in the past, with people wearing low-cut dresses performing acts known to have occurred. These last are often disapproved of unless the author has got the background up to a satisfactory scholarly level and uses it to present an intriguing interpretation of history, as Graves does or Josephine Tey in her famous book about how Richard III was not so bad. But *Young Adolf* is not a historical novel in this usual sense—that is, a dramatization of known events—it is an invention of another kind, a feat of imagination and craft, without definition.

Whatever the real facts of Hitler's life, we believe this account in part because of its manner, detailed and confident, and because it does not insist too stridently in foreshadowing the later reality. Adolf, depressed, hungry, pitiful, driven to expedients, is much like a character in a book by Beryl Bainbridge. That the shirt, the mustache, the uniform, the hairstyle he will later wear, are all acquired during his five-month stay in Liverpool says something, doubtless, about the large consequences of small accidents; and that is characteristic Bainbridge, too. But mostly, when we get a glimpse of the future, the moment veers off into comedy, as when Adolf delivers an excited monologue on a youthful epiphany:

> "That night I struggled free from the dusty membrane of both grub and caterpillar and emerged finally, an airborne creature soaring on iridescent wings above the earth."
>
> For several seconds Adolf remained standing, arm raised in that salute to the heavens. Then abruptly he sat down. Misjudging the position of his chair he fell to the floor and disappeared under the table.

The novel's time unfolds so absorbingly, and with such authority, that we lose our power to hold the future in mind. This is the method of all of Bainbridge's novels, each moment rendered vividly in the mind of one character or another, presented to the reader through his thoughts or his vision. Adolf, watching his brother, "found it difficult to keep a straight face at the sight of his stout brother comparatively naked, garbed in a frayed nightshirt, his plump neck still bearing the imprint of his collar stud as he lolled feverishly among the rumpled pillows, or, desperate for a smoke, scrabbled in the wardrobe for the butt of a forgotten cigar, coughing as he bent over his pot belly, his shirt rising up above his muscular milk white legs."

We are given Adolf's view of Alois here. But often the interpretive consciousness, in this and in others of Bainbridge's novels, misinterprets, misunderstands what it sees, or sees too little. Human limitation is the basic assumption of this novelistic method. Because all consciousness is limited, a number of minds are needed from whom only the reader gathers all. It is because the characters never grasp the entire picture that the gothic and grotesque touches in the earlier books, and the historical game here, have, nonetheless, such an authoritative manner of truth. No moment of realization contradicts the sheer muddle. Each thought seems reasonable, in its context, to its owner. "It sounds reasonable," thinks Brenda, hearing Rossi describe the murder of Freda in *The Bottle Factory Outing*.

A mosaic of personal interpretation reveals the disadvantage humans live under. It also makes Bainbridge's novels very funny. And her way of shifting from mind to mind enables her to escape what would otherwise be the great danger of her method, the danger of slipping into caricature or ridicule. No matter how ridiculous or stereotyped—an old maid, a gesticulating Italian—the immediacy and clarity of each person's perceptions remind us that he is unique, not to be sneezed at, things have happened to him. " 'I was good with the needle', recollected Mary O'Leary. . . . 'You told me', said Bridget; and she tried not to look at the destroyed ribbons swinging from the remains of Mary O'Leary's bonnet." When the characters seem comic to the reader, it is because they seem comic to one another, not to the author, who is virtually invisible in all her work, except for the occasional stage direction. By being only partly perceived, the horror that underlies and threatens in all her narratives seems mere daily horror. The characters have no overview. Marge in *The Dressmaker* giggles at the trouble they have putting the murdered Ira into a bag.

The eventual horror in *Young Adolf* when it is understood cannot be dismissed or forgiven; but none of the characters can foresee it, and we, confined to their minds, can almost forget it. If we refer in our minds to events outside the novel, we perceive Bainbridge's suggestion, no doubt not entirely mischievous, that when the real horror comes, it will have had its origin in the England of 1912. Authorities come in the night to take away some children from poor people living in squalor:

> In every doorway along the length of the street stood men and women, perfectly silent watching the children go. "I don't understand," said Adolf, "there were hundreds of you and not a dozen of them. They didn't even use the police."
>
> "Let the minority act with enough authority," cried Meyer bitterly, "and the majority will walk like lambs to the slaughter."

It is a lesson young Adolf will remember.

Bainbridge is never doctrinaire, seldom so explicit; yet political implications develop logically from her recurring interest in the relation of ordinary people to authority. The characters in her novels are always testing it out. They are usually victims, even if only of the tyranny of social convention, or the tyrannical fear of not being respectable, or the tyranny of near relations over one another, like that of the Dressmaker over her family; and she is fascinated by the complicity of authority and its victims, by the way the victims cooperate, as when Binny, being raped by the intruder, asks whether he doesn't want to touch her breasts.

Bainbridge seems fascinated, also, with the conspiracies among powerless people to defeat authority: that of the Italians at the bottle factory, or, in this novel, when they conspire to save the children or to get Adolf a job. Alois gets him an interview, and, because he has no shirt, they make him look respectable, with "a tray cloth embroidered at the edges with bunches of cherries, which in some fashion he had stuffed into the revers of his black coat." Thus pitiably got up, wet with rain, Adolf waits outside the hotel. "Several times he started to climb the steps towards the Commissionaire who guarded the entrance to the building, and on each occasion he lost courage halfway up and turned back. He couldn't risk a rebuff." Thus we are made to sympathize and pity the monster of the world. It is a complicated exercise in social sympathy that Bainbridge demands of us, and the book is her most ambitious treatment yet of the serious concern and conviction that underlie her comedy.

# Terrorists as Moralists:
# Don DeLillo

WITH EACH DAY'S new terrorist event—in Entebbe or Wall Street or midtown Manhattan—it becomes more natural that terrorists start showing up as prototypical figures in novels; but in novels they do have their uses. They replace the car crash as a means of violent and sudden death, replace psychiatrists and holy men as spokesmen of authority. Like the fools in Shakespeare they are satirical; like clowns, with their air of comic befuddlement, they call attention to the significance of things whose significance we had missed. Until their comeback, some of their powers—for instance, the power to effect retributive justice—had been lost to authors. Perhaps they are the only moral agents anyone can believe in now.

Still, nobody thanks a moralist, as Don DeLillo must know. His brilliant earlier books have been much praised but not so much read, perhaps because they deal with deeply shocking things about America that people would rather not face. *End Zone* (1972) connects football and nuclear warfare; *Ratner's Star* (1976) plays with science and science fiction; and *Great Jones Street* (1973) looks at rock music, nihilism, and urban decay.

In *Players*, his fifth novel, DeLillo wittily deploys terrorists to explore all the secret places in contemporary sensibility. In the prologue, passengers standing in the piano bar of an airplane in flight are watching a film of hippie marauders shooting and hacking to death a band of golfers. The tranquility of a Sunday morning is outraged, the innocent pastels of the golfing costumes are soaked with blood. Without earphones, the passengers cannot hear the soundtrack, so the pianist improvises silent-movie music to go along with the action—sounds of chase, of thrill, of Buster Keaton, incongruously funny for the elaborate physical clumsiness of the screen deaths—bodies plopping, rolling, splashing. The passengers laugh, cheer, clap. It is the terrorists whom they applaud. "To the glamour of revolutionary violence," remarks the author, "to the secret longing it evokes in the most docile soul, the piano's shiny tinkle brings an irony too apt to be ignored." This elegant, highly finished novel does not shrink from suggesting the complicity of Americans with the terrorists they deplore.

Though they give themselves timely airs, novels have never been very good at looking at what's going on in the world; the workbags of novelists are weighted with tricks for avoiding it. The Victorians usually set their novels back a few decades; modern writers adapt the strategies of the Romantic poets and set theirs in faraway or unusual places (banana republics, prisons) or in the flat landscape of timelessness or myth. Recently, people seem to look around for a small town where the people, ostensibly alive today, are not like the people of today but sit in a scene of pumps and privies talking of old times in the style of John Gardner.

This nostalgia, one of DeLillo's many targets, is an implicit comment on the present, but the present gets lost in a welter of antimacassars. A sense of the present also gets lost in novels in the fashionable confessional mode, which, by funneling life through the mesh of private sensibility, do succeed in reducing it to manageable literary proportions but sacrifice any authentic social vision to idiosyncrasy and richness of characterization. (Certain confessional novels, like Joseph Heller's *Something Happened*, manage both richness and relevance.) Not that novels are obliged to look grandly at the whole state of things, but it is significant how few try. It is a measure of DeLillo's bravura that he tries, and a measure of his art that, for all his deceptive simplicity, even plainness, he succeeds.

*Players* is about two Everymen, Pammy and Lyle Wynant, a fun New York professional couple. Since Freud, we've been used to the way novelists normally present a character: looks normal, is secretly strange and individual. In the first of the many inversions of appearance and reality that structure the book, Pammy and Lyle look interesting and seem to do interesting things, but do not interest themselves. The richness is only superficial. Put another way, the novel is not a romantic one about how they don't get along in society, but about how they are *of* society and their normality is what we hate to recognize. The tone is comic, the style is *Candid Camera*. Their smallest gestures are closely observed: "Lyle checked his pockets for change, keys, wallet, cigarettes, pen and memo pad. He did this six or seven times a day, absently, his hand barely skimming over trousers and jacket." We hear not their impassioned but their odd bits of conversation, the ones they actually transact life with: "Goody, cheddar." "What's these?" "Brandy snaps." "Triffic." "Look out." "No you push me, you." Their voices are just distinguishable: Lyle is elaborate, ironic; Pammy credulous.

He works on the floor of the Stock Exchange. She works in the World Trade Center, for a Grief Management firm. They're cool. At home in their apartment they watch television a lot; they don't go out much because "there's nothing out there." Pammy goes off to Maine on a holiday with Jack and Ethan, a pair of homosexual men they know, and Lyle drifts into a terrorist group that is planning to bomb Wall Street. He also covers his bets by informing for the other side—whatever that is—to which, of course, several of the terrorists themselves belong. It doesn't matter to Lyle. Pammy mostly believes the things she's heard, like "follow your instincts, be yourself, act out your fantasies." In Maine she has sex with one of the friends, Jack, who later, for more complicated reasons, pours gasoline over himself and lights it. She comes home.

We know very little about them. DeLillo abandons the ordinary assumption of fiction that action is caused by character and character by experience, some of which, at least, it's the author's duty to suggest. Pammy and Lyle have no history; they are without pasts, were never children, come from nowhere. They worry that they have become too complex to experience things directly and acutely, but the opposite is true. They are being reduced by contemporary reality to numb simplicity, lassitude: "Pornography bored her. Talk of violence made her sigh. Things in the street, just things she saw and heard day to day, forced her into subtle evasions. Her body would automatically relax." You experience the existence of Pammy and Lyle as though they were the subjects of a photo-realist painting, without curiosity or quarrel, the way the world of others is always experienced by the self. Pammy and Lyle: What made them like this? They *are* like this. Society disrupts the cherished relation of cause and effect dominated in fiction by the family; DeLillo suggests that the *Zeitgeist* may count for more than mother love.

Lyle, the urban man, gets involved with terrorists who claim, as terrorists usually do, that they're out to rid society of repressive elements, though it may seem that it is they who are repressive, seeking to substitute one kind of freedom with some order of their own. What's clear in DeLillo's view is that repression is what people (Lyle and Pammy) seek. It's not that the structures of existing society are not repressive, but that these structures are not felt. Society is perceived as a void, an unmanageable chaos in which people must make their own order. Lyle brings home sheets of numbers, because he finds them soothing. Their friend Ethan also likes "filling these little boxes with numbers. Numbers are indispensable to my world view at present. I don't believe I'm doing this. This is some toad's chore. But I genuinely enjoy it. It's so anally satisfying." Pammy likes the predictable and soothing rhythms of her tap-dancing class. The first terrorist, correctly estimating modern proto-fascist yearnings, shows Lyle his guns, his Pento-Mex and ammonium nitrate explosives. "I have this fool notion that once you see this stuff, you're in for good," he says. Weapons compel order.

DeLillo's terrorists want to blow up the Stock Exchange, the way Conrad's in *The Secret Agent* wanted to blow up the prime meridian, ostensibly to cause confusion by destroying these most sacred vestiges of order, but actually and above all as a way of making contact with any structure that remains. Even with the government. Half mockingly Lyle talks about the glamour of the revolutionary life; it is belonging that appeals. He can imagine "Calling some government bureau, some official department, right, of the government. 'I have information about so-and-so.' Or, even better, to be visited, to have them come to you . . . The appeal of mazes and intricate techniques. The suggestion of a double life. 'Fantastic, sign me up, I'll do it.' 'Of course, sir, you won't be able to tell anyone about this, including your nearest and dearest.' 'I love it, I love it, I'll sign.' "

When everyone turns out to be a double agent, it's in a way twice as good. Each side resembles the other in its assumptions, in its respect for Jesuitical reasoning and certain rules. It's a relief to become a player, in any game; for there, where chance operates only within calculable limits, you can grasp the pattern. Terrorist action is not so much an example of lawlessness as a comment on the rules, an aspect of the structure itself.

If urban Lyle has abandoned hope of value, Pammy's bucolic attempt to recover it is DeLillo's pot shot at nostalgia. Pammy and her friends yearn for the primitive life, Maine: "It's simple, maybe, Ethan, but it has a strength to it. You feel it's the sort of core, the moral core." Yet they hate Maine when they get there. Animals live under the house, birds fly into the glass windows and are killed. "I didn't know it would be like this," Jack complains. "I thought swimming at least. Do you believe this water?" Yet their failure is enough to help Jack toward his suicide. His end, faceless, fingerprintless, unidentifiable, implies the fate of individuals in the computerized void.

Few recent novels have found so admirably congruent a form for their subject. The tight, carefully balanced structure, recapitulating the book's idea of people's appetite for boundaries, might have seemed too rigid to contain the unruly, even violent, strangely comic events. Instead, it suggests the ruthless tendency of people to establish order over chaos. Even the trendy touches of such fashionable French thinkers as Jacques Derrida, Roland Barthes, Georges Poulet ("This is a lesson in the intimacy of distance. Space in this context seems less an intuitive experience than a series of relative densities") are not digressive but pertinent; philosophy is one kind of order. DeLillo's attention to detail is masterful. He suggests that though freedom is what people ostensibly want, too naïve a definition of it brings a reaction as frightening as chaos. This is not a fashionable idea, but DeLillo convinces you that it is true. The discoveries of artists do not always—perhaps seldom—corroborate political fashions. But the wit, elegance, and economy of Don DeLillo's art are equal to the bitter clarity of his perceptions.

# How Blacks Should Behave: Toni Morrison, Gayl Jones, and James Alan McPherson

*Natives of poverty, children of*
   *malheur*
*The gaiety of language is our*
   *seigneur*

WALLACE STEVENS'S WORDS might be the epigraph for the work of both Gayl Jones and Toni Morrison, writers very different from each other, whose wonderful richness and vitality of language in a curious way obscure the moral and physical horror of the similar worlds they create or, perhaps, describe. Milkman Dead, the hero of Morrison's novel *Song of Solomon*, has a girl friend who is trying to kill him. He tells a friend, whose only response is to say:

"Would you ask your visitor to kind of neaten things up a little before she goes? I don't want to come back and have to look through a pile of cigarette butts for your head. Be nice if it was laying somewhere I could spot it right off. And if it's her head that's left behind, well, there's some towels in the closet on the shelf in the back."

The flippant tone conceals assumptions common to both speakers, that it is usual for a disappointed woman to come after you with a knife; that you may have to kill her before she kills you. And later the friend will try to kill Milkman.

This novel, and to an even greater extent Morrison's earlier novels *The Bluest Eye* and *Sula*, and the stories in Gayl Jones's collection *White Rat*, like her earlier novels *Corregidora* and *Eva's Man*, entirely concern black people who violate, victimize, and kill one another. Little girls are raped by their fathers, by the boyfriends of their mothers, by neighbor boys. Little boys are drowned by neighbor girls. Women are beaten, mothers burn their sons to death, daughters abandon their mothers. No relationships endure, and all are founded on exploitation. The victimization of blacks by whites is implicit but not the subject. The picture given by both Jones and Morrison of the plight of the decent, aspiring individual in the black family and community is more painful than the gloomiest impressions encouraged by either stereotype or sociology.

It is interesting to notice that despite the chorus of rightly admiring remarks about the power and talent of both writers, little attention has been paid to what they actually seem to be saying, as if the mere execution of work as poetic and vigorous as this— by women, and black women at that—were sufficiently remarkable without the complicating features of meaning or moral commitment. Admittedly fiction is not so well suited to the representation of happiness and goodness as of pain and evil, but perhaps it's more that no one wishes to believe in the unhappy lives they describe. Or it could be because both Morrison and Jones have chosen narrative modes that allow them to keep themselves and the reader at a distance from the content; but mostly it seems that meaning may have been overlooked out of embarrassment, because they write about things whites are afraid other whites may believe blacks do.

Ethnic and social groups, today wishing to assert and even to dramatize their distinctiveness, deny the well-meant assumption, formerly common, that people of different races and creeds are fundamentally the same. They insist upon difference, and although these books are clearly aimed at a general audience with the expectation of being understood, the white reader may experience a few self-doubts. Can a non-black reader understand them? Are blacks really like this? Are these works artistically but not literally true? or merely romantic or sensational? Or—another worry—is one's accepting (or critical) attitude about their content mostly a projection of white racist attitudes?

It's almost impossible to raise questions about black culture without the accompanying lecture about how it got that way, as if explanation were the same as excuse or prediction; but for Jones, Morrison, and James Alan McPherson, history, though immanent, does not seem to be the point. Their attitude seems to be that historical guilt, if indeed people ever feel it, is finally irrelevant, and if it affords history's victims a little amnesty, that amnesty is woefully finite. We are all, including whites, in a world we did not make (to paraphrase Sartre), and the future is the only thing we can affect. If the secret attitude of Anglo-Saxons is that people of other races, charming or menacing primitives, cannot be expected to behave morally, neither Jones, Morrison, nor McPherson takes such a patronizing view. "I can't see how it helps. I can't see how it helps anybody," says Milkman of his friend's revenge cult. Whether the non-black reader confronts or ignores the question raised by these books, the question is whether black people *ought* to be the way Jones and Morrison say they are.

How blacks *ought* to be is not a popular question and it is not one many black writers have asked. Of the many distinguished books by blacks with which most readers will be familiar—by Ralph Ellison, Richard Wright, Eldridge Cleaver (who has in fact been asking the question lately), Malcolm X, James Baldwin, and others, works of fiction or non-fiction, poetic or political—most have been written by men, and men on their way to live in Paris at that, or at least Algeria. Men children in the promised lands, they write about the problems encountered by blacks, usually black males, trying to make it in a white society; that is, they present a criticism not so much of black but of white culture, and that's what gets known as the "black experience." Undoubtedly, white society is the ultimate oppressor, and not just of blacks, but, as Morrison and Jones show, the black person must first deal with the oppressor in the next room, or in the same bed, or no farther away than across the street.

Black male authors who have seldom failed to mention the rape of black women by cruel white masters have not dwelt on the present situation in which the most frequent victims of rape, according to statistics, are young black girls by black men. (And the most frequent cause of death among young black men is homicide.) In a demoralized subculture, everyone is a victim, but women, and especially girls, are actually the most defenseless. In these books, Morrison and Jones present them also as cleverer, more interesting, and eventually more homicidal than men; men are childlike, barely sentient, and predatory. Nearly all the women characters in these works have been sexually abused and exploited, usually as children, a pattern described in Jones's fine story "The Women"; in her novel *Eva's Man*, where a woman is finally driven mad by the indignities she has suffered and murders her lover; and in Morrison's novel *The Bluest Eye*, about the madness of a child who is raped by her father. Defeated and hopeless, men turn first on women. It is little wonder that women's accounts of the black person's struggle should differ from male accounts.

*Song of Solomon* is a picaresque and allegorical saga of a middle-class Northern black family, the Deads, in particular of the son, Milkman Dead, but also of parents, sisters, aunts, cousins, and, when Milkman eventually travels south in search of treasure and family history, of numerous distant connections. The resemblance to *Roots* is perhaps the least satisfying thing about the book; the characters are apt at any moment to burst into arias of familial lore less interesting than their immediate predicaments. There are the sexual problems of Milkman's parents, who required a love potion to conceive him, as if they literally exchanged their sexuality for their bourgeois aspirations. His old-maid sister

Corinthians has a love affair with an old man she meets on a bus; the jealous cousin Hagar attempts murder. A hundred-year-old woman who lives in accumulating filth acts out her long-suppressed hatred for her dead white mistress. Aunt Pilate, six feet tall, with no navel, carries the bones of her father in a sack. There's a hunt for gold in a cave, a murderous band of black terrorists who ritually murder whites, a young girl who dies of either love or a chill, and much more.

Here, as in Morrison's earlier and perhaps more affecting work, human relationships are symbolized by highly dramatic events. In *Sula* a mother pours gasoline over her son and lights it, and, in another place, a young woman watches with interest while her mother burns. But the horrors, rather as in Dickens, are nearly deprived of their grisliness by the tone. It might be a folk tale in which someone cuts someone else's heart out and buries it under a tree, from which a thorn bush springs, and so on. Morrison is interested in black folklore, but in fact the influences of the Bible, Greek myths, and English and American literature are more evident, as in the work of other American writers.

There is a sense in which the use of myth is evasive. Morrison's effect is that of a folk tale in which conventional narrative qualities like unity and suspense are sacrificed to the cumulative effects of individual highly romantic or mythic episodes, whose individual implausibility, by forcing the reader to abandon the criteria of plausibility, ceases to matter. In this way, the writer can imply that hers are not descriptions of reality but only symbols of a psychological condition. Yet if her tales are merely symbolic, the reader can complain of their sensationalism. If they are true, her view of a culture in which its members, for whatever reasons, cannot depend for safety and solace on even the simplest form of social cooperation is almost too harrowing to imagine.

In the work of Gayl Jones one sees other literary influences—of Hemingway, perhaps, or Jean Rhys, highly wrought and economical—but also of those bus-station thrillers in which a female narrator describes her loss of innocence, her sexual exploitation by a relentless string of single-minded lechers. The ancestress of Ursa Corregidora, the abused heroine of Jones's first novel, is the lusty, busty high-yellow beauty so beloved on paperback covers. The difference is that Jones's women, brutalized and dull, seem all too real. It is a skillful exploitation of the stereotype.

The stories in her collection *White Rat* were written in some cases earlier than her novels, so they confirm one's sense of her direction and preoccupations: sex is violation, and violation is the principal dynamic of human relationships. In the sexual relation lie the struggle for power, the means of survival, the symbol of adulthood, the cause of suffering. Where Morrison is an art novelist, who can invoke black speech for striking effect, Jones is a vernacular novelist with a marvelous ear, for whom black speech is the only medium. A boy says to the narrator of "The Women,"

"You got a nice house," . . .
"If you don't got to live in it."
"Your mama keep things around."
"What-nots."
"Yeah, my mama got those around too. She paint pictures and put them up on the wall. Daddy tell her take 'em down. She say she don't like look at the bare wall."
"Aw."

The monosyllables with which the characters conduct their lives suggest their defended isolation. It is as if there were only so much information to go around, and each person, jealous of the advantage it confers, is reluctant to share his. The jazzy banter that Morrison and McPherson both portray so well has the same back-to-the-wall quality. Though ignorance these days has lost much of its traditional status as a routinely stigmatized enemy of human happiness—indeed, it is often admired—the plight of these characters renews one's sense of its virulence.

The women characters in Morrison are all eccentric, brave, and resolute. Gayl Jones presents women who are stunned and withdrawn. But both writers arrange their narratives in such a way as to avoid preachiness and, perhaps, to avert accusations of disloyalty. Morrison often lets a character have a say, like Lena, in *Song of Solomon*, who asks her brother, "Where do you get the *right* to decide our lives? . . . I'll tell you where. From that hog's gut that hangs down between your legs. Well, let me tell you something, baby brother, you will need more than that."

Moral comment in Jones is more oblique. Ursa Corregidora, asleep, dreams resentfully of her possessive lover, "talking about *his* pussy. Asking me to let him see his pussy. Let me feel my pussy. The center of a woman's being. Is it?" When she wakes up she denies her resentment. "The shit you can dream." (His beatings have required her to lose her womb.) Because she writes entirely in the first person, Jones seems to record what people say and think as if it were no fault of hers, and Morrison seems to assert no more control over the exotic events of her narratives than the teller of a tall tale does. Perhaps art is always subversive in this way.

If there is always disparity between male and female versions of a culture, it is certain that the Authorized version will always be male and, hence, familiar. In the stories of James Alan McPherson (*Elbow Room*) the ordinary white reader will at first feel at home. There are some men's-magazine tall tales about romantic barroom types—the "bullshitters and goodtimers," like Billy Renfro, the one-eyed car-payment collector—which could have been written by any American with an ear for dialect and a satirical gift:

> At the murder trial, the defendant, Robert L. Charles, after having sat four days in silence while his court-appointed lawyer pleaded for him, rose suddenly from his chair during his counsel's summation and faced the jurors. "It wasn't no accident," he told them in a calm voice. "I had me nine bullets and a no-good gun. Gentlemens, the *onliest* thing I regret is the gun broke before I could pump more than six slugs into the sonofobitch."

But McPherson writes about real people, too, mainly middle-class people with middle-class reactions, making one wonder whether the savagely angry women, the failed women sliding off into madness (in Morrison and Jones, as in so many stories by other women writers), are, like Robert L. Charles, Billy Renfro, or Dead-Eye Dick, romantic exaggerations. Where is the real view? Or are there disparate views, all true, irreconcilable?

McPherson's stories, absorbing and sensitive, seem at first glance colorless. The narrator of many is intelligent, analytical, and uncomfortably out of place in the settings of his stories. He thinks himself too good for the "street niggers." ("Black guys like you with them funny eye-glasses are a real trip. You got to know everything. You sit in corners and watch people," someone tells him.) But he also despises Paul, the white husband of a black friend of his, because he can't quite be a "nigger." He despises Professional Blacks, too, describing the current scene as one where "even the great myths floated apart from their rituals. Cynical salesmen hawked them as folklore. And language, mother language, was being whored by her best sons [n.b.] to suit the appetites of wealthy patrons. . . . Black folk were back into entertaining with the time-tested acts."

Fastidious, leary of climbing on the soul train, McPherson makes explicit his sense of his artistic problem:

> *You are saying you want to be white?*
> A narrator needs as much access to the world as the advocates of that mythology.
> *You are ashamed then of being black?*
> Only of not being nimble enough to dodge other people's straitjackets.
> *Are you not too much obsessed here with integration?*

Maybe he is, maybe he isn't. A white reader, at first sympathizing with his stiff discomfort, and perhaps disappointed at his straight prose, may wish he would hop on the soul train and have a little fun. But perhaps that would be bad advice. Perhaps what is exciting about the violence and depravity in Jones and Morrison is that they confirm white fears, the way the violence and depravity in *Looking for Mr. Goodbar*, say, confirmed cheap, antifeminist prejudice. It's easy to say, comfortably or dismissively, while enjoying the rich, wild speech in Jones and Morrison: That's how those people are. But maybe the plain, anxious people in McPherson's stories, mapping out their future lives in "blocks of years, stepladders of subgoals," are what more people are really like. Morrison and Jones are more convincing.

# The Obligation of Ethical Judgment:
# Doris Lessing

IT HAS BEEN more than fifteen years since the first exultant admirers of *The Golden Notebook* began to urge it on their friends, make of it a cult classic, claim Doris Lessing as the leading feminist writer of our time, and, with all this, qualify her real stature. When a novelist seems to speak loudly or newly or with special clarity on important subjects, few people hear the low notes. Many—very many men, it is to be feared—imagining her to be that nonexistent entity, a "woman's novelist," did not read her and have never read her. Others were put off by her books about Marxism or mental illness, those two most potentially boring of subjects. And the excitement and relief that women felt at being written about so understandingly kept them from noticing that she also understands men, politics, social class, striving, religion, loneliness, and lust.

It is not Mrs. Lessing's fault that, among the many secrets she knows, her knowledge of women's anger and aggression, even more than of their sexuality, took people by surprise and categorized her. That is the fault of our times and of history. But this new collection of all her short fiction (except her African stories) should repair any misunderstanding of her timelessness, the breadth of her sympathy and range of her interests, and, above all, the pleasures of reading her. Rereading these stories is like returning to a Victorian novel one loves, and affords the same delightful feeling of self-indulgence combined with self-improvement.

Mrs. Lessing is the great realist writer of our time, in the tradition of the major Continental novelists of the nineteenth century, particularly Stendhal and Balzac, but also Turgenev and Chekhov—a masculine tradition with which she shares large moral concerns, an earnest and affirmative view of human nature, and a dead-eye for social types. Hers is a conscious allegiance. In a 1957 essay, A Small Personal Voice, she said that she believed realist writing to be the highest form, "higher than and out of reach of any comparison with expressionism, impressionism, symbolism, naturalism, or any other ism." And it is true that she has not had recourse to any of these isms to render the murkier, more furtive moral climate of our day. She has remained faithful to the difficult realist aesthetic (no recourse to graphics or muddle) and also to the obligation of ethical judgment, which her fictional predecessors believed to be inarguably the writer's right and duty, but which many writers since have refused. She has never been fooled into the kind of moral determinism that characterizes the resolution of much nineteenth-century fiction. She never confuses what should be with what is, and that is a very forbearing thing in a moralist.

Margaret Drabble has made the apposite remark that Mrs. Lessing "is one of the very few novelists who have refused to believe that the world is too complicated to understand" and, one might add, to describe. For dealing with the subtlest nuances of the human personality she has a style so plain it is almost affectation— has, it seems, something like disdain for figurative language, and her plainness includes the deceptively forthright way of telling a story from beginning to end with nothing left out, in the author's particular, somewhat chilly and omniscient voice. A man's marriage, for instance, "was not at all the unique thing he had imagined. It was nothing more than the experience of everyone in his circle. And presumably everybody else's circle too? Anyway, round about the tenth year of his marriage he had seen a good many things clearly, a certain kind of emotional adventure went from his life, and the marriage itself changed."

The people in her stories make their own mistakes, but it is clearly Mrs. Lessing who takes responsibility for singling them out. Hers is a real authorial presence, with the welfare of real readers in mind. This is what happened, and then that, and this is what it felt like: "This is a story, I suppose, about a failure in intelligence: The Rawlings' marriage was grounded in intelligence." No irony here. This magnificent story ("To Room Nineteen") is about, among many other things, a failure in intelligence. A woman who has everything is drawn to a bleak suicide. Perhaps only Mrs. Lessing could make such a mysterious and irrational conclusion so inevitable—above all, so recognizable.

Collections of stories are often praised for their variety, their range of technical effects, the versatility of the writer; and certainly Mrs. Lessing is various and versatile. But what is impressive about these stories is a cumulative coherence. They have, even as they particularize human experience, almost the gathering suspense of a novel—a novel of sensibility, about itself as much as about the nearly arbitrary (it seems) subjects whose stories the author has chosen to tell. Into what new areas of human feeling will this amazing guide next take us?

Although she might choose to tell any story at all, she has in fact chosen these, of Maureen, who has to cope with a beautiful face and a bad accent, or of Jerry, who goes swimming and almost drowns, or of Judith, who loves cats more than people. A woman discovers her heart in her hand, wraps it in tinfoil, and leaves it on the underground. A woman with a new baby suddenly wishes her husband and her best friend would sleep together and let her alone. An aging actress writes an affecting letter to a man she has fallen in love with. Thirty-five stories. To each of the small and great subjects—gardens, nameless grief—Mrs. Lessing brings that rarest of narrative gifts, the ability to fascinate. With an interest reserved, usually, for ourselves, we attend the resolution of George's sexual ennui, wonder whether old freethinking

Jack Orkney will get religion after all, or whether Mary and Tommy Rogers will go back to the Belle Vue for their holiday next year, or whether Susan Rawlings, with everything to live for, will shake off the so inexorable grip of despair.

With what nerveless serenity she leaves people like Susan Rawlings to their fates, or allows Graham Spence to humiliate himself (in the brilliant "One off the Short List," surely one of the most devastating revenge stories ever written). On sex Mrs. Lessing has few equals in understanding not only desire, but the rest—boredom, disappointment, erotic fury. Perhaps vanity is at bottom her great subject, but on every subject there is a selfless, composed quality about her writing, a special combination of indignation and compassion. She uses her own life with the dispassionate relish of an evangelical after new converts to her world view, and in hers we recognize ours.

Of course, in the long run, it really isn't possible to anatomize genius. Mrs. Lessing is the great novelist of the unspoken thing, of the part a husband and wife cannot tell each other, of the mysteries that have no name and the little things people are simply reluctant to talk about—disapproval, grudges, vague longings, disappointments, the promptings of the self in all its guises. She seems to know everything and to forgive it, or, in the overview, to see nothing to forgive. She has been the most political and involved of all literary figures, a Marxist, socialist, outspoken foe of South African racial policies, women's lot, and nearly all social ills. Yet, taken together, her work is suffused with a calm charity that reassures, heals, and encourages.

# Should Novels Have a Message?
# Joan Didion, Bertha Harris,
# and Erica Jong

ABOUT THE RESPONSE to Erica Jong's novel, *How to Save Your Own Life*, it is hard to guess which emotions will prevail on the part of people who admired or liked her exuberant *Fear of Flying*. Stupefaction, chagrin, the feeling of having been had? Or pity? The feeling that it is after all Erica Jong who has been had, who has trusted people too far, as in a scene from a horrid film in which thin, cruel sorority girls tell an unlovable fat girl over and over that she is talented and loved, that she writes like Chaucer and John Keats, ply her with presents and compliments about her beauty, encourage her to take off all her clothes and confide her most fatuous secrets: then they all laugh and turn away.

Of course, if pity is what people decide to feel, it will be mitigated, as pity always is, by thoughts of all the money she'll be making. There is no point in talking about *How to Save Your Own Life* as a serious didactic work, despite the title, or as art, or as entertainment; but it does provide an opportunity to observe the biological structure of the world of books. Without claim to art or interest, the book is like an inert substance, say purple dye, which, dropped into the water of the publishing pond, creeps up various stems, empurpling now this petal, now that, indelibly tracing the cellular relations of things that grow in this rich pool of huge advances, eight-by-ten glossies dispatched in kits to potential reviewers and interviewers along with lists of questions to ask Jong if—as seems likely—she comes by, excerpts appearing in *Vogue,* and the rest.

There are in fact some good or at least interesting things about the book. In some respects it is an improvement on life. For instance, in life, at an inevitable point in the divorces or psychoanalyses of our friends, we find ourselves avoiding them, ashamed that we can't any longer endure the self-engrossed and repetitious monologues into which they have descended, angry with them for having brought out these bad qualities of impatience and disloyalty in our character. But Jong's book, which resembles in every way the ramblings of the deserted friend who has taken to the tape recorder and submitted the unedited transcript, has the virtue that we can abandon it without hurting her feelings or damaging our own self-regard.

*How to Save Your Own Life* appears to be a mostly autobiographical work about Isadora Wing, now the author of a best-selling book that has changed the lives of women everywhere: her heroine, Candida Wong, had "turned out to be amanuensis to the Zeitgeist. . . . As Candida felt, so felt the nation." Despite the riches and fame Candida has brought her, Isadora is not happy, because she is still unfulfilled, stuck in a loveless marriage with the unpleasant psychiatrist Bennett Wing. She suffers and feels guilty and goes around complaining to her friends. Presently she goes to California in search of the Hollywood dream, there meets a nice Jewish boy, and finds happiness.

In short, a plain, wholesome American story, containing as it does that peculiarly American and purely literary substance Fulfillment, modern equivalent of fairy gold, so gleaming and tangible you can even put it in your pocket and carry it from coast to coast. The novelist is adroit in combining all the clichés of two types of regional novel which had formerly seemed distinct, the Manhattan and the Hollywood, in such a way as to reveal that Hollywood is simply a cultural mutation of New York. She says, with characteristic delicacy, "California is a wet dream in the mind of New York," which perhaps we ought to have seen all along, though from the Western point of view certain differences seem to persist, which are not discoverable if you get no farther than the Polo Lounge. East or West, the nature of her prescription for saving your own life is finally unclear: divorce? lesbian encounters? love? best-sellerdom? So it is hard to say of what use the unfulfilled will find it.

To those who won't like Ms. Jong's novel as much as they had hoped to, I suppose will be added many who won't like Joan Didion's novel as much as they feel they ought to. But it should be emphasized that there is really no comparison to be made between these books beyond the hardly accidental sense in which they both, together with Bertha Harris's *Lover*, and with many other books today, concern strategies that women are devising to survive or adapt ("seeking fulfillment"). To the satisfaction of English departments, the novels of any period do share preoccupations which ultimately define them, or at least afford matter for the historian which mere demography conceals. So it is just possible to discern a pattern here.

*A Book of Common Prayer* concerns, in the narrator's summary, Charlotte Douglas, a San Francisco "socialite" (as they are called locally), who "left one man, she left a second man, she traveled again with the first; she let him die alone. She lost one child to 'history' and another to complications . . . she imagined herself capable of shedding that baggage and came to Boca Grande, a tourist." The narrator's account, so spare it might almost be a screenplay, can be amplified somewhat. Charlotte, after her daughter, Marin, hijacks an airplane, is disoriented, gives birth to a child who dies of hydrocephalis, wanders off with her first husband, winds up in Boca Grande, a Central American republic, where she sleeps with a few of the influential locals and hangs around the airport, and eventually gets killed in one of the frequent revolutions.

Charlotte's story is told through the formal device of a more-or-less disinterested narrator, an observer, a kind of new novelist by temperament—Grace Strasser-Mendana. This elderly, dying woman, and real power in Boca Grande, follows Charlotte's movements or collects accounts of them with the cryptic dispassion of a private eye. Through her we know what Charlotte says: "Gastro-intestinal infection is the leading natural cause of death in this country," and other trivia. We know what she does: "Here is what Charlotte Douglas was said by Elena to have done with the twenty-four white roses Victor sent her on Christmas eve: left them untouched in their box and laid the box in the hallway for the night maid." We even know what she wears on most occasions; and about "the safety pin that puckered the hem of the Irish linen skirt, the clasp that did not quite close the six-hundred-dollar handbag." Didion's descriptions are a marvel. But it is rather a case where one might say, "I see the clothes, now where is the emperor?" We never get to know or understand Charlotte Douglas at all.

Partly at fault is the overbearing objectivity of the super-cool Sra. Grace, who functions in the narrative like a kind of Intourist guide, rebuffing attempts at penetration while providing an official version of the events which unfold before you as in a movie. And you feel for her the same antagonism. You are constantly wanting to slip away from her and find out what Charlotte is thinking; hoping that, if you can just slip away from Sra. Grace, you will luckily meet up with Joan Didion, a penetrating and brilliant understander and explainer of things (*Slouching Towards Bethlehem*) as well as a brilliant describer of them. She might let you know how Charlotte Douglas feels when her baby dies, what she really thinks about Marin, what she sees in that boring drunk, Warren.

As it is, one can invent the meaning for oneself (one reviewer believes it to be a story of maternal constancy). Probably the meaning is meaninglessness, or delusion, as Sra. Grace says. Didion seems to write under the rubric of Robbe-Grillet's dictum that the genuine writer has nothing to say, but has only a way of speaking. "Art is not a more or less brightly colored envelope intended to embellish the author's message," said Robbe-Grillet, intending to emphasize that "the work of art contains nothing"— like an empty box—and unwilling to admit what is apparently true: that if the reader opens the box or envelope and sees nothing there, or doesn't understand what is there, he will adapt this bright container to his own uses, and feel the more pleased with it, the more useful it is.

For a century or more, art has been trying to clear its skirts of didacticism and exist for its own sake; poems have tried to not mean, just be; the stark artifacts washed up by the *nouvelle vague* try to repel attempts to riddle them. Yet nothing has succeeded in averting the ineluctable tendency of narrative fiction to mean something, even in spite of the writer of it. It is almost as if the interests of writer and reader were opposed, like the forces on a dam.

The utility, for writers, of fiction that eludes meaning is evident. Things that mean something are thought to have messages, and the composing of messages, like child care, seems to be a duty that, in most societies, no one really wants. It gets left to those who can least avoid it: the old, younger sons, and women. "There is not a war in the world, no, nor an injustice, but you women are answerable for it: not in that you have provoked, but in that you have not hindered," said Ruskin. That's how it works. George Eliot did not mind, and it is the tradition Erica Jong is writing in.

But no wonder Lina Wertmüller complained somewhere recently that she was not a woman director, only a director. To be a woman writing, like a woman directing, is to be expected to have a position toward woman's lot, whether she has one or not, and any book falling from the hand of a woman, however it may have been conceived in purest androgyny (even if that were possible or desirable), will be perceived by reader and critic in the light of the author's womanhood, something that has in the past prompted some famous stratagems of self-disguise. Today it is not so necessary to call yourself George, and there can also be advantages, as Jong points out: everyone watches you and you get rich. But it is not surprising that Didion has tried to avoid the intensely subjective mode that seems to predominate in recent fiction by women and has tried to make herself vanish with the Tarnhelm of Art—or the rainbow cloak of Manner.

Should novels have a message? And the other great unresolved question in modern fiction has to do with character. No objections have yet been raised to the presence of characters in novels, of course; the worry is over whether it is allowed for us to like and care about them. Over whether it is necessary at least to identify with them in order for a fiction to "work." Few people can have liked the narrator in Joseph Heller's *Something Happened*, for instance, but most could identify with him, and few would deny the power of that fiction.

Still, the relationship between literary character and reader is as yet little understood. The interesting formal innovations in modern fiction, its preoccupations with language and with the texture of text, have been held, perhaps wrongly, to preclude or discredit these mysterious processes of sympathy and identification. On the one hand, people seem to feel uneasy about their own wish to read about people they care about, as if there were something essentially unmodern, suspect, sentimental about such wishes, something that will lead to sloppy crying jags in bars. On the other, the fact remains that people did like and identify with Isadora Wing, at least in *Fear of Flying*, if only because she seemed to have been experienced in some vital way by the author. Because you can't really know her, your feelings about Charlotte Douglas are much more qualified. What isn't settled is whether this matters.

Writers lately seem to share a suspicion of sympathetic models, perhaps because, finding so few around in life, they have begun to believe they are only found in fiction, and whatever their aesthetic, writers have some allegiance to mimesis. So we find modern fiction avoiding old-fashioned likable characters in various ways. One is to give them goofy names, as in Vonnegut or Pynchon, subtly depriving them of probable histories—which would imply parents who would actually give them names like Oedipa Maas—and thereby of their "life."

Or a writer may consider the characters in his novel according to their function instead of as individuals, as in Jong, for instance, where they are divided up into four categories: men, distinguishable by "cocks," women, distinguishable by "cunts," Jews, distinguishable by "warmth," and WASPs, distinguishable by "coolness." The function of the first group is to symbolize authority and to oppress or placate the good character, and of the last to symbolize materialism and introduce the good character to dope and orgies.

Or a writer can do as Didion does, invent characters who are altogether real (who indeed will seem, to some, to have been drawn from recent history). They have pasts, minutely particularized; their peculiarities are their own, elaborately studied, consistent, unique; they even have real addresses and real labels—always good labels—in their clothes.

But Didion does not wish to intrude on what the French call the *mouvements intérieurs* of these characters, a phrase that suggests, to the English speaker, the queasiness with which matters below the surface are viewed. No polite person should wish to intrude upon a *mouvement intérieur*. Yet the transaction between reader and character, whatever it is, seems to involve the character's confidences about his emotions. Without them, Didion's book is like a serious, exciting, but strangely silent film; the motives, anxieties, passions, and delusions are all presented in pantomime.

It's hard not to be of two minds about this. On the one hand one feels it's appropriate enough for an age when meaning, like value, has abrogated its claim anyway and only surfaces remain. On the other is the undeniable fact that this starved, lean prose is like a high-protein diet. Didion's writing is high protein, but leaves the reader a little hungry for the starchy pleasures of the inner life.

On balance, the form of Didion's presentation of Charlotte Douglas is the truest one that she could have chosen as a mirror of contemporary reality, where women behave somewhat as Charlotte Douglas behaves, strangely, without being able to explain themselves or be understood. Things are going on that no one understands. Through Grace's eyes, that is, the eyes of an old woman who has outlived the problems attendant upon her wom-

anhood and gained an honorary neuter voice, we view a woman
of about forty, the generation hardest hit. How wise Didion was
to avoid the mind of the girl hijacker, Marin. To the really alienated woman in her forties, the Marins, the Nancy Ling Perrys,
the Leila Khaleds are not only mysterious; they seem, in their
assumption of equality, in their faith in political process and protest, like naïve collaborationists.

Charlotte Douglas seems not to understand, but perhaps,
rather, to admire, her daughter, Marin. Caught without prepa-
ration in the generation of change, she is a romantic version of
the millions of women who decide to go back to school and take
some courses, and whose daughters are living with someone, with
the mildly complicitous admiration of their mothers. In the drama
of evolving consciousness, it is Isadora Wing—patriarch-ridden,
victim of sex-in-the-head, barely out of the harem—who is the
old-fashioned girl. Charlotte Douglas is the next step, has freed
herself of guilt and does as she pleases. (It helps that she's nearly
as rich as the people Truman Capote and other silver-fork novelists
write about.)

Female power. Didion's woman narrator, by controlling a
trust, controls the republic of Boca Grande, even though it's ostensibly run by her male relations, whose childlike *machismo* she
does not take seriously. Charlotte takes neither of her husbands
seriously. Her daughter is a successful hijacker whose male companion is apprehended and hangs himself. Both Charlotte and her
daughter exist in the vivid yet dreamlike world of romance, where
women are accountable to no one; they have in fact replaced the
men. Despite the formalism of Didion's presentation, hers is the
world of Conrad and Graham Greene, but now it is women who
have obscure crises of spirit in seedy hotel rooms and die forlorn
and solitary deaths in warm climates.

It makes a change from the fictional world (or the real one)
where husbands do not understand you, wives are not fulfilled,
children are tiresome, and that includes all the other details of
female despair which, without surrendering their authentic claim
to our attention, are not such good reading either.

Bertha Harris, too, has created a woman's world *(Lover)*, as relaxed and sisterly and funny as Didion's is tense and controlled. The rhetoric of significance reverberates perhaps a little too loudly in Didion's unpadded prose. Harris's is overstuffed; hers is a crowded female menage so full of characters, mostly wise and witty women, that one can hardly keep them straight. And each has stories, thoughts, emotions, and views, presented somewhat haphazardly in a series of monologues and anecdotes separated by little *exempla*: "Petronilla, who did not wish to marry Flacco, obtained the grace to die; and was buried before his eyes." It is a kind of burlesque show, the subject of which is all literature and all life, put on for the cheery inmates of a happy lesbian safe house—the grandmothers, Veronica and Samaria; a granddaughter, Flynn; the mother, Daisy; many many others.

A few male characters are brought on for ritual slaughter. There are Bogart and Boatwright, pitiful twins whose mother tries to convince them she is not their mother: "I wish you would rid yourself of that irksome fantasy—in your best interests. It only holds you back." They will be murdered (while dressed as girls) by the other male character, the Murderer, who lurks from chapter to chapter and is a compendium of macho hangups, violent behavior, and all-too-familiar rhetoric. He will be murdered by Veronica and Samaria, in self-defense. There is about him something at once unfair and queerly plausible; he is a deserving companion to all those misogynist stereotypes—the earth mother, the prostitute with heart of gold, the innocent, pure maiden— who have dominated the literary tradition for so long.

Every aspect of literary and social tradition comes under examination, as in the novel within the novel one of the characters plans to write, which begins with "rejection by Father, no good at baseball, seduction by horny rustic grandfather, gangbanged by California motorcyclists, likes it (?). *Chapter Two*, identity crisis, memory of Mother deliberately (?) parading past in black lace nightie, the march on Selma . . . ," all the way to the last chapter, which is to end with "grace, retreat into the wilderness, solitude (insert lines from 'The Pulley' by George Herbert), conversion to Catholicism, love, death." Everything is to be included, and if Harris sacrifices traditional narrative qualities like coherence, it is all so funny and inventive that it is impossible to mind.

Erica Jong, the realist, presents a view of women as insecure, dependent, banal, and demanding; Joan Didion makes them as powerful and mysterious as the heroes of romance. Bertha Harris presents a utopian vision of a world where women are in charge of themselves, and where, it is nice to note, they are very good company indeed.

# Saul Bellow as Reformer

ERNST GOMBRICH IN *Art and Illusion* talks about those pictures which appear to be one thing until you perceive a different pattern, whereupon the rabbit turns into a goat, the can-can girl into a hag in a bonnet. Once you've seen both, you can then have either perception, but not the two at once. Saul Bellow's novel, *The Dean's December*, is like this, a novel about Albert Corde, an American spending December in Rumania, or a novel about conditions of American society presented through the meditations and conversations of the same character, removed from the scene, in a situation that affords certain opportunities for comparison and reflection. Either novel disappears when the other is focused on. The pattern of the social novel is the more insistent and interesting, but the Corde novel rivalrously endangers it.

The Corde novel suffers from the author's satisfaction with his creation, Corde, a former journalist, now a college dean in Chicago. Dashiell Hammett once wrote of a book he was reviewing that its hero "thought he was a giant. His wife thought he was a giant. That is all very well. But when [the author] agreed with them, he spoiled his book." Bellow's approval of Corde is so immense, and he takes so little trouble to convince us of his view, that the reader feels excluded; it's like embarking on a long train journey alone with two people who have just fallen in love with each other.

Moreover, it's not easy to see what Bellow and the other characters see in this love object. Corde is just a plain person—smart, but very plain and calm. He visits his dying mother-in-law in a Bucharest hospital: why should her vital signs galvanize when she is advised by this son-in-law, whom she hardly knows, that she is loved by him? Or why should he be the talk of Chicago? Why do the Rumanian cousins worry about his diet, and the curious contrive to meet him? A Nobel Prize winner they might, maybe; a dean, no. Yet Corde feels himself constantly the object of attention, like a wonderful object under glass, which confuses the reader's perception that this novel is not about him; he is only the interpretative consciousness in a novel about much larger matters.

The reader will have other complaints. Most of the characters are not especially interesting; they have the faded, anonymous aspect of old photos of someone else's ancestors. The Rumanians are as understandably subdued and grim as their Rumanian situation compels, and the potentially more colorful Chicagoans lose color from being rendered discontinuously from Middle Europe in Corde's meditations as he passes the time. Partly the collective pallor is owing to the fact that the minor characters have very few lines, and none of the fantastical exuberance of, say, Henderson's African king, and none of the dignified learning of the elderly Jewish gentlemen Bellow does so marvelously.

It's hard to remember that Corde himself is a WASP, a Huguenot from a distinguished old family. He and his family seem like nice Jewish characters, as usual. There's a cousin Maxie, a horrid nephew Mason, a nice sister Elfrida, married to a judge. Corde feels Herzogian guilt for his past doings, and welcomes his own satisfaction with his new domestic stability, and there is a lot of mention of digestion. Probably Bellow got tired of his old characters and of being expected to stick to them—the disadvantage of a specialty, the same disadvantage that women novelists find, say, when everything they write gets read in the light of womanhood whether or not womanhood has anything to do with what they are writing about. Corde's ethnicity has nothing to do with his observational powers, but it's interesting to wonder at the connection, for the author, between Corde and that other, more wonderful non-Jew, Henderson.

Like the earlier Mr. Sammler's, Corde's mission is to be at the moral center of the book, the worried and thoughtful person. And at that he is splendid. He is in Rumania to attend the deathbed of his wife's mother, formerly an important woman there, now out of favor. Corde's astronomer wife Minna and he are kept waiting around, arbitrarily prevented from visiting the intensive care unit by petulant officials who resent the dying Valeria and Minna's defection. They connive visits, and the rest of the time sit around the cold apartment, eat bleakly, and talk.

Corde is following the progress, back home, of a court case involving the murder of a white student. Two blacks are accused of pushing him out of a window to his death. They claim he fell, and that he had anyway been asking for trouble. Corde has encouraged their prosecution, but without his interest the case would probably have gone the way of other such cases—postponement after postponement until the witnesses died or moved away, and eventual freedom for the killers. Some, including his nephew Mason, feel that Corde is failing to allow for the social conditions which led to the depravity of the black killers. Increasingly appalled by what he has been finding out about the legal system, hospitals, slums, social conditions generally, and the outlook for black people, Corde has written some controversial articles in *Harper's* telling what he sees.

The action of the novel proceeds simply, without suspense. The mother dies, is cremated, family members gather. Minna and Corde return to Chicago. If the blacks had not been found guilty, Corde would have been in difficulty at the university. But the accused have been tried, convicted, and given sixteen years. Nevertheless Corde resigns his academic post and plans to devote himself to journalism.

His *Harper's* articles are mostly descriptive. Detectives shoot an escaping young prisoner ten times in the head. In the slum housing project, people, "being afraid to go at night to the incinerator drop on each floor," drop their garbage down the toilets and break them. There are "young men getting on top of the elevator cabs, opening the hatch and threatening to pour in gas, to douse people with gasoline and set them afire." Snipers, rapes, revolting murders, terrible despair—a huge American underclass which is not attached to life, and no one can suggest how to attach it (n.b., "Corde").

People don't want to read about this. The *Harper's* subscribers are angry. Student militants demand an apology to "Black, Puerto Rican and Mexican toilers" for making them look like "animals and savages." Corde observes that in our society the truth-teller needs a lead apron against the radiation and shock waves set off by mere objectivity—and the complicated formal arrangement of the novel is perhaps Bellow's lead apron.

If there is a lie at the heart of the book it is here, in assuming or pretending that there would be a great public reaction to objective descriptions of American social conditions. Perhaps we are beyond outrage. People do try to write angry descriptive articles and outcries are seldom raised. It's wishful thinking to imagine that one commentator, even Albert Corde, speaking of "superfluous populations," "written off," "doomed peoples," might get through to the rest of us, but it's an honorable wish, and the novel an honorable outcry. Corde himself is concerned about the thickness of our rhetorical insulation and of the self-satisfaction of liberalism:

We sat there explaining evils to each other, to pass them off somehow, redistribute the various monstrous elements, and compose something the well-disposed liberal democratic temperament could live with. Nobody actually said, "An evil has been done." No, it was rather, "An unfortunate crazed man destroyed a women, true enough, but it would be wrong of us to constitute ourselves judges of this crime since its causes lie in certain human and social failures."

In a sense, Bellow has written a novel about how nobody will read or accept the novel he is writing, any more than the people Corde talks to believe *him*, and it is always easier for critics of novels to talk about language or form than about what the novel is saying. It's by no means agreed that novels should say anything.

Corde reflects upon Rilke's idea that you shouldn't talk about horrors, because you can only talk about them in "newspaper expressions" which trivialize them. Corde himself is on the side of "so-and-so, who said that you departed for the eternal only from Grand Central Station . . . that the contemporary is your only point of departure." One might contrast this view with, say, the practice of E. L. Doctorow, who, also writing about society, uses history for a point of departure, presumably for Rilke's reason. History, especially in Doctorow's hands, is wittier, but has the disadvantage of retaining its emotional power unevenly; different myths have different half-lives, while the contemporary world holds its present in common. It is interesting that an initial connection to the contemporary, in Isherwood's Berlin stories, for instance, retains in the names of cabinet ministers now dead and vanished streets an immediacy that seems to resonate in the very words and names, transcends the passage of time, and does not date.

Corde suggests, not playfully, that "perhaps only poetry had the strength to rival the attractions of narcotics, the magnetism of TV, the excitements of sex, or the ecstasies of destruction" in trying to reclaim the doomed American underclass. His is the Arnoldian view that people can be attached to life by culture—but there is no culture in the city, in the wasteland. He is defending humanistic Western culture against the conventional liberal institutions that have failed to maintain it. "Public discussion is threadbare." The communications industry "breeds hysteria and misunderstanding," academics make no effort to lead the public, "the intellectuals have been incapable of clarifying our principal problems."

John Updike's recent novel *Rabbit Is Rich* is a picture of the moral and spiritual situation of a modern middle-class American man. Bellow's novel is only a picture of a man thinking about the spiritual situation and its actual correlatives; that is, it is abstracted by a process of diffraction through the minds of Corde, of his friend Dewey, of other people he talks to. It would have been possible to dramatize the Chicago novel another way. The Dean is awakened one night to learn of the murder of one of his students. He enlists the help of the university in seeing that the killers are brought to justice—and attempts are made to dissuade him from seeing justice done. His ambitious cousin Max is attorney for the defense, etc.

This would have provided a dramatic, active, involving novel with a climactic courtroom scene, or whatever. But it is not the novel Bellow, a masterly novelist, chose to write, perhaps because it would have deprived him of Rumania, and the implicit contrast of a regimented society with our chaos, but also perhaps because this more conventional structure would have required a resolution, some ending, unhappy or happy, to suspense; and that in turn would provide a satisfaction that would belie the view of contemporary life he is taking here. If the formal success of a work of art lies in part in the resolution of the tensions and problems with which it deals, if only in the form, then this novel could be said to fail. Yet to resolve the huge problems that engage Corde, by prescription on the one hand or catharsis on the other, would produce a reassuring work. Perhaps art is meant to be reassuring at the same time that it disturbs. But reassurance, more suited to the matters of the individual soul than to the body politic, would falsify the subject here. So Bellow has chosen a strategy more akin to that of an essay, which leaves questions, and his language is the plain meditative language of thought, in place of the exuberant language he has commanded elsewhere.

Perhaps Corde overstates the failure of press and academy, but it doesn't seem so. The American novel, which has always waxed private and public in turn, has been stuck for three decades in a mode of private confession now very worn, or of experiment, the more vital strain with too few practitioners. Breaking away, as he does, from the confessional mode, Corde is perhaps, as he puts it, "objectivity intoxicated." But he seems nowhere wrong. If the role of art is somehow, as Arnold Hauser suggested, to make you feel that you must change your life, then this novel succeeds by recommending—no, by showing (for novelists are always being enjoined to show, not tell, and Bellow has not forgotten this injunction)—an American in the first stages of change, that is, the describing stage, the stage of admitting how things really are in the world beyond the self.

# The Righteous Artist:
# E. L. Doctorow

LIKE THE WRITINGS of many prophets, the writings of E. L. Doctorow contain texts to interpret them by: "We will overthrow America in images." "He [God] enlists the help of naturally righteous humans who become messengers or carriers of his miracles, or who deliver their people. Each age has by trial to achieve its recognition of Him . . ." *(The Book of Daniel)*.

The special trial sent to Doctorow is to be not only righteous but also an artist, thought since Victorian times to be antithetical; either the artist must "sit as God holding no form of creed, / But contemplating all," in the words of Tennyson's poem, or do a little peace marching, but to try to do both together is to start with a special handicap, like a sack-runner in the regular race. Doctorow is an artist struggling in a message sack, or a messenger beguiled by a sackful of artist's playthings—possibilities of language and form—but all the same he runs a swift race.

That is to say, *Loon Lake* is a work both formally ambitious and doctrinaire. It is narrated mainly by Joe Korzeniowski, aka Joe of Paterson, the son of parents defeated by their ugly and poor urban environment, a bad kid who robs the poor box, beats up priests, and lives without compunctions by his wits and good looks. Eventually, after the events of this book have taken place, he rises to such establishment positions as head of the CIA, chairman of industrial boards, heir of the rich capitalist F. W. Bennett. The action is simple, though the structure of the work is not. Joe leaves home, tramps around, works in a carnival, and during his picaresque wanderings near Loon Lake, Bennett's private retreat, he is attacked by savage dogs. While convalescing there, he meets Warren Penfield, failed poet and drunk, son of poor miners, and now "poet-in-residence." Other characters are Bennett's wife, Lucinda, an aviatrix who reminds us of Amelia Earhart; Clara, mistress first of a gangster guest at Loon Lake, then of Bennett, later of Penfield and Joe; and the Jameses, Sandy and Red, whom Joe meets after escaping from Loon Lake with Clara. He lives with Clara for a time and works in a factory, where he is impressed with the beauty of this "complex society with standards of conduct honor serious moral judgment." After Red, an apparently nice union guy, is unmasked as a company operative and murdered, probably by other company men, Joe befriends, but later deserts, Sandy, then returns to Loon Lake and the sponsorship of Bennett.

The narrative projects events up until the time of writing (1970s) and backward into the childhoods of Penfield and Joe, with the main action set in the 1930s. Joe's account is presented in both the first and third person:

> I stand poised on the edge and dive into the water. With powerful strokes learned in the filth of industrial rivers Joe swims a great circle crawl in the sweet clear cold mountain lake. He pulls himself up on the float and stands panting in the sun, his glistening white young body inhaling the light, the sun healing my scars my cracked bones my lacerated soul.

The passage aptly conveys Joe's calculation, his ability to objectify himself.

Joe's story alternates with the recollections and poems of Penfield, which Penfield has left him at his death. Penfield's memories are presented in the third person:

Warren felt the rough hand of the armed guard on his neck and then the coolness of the night air as he flew from the top of the rail-car step to the graveled ground. His knee was embedded with bits of stone as the miners had been peppered with coal fragments, so he understood that feeling. To understand what it meant to be buried alive in a mountain he sat later with his eyes closed in the night and his hands over his ears and he held his breath as long as he could.

Penfield's poems, also printed here, are narrative and descriptive; it is these writings which articulate the central moral preoccupations of the book—capitalism and its metaphorical correlatives: nature, personal space, and sex. Sometimes the voices of Penfield and Joe, sharing an analogical matrix of the language of economics, tend to merge and to become Doctorow: "The rescue work was commanded from the private railroad car, a property like the mine and like the miners . . ." (Warren). "Everything in this room, unlit and still, seemed more awesome than from the distance of the night, for it was quite clearly owned. That was the main property of the entire car, not that it was handsome or luxurious but that it was owned" (Joe).

Like *Ragtime*, *Loon Lake* concerns itself with capitalism in general and with the history of union struggle in the early part of this century. Most modern writing has tended to focus on private experience, and if an occasional didactic impulse comes on him, the writer sets up a lot of real-looking shrubs in which to hide it, in hopes that it will appear to be an aspect of the natural world. We call these realistic novels. Doctorow, impatient with ambiguity, sets up ideas like little black and white figures on top of a wedding cake, all decorated with the icing sugar of art—Warren's little poems, for example, restfully prosaic though they may be:

> *He talked about the unrest in the*
> *country*
> *and the peculiar mood of the*
> *workers*

*and he solicited the gangsters' views*
*over brandy*
*on the likelihood of revolution.*

The result is a special and characteristic concoction, not realistic and not self-consciously surreal but, rather, like an epic or a morality play, in which the poet celebrates the good, deplores the bad, and develops in a musical way the meaningful themes of his society as he sees it.

The sexual relationships in *Loon Lake,* therefore, are developed in sadistic and economic terms, as is usual in Doctorow's work. (Is it the sadism he means, in an interview, when he says that this "is the fullest exploration I've made of love in America"? Or is it the cash nexus?) Anyway, all the sexual relationships involve money, and the ultimate metaphor for private enterprise is the carnival, that time-honored image of society, where the rubes line up every night after the show to fuck the freak-show fat lady, and tickets are sold for a final, disgusting orgy as she dies. Joe runs off with the entrepreneur's wife, Magda ("this thieving crone bitch"), who's got the profits. "At one point the coins sticking to the wet ass, the wet belly, I invented a use of Magda Hearn so unendurable to her that with the same cry that must have come from her the day she fell twisting from the trapeze, she flung herself off the bed." When Magda drops into exhausted sleep, Joe takes the orgy money and scatters it to the wind; but he's not usually so quixotic.

Nature itself is an aspect of social injustice. Joe, in the last pages of the book, plunges into the icy waters of Loon Lake and comes up smiling. Nature is ice is capitalism. Loon Lake is "a cold black lake," owned, loons preying on fish there, the shores haunted by the ghosts of dying Indians. It is a reflex of capitalist society and a form of selfish luxury. To the urban romantic, like Doctorow, the romantic poet of nature is a poseur. In the Adirondacks "one summer after the May flies painters and poets arrived / who paid money to sit in guide boats and to stand momentously / above the gorges of rushing streams. / The artists and poets patrons seeing and hearing their reports / bought vast tracts of the Adirondacks very cheaply and began to build elaborate camps there thus inventing / the wilderness as luxury" (writes Warren). Elsewhere, Joe "understands what wealth is, the desire for isolation."

But nature, which seems to an urban sensibility emblematic of spiritual desolation and selfishness, seems to the product of rural culture emblematic of goodness. Because we are not universally urban, and because the idea of nature as good (and of society as vain, bad, crowded, indifferent, etc.) is basic to a strain of Western literature since Virgil, the artist must struggle uphill in his sack. *Ragtime*, comic and working with simpler material, risked less and succeeded, but one could complain of the stately and ambitious *Loon Lake* that, by attempting to look more broadly at American history, it seems the more constrained by an ideology that explains or convokes the experience of only some Americans, without having the exemplary power of an ambiguous fictional world to expand the experience of others.

The effect of this fiction to some extent depends, then, on one's assent to the validity and explanatory power of its underlying myth of American capitalism. There are many accounts of creation. The view of American history each of us has is probably, as Frances FitzGerald has suggested, strongly conditioned by our third-grade textbooks—in some communities they're still fighting the Civil War, or celebrating the romance of religious freedom. Doctorow is particularly compelled by the stories of union brotherhood and by how poor immigrants, especially Jewish immigrants, upon arriving in America around the turn of the century, were routinely mistreated, given names they didn't like, and made to live in unspeakable conditions forced on them by an exploitative ruling class.

We have other stories, too. A recent French TV documentary reconstructed the French view of America from footage on America in French TV film files: almost entirely fat sheriffs wearing sunglasses handling Dobermans which they are about to release on blacks. Blacks rioting, bleeding New Yorkers being taken to emergency rooms, and Middle Americans wearing foolish costumes at a variety of assemblies—political, Klan, religious, or self-improvement groups. America lends itself to simplification and caricature, but each of our stories is differently affecting. For each of us there are things that prompt a special swell of indignation or an inexplicable tear: Appomattox, Chicago, Mother Machree.

Like any other idealistic and perceptive person, Doctorow has a complaint about history, that it contained brutality and villainy. The indignation that breaks through the lyricism or funny bits in all his work suggests despair about human nature itself (and why not?), but also a demand for some sort of apology, and it is here that a question arises of how the tone interferes at times with the narrative. Unless you are descended from an Ellis Island customs official or a railroad baron, you may find yourself wanting to assure the writer that all this wasn't your fault, or that history is just history, and that there is misery enough in the actual world, without its being retroactive. The twentieth-century American working class was not Earth's most pitiable group. But no doubt Doctorow pays America a kind of compliment by believing we could have been better.

He is apparently dismayed by our plurality of incongruous myths, the differences in American social conditioning which exaggerate the divisions in our national life and prevent political communion. This is the preoccupation of Penfield, in *Loon Lake*, who recalls being in Seattle during the great general strike of 1919, talking to his landlady, a woman "proud to be free and beholden to no one." He is sorry that she can't understand "the incredible tangible emotion of solidarity key word no abstract idealization but an actual feeling" about collective effort and the labor movement and cooperation (instead of competition as exemplified by Bennett and by Joe, who gets to the Top through crime, by using the system, and by literally and figuratively screwing everybody). He's right, she can't feel it. If we are, as in the currently fashionable view, still connected to our roots, this "big woman large jaw blue eyes taller" (than Penfield) was constrained by the love of solitude her ancestors felt herding their reindeer in some vast landscape. The landlady points out that the Huns had warm feelings of group solidarity. "Nobody knows what human nature is in the raw it's never been seen on this earth," Warren has to admit. Defeated by the fear that even the triumph of labor would not bring utopia he goes off to Japan and studies Zen, becomes a parody of the self-involved dropout American artist. Penfield is Doctorow's wittiest invention here.

Penfield's coal-miner father had wanted him to work in the mines and to bear witness to the human suffering there. Penfield is punished for his failure of social commitment by alcoholism and violent death, twin destinies of American writers of the period. In *Loon Lake* as in *Ragtime*, punishments and rewards are appointed not by considerations of realism and not by fictional conventions of retributive justice but by Doctorow's personal scheme. In *Ragtime*, the inoffensive Father, a WASP flag manufacturer, is given sexual inadequacy, diffidence, an inability to converse, long self-exile in the frozen arctic, where parts of him become frostbitten, and finally death by drowning in an icy sea—images of ice and frigidity inundating him as they are apt to do to other non-Jewish or non-union characters. (It is notable that enthusiastic sexuality, in all the works, is a property only of those committed to the class struggle.)

Tateh is the wickedest character in *Ragtime*, risking Doctorow's vengeance by pointing "his life along the lines of flow of American energy. Workers could strike and die but in the streets of cities an entrepreneur could cook sweet potatoes in a bucket of hot coals and sell them for a penny or two." But Tateh has paid his dues by being a Jewish immigrant and an artist to boot, and is rewarded by happiness, a remunerative gimmick, and the hand of Mother. Joe, in the present work, having paid his dues, is rewarded by wealth, though not, we are to assume, happiness.

It's a danger, with flat characters (in Forster's sense), that if, like broken parts of a machine, one or another doesn't work, the fiction may come to a halt. In *Ragtime*, where their flatness is part of the design, the audience knows, as at a morality play, the stereotypes: union people are good, cops are bad, WASPs are neglectful of their children, Jews are sexy, blacks are flamboyant, the rich are kinky, and so on—there's a stereotype to offend everybody, and that's the fun. The villains and heroes, equally charming, dash on and off stage in bright costumes, dramatizing the simpler dichotomies of American history.

In *Loon Lake*, the characters are rounded by the process of speaking for themselves. It's hard to be flat in the first person. None has the convincing poignancy of the brilliant characterization of Daniel in *The Book of Daniel*, but because Doctorow can only write wonderfully, even the bad Joe endears himself by his felicitous phrases, by his complexity, and by the splendid intelligence his author can't help giving him. Still, the exegetical function of the characters does somehow impede the action: the real drama lies behind the action, as in *Pilgrim's Progress*—lies in the great fable (or in this case the great program) being played on the writer's "secret boards," in Emerson's phrase, to be reconstructed by the audience in part from the typology and in part from the rhetoric itself.

Philosophy is hard to illustrate, but William James devised as frontispiece to one of his father's many works on Swedenborg a picture of a man beating a dead horse. The reader may become restive, even combative, slyly imagining, under the stern gaze of the master, alternative scenarios involving cheery cops, bad union men, spontaneous, affectionate Episcopalians. Doctrine begets revisionists. The author's impatience with the moral confusion of American orthodoxy may tap a vestigial patriotic vein and release a trickle of nostalgia for our villains, tycoons like Bennett, for example, who, although wicked, were at least effective, and whom, now that we fear ourselves to be a nation of bunglers, we may remember, *pace* Doctorow, with a certain wistful admiration.

But Doctorow's faith in his version of American history, and his willingness to run the large artistic risks involved in asserting it, make him one of the bravest and most interesting of modern American novelists, flying in the face of the self-indulgent fashion for confession to write *about* something, reviving the discredited function of artist as judge, and working to find the forms for judgment. It is interesting to notice that a strong ideology often, in literature, has had the paradoxical effect of stimulating formal experiments (in Whitman and Dos Passos, for instance), but also, in this respect, one senses in *Loon Lake* Doctorow's need to interest himself.

The risk is of a retreat into manner. One can picture the rival counselors who sit on his shoulders, whispering in his ears, vying for his attention—one a kindly Marxist rabbi, the other an elegant, suavely smiling rascal, maybe somebody like Oscar Wilde. Each is nearly satisfied with *Loon Lake,* but one wishes they would go away together and leave Doctorow alone.

# Possibly Parables:
# Donald Barthelme

MANY WRITERS HAVE tried to write like Donald Barthelme; it is
said he has more imitators than anyone since Hemingway. Literary history shows that either the avant-garde of one period is the
norm a few decades later, the way four-letter words are now the
norm, or else the highly original writer, his imitators fallen away,
is left in the isolation of his special gift—standing, one might say,
in the altogether. This sixth collection (*Great Days*) is bare Barthelme at his best, quite inimitable, with a new kind of calm
confidence, a new depth of subject, and no pictures. And, one
hopes, his imitators in disarray; for it should now be clear to
everybody that nobody can write a Barthelme story as well as he
can.

What are his stories about and what are they like? It seems a bit
unfair to Barthelme to describe them (as the hard-cover publisher
does) in ordinary terms: One story, we read, "explores the tragic,
ambiguous relationship between Cortés and Montezuma," which
would lead all but veteran Barthelme readers to expect more ex-
position and development than they are going to get. Two
pieces—the one about Cortés and "The Death of Edward Lear"—
have historical referents. One piece, the author says, is an *objet
trouvé* from *Godey's Lady's Book*, 1850, slightly altered by him.
One, "Tales of the Swedish Army," seems like an earlier, wackier

Barthelme. A number of stories impressively challenge formal problems—for example, "Concerning the Bodyguard."

The bodyguard: new fact of modern life, therefore typical Barthelme subject. An ordinary writer of fiction, imagining a bodyguard, would give him a name, a past, would follow his life, report his conversations and thoughts, invent a little disturbing event or two to dramatize his spiritual condition, and end with a climax of triumph or failure, some moment of bodyguard truth. Barthelme instead writes six pages of questions:

> After leaving technical school, in what sort of enterprise did the bodyguard engage before accepting his present post? Has he ever been in jail? For what sort of offense? Has the bodyguard acquired a fondness for his principal? Is there mutual respect? Is there mutual contempt? When his principal takes tea, is the bodyguard offered tea? Beer? Who pays?

Six pages of questions, of which the reader, whether he likes it or not, is both the wonderer and the one who must supply the probable answers. Beer, you think, and the principal pays. This is the kind of transaction approved of by French critics; you might call it a stone-soup method of writing, recalling the folk tale in which a wily stranger puts a stone in some water, announces that he is making soup, and invites the villagers to improve the flavor by putting in carrots and onions of their own. Of course Barthelme, unlike the stranger, is far from destitute—is, rather, a miracle of variousness and vigilance in the matter of our times— and he puts strange objects in instead of stones. This, of course, is the normal way of poets.

But where one is content to let poets do the work, here one is involved in a struggle—it is the struggle that accounts for some of the effect of Barthelme's work, even if the effect is of puzzlement. His method at its purest wants you to put in all the onions, and you want him to. (I take this to be an irreversible readerly tendency.) But he tricks you into putting in your onion every time;

you will find attitudes under his attitude whether he put them there or not, as in the story of Hokie Mokie, the new king of jazz, from Pass Christian, Mississippi:

> Can you distinguish our great homemade American jazz performers each from the other? somebody asks somebody.
> —Used to could.
> —Then who was that playing?
> —Sounds like Hokie Mokie to me. . . .

Then a young Japanese musician comes to the gig, shows Hokie up, and is the new hero and king until Hokie pulls himself together and, diffidently standing at the left (the left! Is that significant?) blows an all-American sound, "like beavers chewing trees in an Appalachian marsh," like "a mule deer wandering a montane of the Sierra Nevada" and so on. Hideo steps down: "I see I have many years of work and study before me still." "It happens to the best of us," Hokie assures him, "Or it almost happens to the best of us."

Now, to avoid detecting a parable in this—something, say, about Western industrial productivity—you have to be a very deep, serious reader indeed, like one of those mathematical geniuses who understand relativity but not addition. Anything you make it, maybe it's okay with Barthelme. Certainly it isn't a fault to write a parable, although it's confusing when people pretend parables aren't. It's nice that Barthelme's stories are equally fun for the light reader browsing through *The New Yorker* looking for fables, laughs, punch lines, and also for someone who wishes to brood, reread, and make connections. Good writing, like religion, no doubt, develops complexity and interest in proportion to the attention you give it.

But the old-fashioned reader, casually reading for profit and pleasure, will find parables, will try to make out what Barthelme is up to, and will not believe that he is only, say, providing (to quote the jacket again) "an account of zombies out on a wife-buying expedition." The story says "The women do not want zombies, but zombies are their portion. A woman says to another woman 'These guys are Zombies' 'Yes,' says the second woman, 'I saw a handsome man, he had his picture in the paper, but he is not here,' " Ah. The whole thing becomes intelligible. At least to female readers.

Readers will read for profit; they will also read for prophecy. So uncannily tuned is Barthelme's sense of what's happening in our times, in our world, he even picks up eerily on what will happen, as in one dialogue, "Morning," one of the seven dialogues that form the substance and principal distinction of this volume, where two characters discuss, from some kind of hot place of exile, some kind of event:

> So I decided it was about time we got gay. I changed the record, that helped, and fiddled with the lights. . . . Fixed up the Kool-Aid with some stuff I had with me. Complicated the decor with carefully placed items of lawn furniture, bird-baths, sundials, mirrored globes on stands.

The interlocutor asks how the party ended.

> I wasn't there. Got to scat, I said, got to get away, got to creep, it's that time of night. . . .
> —Say you're frightened.
> —Less and less. I have a smoke detector and tickets to everywhere. . . . After a while, darkness, and they give up the search.

These dialogues reflect a solemn mood in Barthelme, and his eye on Great Subjects (fear, faith, hope, sexual contention). They are naturally different from the works of two other writers in this form that come to mind, Pinter and Beckett, but like them remind us of how curiously well adapted the dialogue is for displaying a writer's particularity. In Pinter, who comes from a society in which people still converse, the voices engage, contend. Here the voices are dreamy, parallel, each probing personal

memory, and the contents of memory have not the fiercely ego-
tistical humanity of Beckett but instead comprise the things of our
society—"There's lots of green furniture you know with paint on
it. Worn green paint. Gilt lines one quarter inch from the edges."
Or the people: "Joan Armatrading." "Aretha Franklin." Or issues:
"What about Z.P.G.?"

You wonder, if these dialogues were spoken aloud, would the
dynamics of the conversations be easier to follow than they are on
the plain page without "he said"s and names. For instance, in
"The Leap," it is the character who initiates the discussion—"Today we make the leap to faith. Today"—who eventually can't go
through with it; but to figure this out you may have to count
down from the beginning.

The voices, male and female, hopeful or reflective, are funny,
sad, smart. They fit together. It's possible that all of Barthelme's
stories fit together, like a wardrobe of well-chosen basics; but they
provide in combination something more than a sum of the parts.
By denying himself the full-dress trappings of the conventional
novel, with its resources (plot, characters) for self-concealment,
the author, bare, scuttles speedily across a stage empty except for
these austere pillars, marked "The Leap," "Morning," and so
on, hiding behind first one, then another, yet seen—funny, sad,
smart. His sensibility is the game, and to mark him as a banner-
carrier in some new legion has been rather to belittle his accomplishment. It's also unfair to construe a writer's phrase in another
context as a comment on his own work, but in this volume he
has one character say, "I'm some kind of an artist, but I'm conservative. Mine is the art of the possible, plus two." It seems
apposite.

# III

---

# The Real World

# Ah, Wilderness:
# Texas and Alaska With
# Kramer and McPhee

"AMERICANS," WROTE TOCQUEVILLE, "are insensible to the wonders of nature," and only bent on subduing it. Now, it seems, whatever our intentions to nature itself, we cannot get enough of reading about its wonders. The new abundance of wilderness literature in America,* which seems to exceed what can be accounted for by transitory romanticism, reflects, I take it, both the disappearance of our frontiers and our dawning sense of their primal significance to us. As I write this (in February 1978), John McPhee's richly detailed account of Alaska (*Coming into the Country*) is the best-selling book of non-fiction in a number of Eastern cities, something usually reserved for works on sex or self-improvement; this suggests that the new American feeling about wilderness springs from some similar deep source of anxiety and hope. In the matter of Alaska, some of the interest may also arise from responsible citizenship, since we are on the point of having to decide what to do with this vast state. Alaska, like a late baby to elderly parents, is a matter for both surprise and obsessive solic-

---

*In three days, without effort, I came across: a *Sports Illustrated* spread on Alaska; another in the *Smithsonian* magazine; a report of The Wilderness Project from the University of Montana; two books from a friend who works for a press in Seattle which every eleven days prints a new book on the wilds: *Fog Swamp: Living with Swans in the Wilderness* and *Harvest of Salmon: Adventures in Fishing the B.C. Coast.*

itude, a last frontier which provides an occasion for reviewing the mistakes that have blighted other, older, frontiers, like the one described by Jane Kramer in her book on the Texas Panhandle (*The Last Cowboy*).

There are many reasons for the enduring popularity of travel literature: the dreamer is led out of the confinement of his daily life on primitive adventures from a legendary past; he indulges his dreams of a future life of freedom. At the same time, most travel accounts reassure him that where he lives is really best. The city-dweller, reading McPhee or Kramer in his *New Yorker* about the sixty-below winters of Alaska, the bullet-riddled signposts of Texas, will feel grateful for the locks and bolts that may at other times seem oppressive. Out there be dragons.

We are always grateful to redoubtable travelers, from Marco Polo to Kramer and McPhee, for braving our rigors for us. It is interesting to remember that the most entertaining, accurate, and cruelly analytical books about America used to be written by and for Europeans. Themselves urban, without frontiers, they devoured Anthony Trollope on the giant "Wellingtonia" trees of Yosemite, or his mother on our atrocious domestic manners, or Dickens's account of his visit, or the dozens of Gold Rush tales. Busy, in the middle of their adventure, Americans on America were given to boosting and boasting.

But now the best books on America are written by Americans. Far from being leveled by television, we grow more and more unlike one another, more conscious of diversity and more interested in it (a recent public-television series on American families provided subtitles for the speech of rural Georgians, on the assumption that their dialect was not intelligible). The traveler from New York, teetering around the Panhandle in new cowboy boots, is in a foreign land and yet in a familiar one. With access to a common heritage of American traditions and myths, she knows what questions to ask, and yet retains that slightly condescending sense of wonder on which the liveliest travel literature depends.

In fact, Europeans seem to understand us less and less. Perhaps we no longer resemble the open, uncomplicated Jamesian Americans we were once supposed to be, so much as the mysterious Europeans we, like James, so admire; perhaps complexity arises not so much from character as from having a complicated place to be in, and that is what Americans are now finding out about. At present, at any rate, certain American things appear to be mysterious to Europeans, in particular American environmentalism. Most could not seem to imagine that grass-roots opposition to the Concorde, for instance, was not a U.S. government or aircraft-industry plot—any more than we can imagine, say, why the English would allow operagoers to blight the exquisite rural peace of Glyndebourne by arriving in helicopters.

Jane Kramer, an adaptable and shrewd reporter of diverse cultures (Morocco, Italy, Yugoslavia, Ireland), focused her study of Texas on one representative cowboy, Henry Blanton; his wife, Betsy; their family and friends. Henry is the foreman of a large ranch in the Panhandle, and, at forty, is something of a burnt-out case, facing the likelihood that he will never have a place of his own, or the independence and self-pride that his understanding of the American dream, Western-style, has led him implicitly to expect. To Kramer, but also to Henry himself, he is the last of a "disappearing breed" of American. He is still a cowboy who uses traditional methods of handling cattle (range, rope, horse, corral, brand) in the face of developments that mechanize, depersonalize, and brutalize the production of beef, and dispossess people like himself. But he and people like him are disappearing also because they are poorly adapted for survival in America. They have accepted certain myths about the West, and extrapolated certain expectations and ideals of personal conduct which, like lethal mutations, put them at a disadvantage in the great struggle for existence. "The way *we* live; it's just people helping people. It's people neighboring. Like when a cowman has a grass fire, . . . why you just get everybody out there helping. Whereas I heard for a fact . . . that when certain farmers have a fire they have to go and call the firemen."

"Myth" is a word with at least two common significances, one of them referring to a cherished core of ostensibly historical stories

(Kit Carson, Paul Bunyan) that serve to explain present beliefs and practices; more and more it comes to be used in the sense of delusion. Kramer sees the myths Henry Blanton lives by in this second sense:

> It took . . . the imagination of Easterners to produce a proper cowboy—a cowboy whom children could idolize, and grown men, chafing at their own domesticated competence, hold as a model of some profoundly masculine truth. . . . The proper cowboy was a fiction appropriate to a frontier so wild and inhospitable that most Easterners regarded it as a landscape of Manichaean possibilities. He became for those Easterners the frontier's custodian. They made him Rousseau's Émile with a six-gun. They turned man-in-nature into a myth of natural man, and added natural justice to ease the menace of a place that lay beyond their hegemony and their institutions. They saw to it that he was born good, and that if he died violently, he died wise and defiant and uncorrupted. They set him against outlaws and spoilers, card sharks and Comanches. Their fears became his own sworn enemies.

Kramer's point is that Henry Blanton and others like him, believing his myth, believed in a West that never existed, "a West as sentimental and as brutal as the people who made a virtue of that curious combination of qualities and called it the American experience." In the real West, where cattle is big business run by people who live in London or Pasadena, literal, trustful people like Henry are destroyed by their naïveté.

As we would expect, Kramer approves of neither sentimentality nor brutality, and deplores their association with the American character. She is sorry that Henry Blanton totes guns and acts up in barrooms and is so foolish as to believe that a handshake seals a bargain. Henry has been done out of several good deals in his life because he doesn't think you should have to get things in writing. Kramer's lack of sympathy for Henry's credulity is in itself somewhat unsympathetic; credulity, of all human follies, is after all the easiest to spot, in other people. And, in her affectionate impatience with him, she perhaps does not do justice to the decency and desirability of some of Henry's beliefs, to principles of conduct that will only be acted on as long as people believe in them.

People seem always to have had the sneaking suspicion that we need exemplary myths—noble lies, as Plato called them—defending their beneficial effect on the conduct of the unenlightened, the way enlightened Victorians who had given up religion nonetheless recommended it for the average person. Like it or not, we as Americans have had a deeply formative body of exemplary myths, of which the movies of Glenn Ford and John Wayne are some recent expressions; and one would have to agree with Kramer that the values they communicate, like those of many religions, do not seem any longer to serve the interest of the individual who holds them. But if Henry's values (cooperation; a man's word is his bond; responsibility to family) are dismissed without regard, society loses yet more props to its teetering structure—the "breakdown" so complacently predicted by all.

Betsy Blanton's values are a little out of fashion, too, and Kramer's impatience with her shows. She perhaps describes Betsy's bathroom in too great detail. Betsy, sunk in her own crisis of becoming forty and wondering what it all means, finds relief in action, as Matthew Arnold would have advised; she redecorates her little house:

Two satiny blue shower curtains went up, drawn back on either side with velvet bows to frame the bathtub. Soon plastic ivy drooped from the ceiling. Plastic chrysanthemums, in little gilt pots, sat precariously around the rim of the washbasin and the tub. The room took on a wet, heady smell, which came from steaming bathwater and too much Airwick Herbal Bouquet, and one morning, after searching in the mist for half an hour, Henry was horrified to discover his toothbrush in a bud vase and his razor and shaving soap in a Maxwell House coffee can disguised by grosgrain ribbon and paper lace.

Kramer does not patronize—she is too kind, and too good a reporter for that. But one senses her lack of sympathy for that brave plastic ivy. Much could be said of the poverty of poor Betsy's alternatives, in the Panhandle society of unreconstructed male chauvinists of vigorous sincerity: "I hear them liberated women don't want no separate rest rooms. Well, I say fine. Let them fight in the wars, too. Let them have the same jails as what the men have. Let them play football. . . ." Kramer wisely forbears to comment. Hers is the touch of a novelist and a satirist; her writing, although admirably economical, can seem a bit as if she is working hard to keep powerful dramatizing and shaping impulses under control.

The Last Cowboy is in fact so like a novel in many ways that it makes you wonder, as people have often wondered before, just why a work is or isn't one. If you wrote the story of the people next door as factually as possible, but changed their names (just what novelists are always doing), you could call your book a fiction. Henry and Betsy Blanton are not the real names of Kramer's cowboys. Perhaps The Last Cowboy is non-fiction because it contains true facts about the cattle industry—the way Moby Dick contains facts about whaling. Anyhow, this shapely narrative has the dramatic and suitable ending of a novel: the essentially gentle Henry, frustrated by yet another defeat in his wish to have a few cattle of his own, his own place, independence, vents his disappointment by castrating a neighbor's bulls, who have got loose among his cows. The distinction between genres of fiction and non-fiction is perhaps only of interest to librarians and literary critics, but novelists are entitled to complain, I think, of the politer way writers of non-fiction are treated, being allowed, as the novelist is not, to say, "That's the way it really happened." No one yet understands, I take it, why the serious reader of today, as much as the Puritan reader of Defoe, feels more trustful of "reality" than of imagination, which is often so much truer.

In some cultures, like Japan, people, by putting the best possible face on disaster or failure, perhaps thereby develop a certain actual imperviousness, but this is not given to Americans. Kramer's cowboys are ashamed of themselves because, by not being successful the way they had been led by Saturday-afternoon Westerns to believe they would be, they have let America down. And America has let them down. Henry is resentful, but he is mostly sad and confused. He has no alternative skills or articles of faith to make another start with, but with other skills—and a more skeptical nature—he might go to Alaska.

If you live in the Western United States, you meet many Alaskans, and people who are planning to go there or have been there, some expecting to get rich, but most looking for a place where a deal can still be sealed with a handshake—where ideals of independence and voluntary cooperation are still functional. Last year I floated the Snake River in deer season; the scenery was matchless, there were no other humans in sight; but owing to the peculiar acoustics of the canyon, you could hear the voices of hunters at every turn, and finally the raftsman, a young local guide and sheriff's deputy, burst out, almost tearfully: This country is ruined. A man like him can now no longer ever expect to own an acre in the Tetons, or a foot along the river: all is overrun, full of strangers, expensive, impossible. He was going, he said, to Alaska. College kids go up there summers for the lucrative fishing. San Francisco architects will build the new capital. The point is that for many people, especially in the West, Alaska is an actual and possible frontier. For Easterners, one guesses, its significance is mostly metaphorical, and this profound difference is reflected, too, in the more conservative, romantic, and individualistic politics of the West.

For some people Alaska could mean immense profits in timber, land, minerals, and oil, and the sacrifice of the private individual and the public interest. John McPhee, a writer who is able to be interesting on almost any subject, is particularly skilled at presenting the dynamics of those complicated conflicting forces. An outdoorsman, romantic but also astute and accepting, he understands the wilderness, he appreciates naïveté, and he also sees who will sell out whom.

The writer of recent nonfiction chooses his role in his narrative as carefully as a novelist does. Jane Kramer, after explaining her presence in Texas and admitting to uneasy dreams of rattlesnakes and tornadoes, fades gracefully out, leaving the reader to wonder how she managed to overhear those misogynist cowboys on subjects they would not consider proper for women to hear. McPhee is more vividly present throughout his book, asking questions, commenting, making himself the butt of an occasional joke or misfortune, admitting to scary dreams about grizzly bears. He has a fine instinct for knowing when his corporeal presence is essential, as here, in a wilderness of unimaginable vastness and coldness, where to see him squatting apprehensively over a campfire or huddling in a deserted cabin is to have the unimaginable made accessible to us.

*Coming into the Country* is in three parts, beginning with an account of a river trip by canoe and kayak in northern Alaska that McPhee took with four other men. Here he tells us something of the size and climate of the state, and a few of its myths. One myth, a friend tells him, "is that in Alaska there's a fish on every cast, a moose behind every tree. But the fish and the moose aren't there. . . . To get to the headwaters of a river like this one takes a lot of money. The state needs to look to the budgets and desires of people who cannot afford to come to a place like this."

In the second part, McPhee flies over Alaska with people who are appointed to choose the site of a new capital, which will (perhaps) be built from scratch because political factionalism prevents the small Alaskan population from agreeing on which of the already existing cities would do. The search provides McPhee an occasion for discussing the positions of each party: natives, old-timers, environmentalists, developers, and Feds squaring off for the biggest land grab in history. Alaska consists of 375 million acres. Forty million have been settled on native Alaskans. The fate of the rest is largely undecided, but some eighty million acres have been proposed for national parks and wilderness area.

In the third and longest section of his book, McPhee talks to people in Eagle, Alaska, in the Yukon. It is a kind of chorale for Alaskan voices, and gives the reader a strong sense of the kind of original, skeptical, resourceful people who have come here. With what patience McPhee records, and with what fascination one reads, the minutiae of the Alaskan diet or dwelling: "Boone chinked his walls and insulated his floor and ceiling with moss collected by his children, planning to supplement it with cement and lime, while the Greenes used fibre glass between their logs. With their heating stove and cooking stove, the Greenes had powerful defenses against the coming cold, almost enough to drive them out into the snow, because if their cabin was handsome, it was ten times as snug. A lighted match could make it warm. The Greenes burn wood at the rate of four cords a winter. The Boones, with their larger cabin, use fifteen." "Jack Greene has built an efficient cistern, with an adroit plumbing system that services a kitchen sink and a solar-heated shower." There are about 250 pages of such information—Alaska as utopia, albeit a utopia with population problems and littered with old rubber tires.

Gaston Bachelard, in *The Poetics of Space*, writes of the human love of musing on primitiveness: "restored, desired, and experienced through simple images, an album of pictures of huts would constitute a textbook of simple exercises for the phenomenology of the imagination." McPhee's book is, in a way, such an album, for the hut-dreamer, for the city-dweller. Even the coldness of Alaska is of primal importance: "a reminder of winter strengthens the happiness of inhabiting" the warm flat. McPhee, at home in Alaska in a way that Kramer is not in Texas, is sympathetic to simplicity, and his is a communicable sympathy. "What a striking thing it is that a mere image of the old homestead in snow-drifts should be able to integrate images of the year one thousand in the mind of a child," exclaims Bachelard. If you loved *Swiss Family Robinson*, you'll love John McPhee.

The people McPhee talks to point out that Alaska is our last-chance wilderness, meaning either that it is our last large unspoiled area, to be preserved from development and environmental exploitation, or that it is the last place a man like Henry Blanton can go when he is pushed out of the Lower Forty-eight by industrial or corporate or governmental interests that have no regard for him. At the moment the wilderness preservers, with the federal government as an ally, seem to prevail. Until 1958, the settler could acquire federal land by homesteading, but now it is hard for a private person to buy land in Alaska. People are huddled together on small lots in cities, and urban crowding is a matter of genuine concern. The federal agent makes the solitary trapper leave his little hut, and the trapper and squatter have come to see the Fed as the enemy, the same kind of enemy big cattle interests are to Henry Blanton. Behind the federal agent is the big-city dreamer with his sentimental yearning for the primitive wilderness. Alaska is not for private interests, say the preservers, but for all Americans, and therefore it cannot belong to Henry, or to the sheriff's deputy from Wyoming, or to the alienated college kids who wish to recover the good American myths, who want to get away from cities, from regimentation, and from politics. (Even Western politicians want to get away from politics, like Paul Hatfield, the new senator from Montana, whose initial remarks at his swearing-in last week expressed the common Western view: "I have been increasingly concerned about the continuing infringement of federal activity on the sovereignty of the states and the lives of the people.")

Between the ecologist and the lone trapper there need be no antagonism, for neither will do the other much harm, and it will be too bad if these factions become locked in an opposition so intense that they cannot combine forces against the much more powerful oil, mineral, and real-estate interests who care for neither of them, nor for the wilderness, nor even for the idea of the wilderness. And one cannot help questioning the motivation of the U.S. government, suddenly so conservation-minded, where only four hundred thousand people are concerned, when it does so little to preserve the environment of millions of people in the Lower Forty-eight against entrenched private interests. Alaska presents the government with a cheap way to placate environmentalists without offending big real estate or big oil or big timber by trying to protect the more accessible, rarer, and therefore more precious areas in the rest of the U.S. We've given you eighty million acres of wilderness preserve, it can say; what do you want to worry about Lake Tahoe or the Everglades for? And meanwhile the Alaskan wilderness is inaccessible even to Alaskans. "We need parks near our cities," an Alaskan told me. "Go fishing near Anchorage, you'll get someone else's fishhook in your eye. To get away from other people you have to charter a plane."

McPhee's own prescription for Alaska seems sensible:

> Only an easygoing extremist would preserve every bit of the country. And extremists alone would exploit it all. Everyone else has to think the matter through, choose a point of tolerance, however much the point might tend to one side. For myself, I am closer to the preserving side—that is, the side that would preserve . . . [the lone trapper, or Henry Blanton]. To be sure, I would preserve plenty of land as well. My own margin of tolerance would not include some faceless corporation "responsible" to a hundred thousand stockholders, making a crater you could see from the moon. Nor would it include visiting exploiters—here in the seventies, gone in the eighties—with some pipe and some skyscrapers left behind. . . . Alaska . . . by virtue of its climate, will always screen its own, and will not be overrun. If I were writing the ticket, I would say that anyone at all is free to build a cabin on any federal land in the United States that is at least a hundred miles from the nearest town of ten thousand or more—the sole restriction being that you can't carry in materials for walls or roofs or floors.

"In the society as a whole," says McPhee, "there is an elemental need for a frontier outlet, for a pioneer place to go—important even to those who do not go there." This proposition, which most Americans would accept without argument, may have some things to be said against it. Societies without frontiers are different from those that have them, and perhaps have advantages. Just as life in prison is said to be more endurable when there is no chance of escape, so perhaps will we only learn to live in our cities—the real places Americans have to learn to live in—when we cannot dream of escape. Without a frontier we would have to address ourselves seriously to living with what we have, something that the attitude in Congress toward energy makes clear we are at present unable to do.

A society without frontiers must devote itself to politics; politics means factions, divisions—or, to put it positively, engagement. To the Westerner, those are qualities of Eastern American life he would avoid, and he feels them coming west. The Easterner is suspicious of the laid-back Westerner, and may feel that his myths are degenerate and brutal, associated with things like guns which our society would be better off without.

If the urban civilization is ripe or inevitable, it could be that keeping Alaska in wilderness, or as a last frontier, may be just an unnecessary cultural luxury, slightly fake, like a giant Disneyland Wilderness Visit temporarily closed for repair; maybe we would do better to subdue it at once, incorporate its riches, abandon our individualist philosophies, and resign ourselves to our perimeters. But most of us would agree, I think, with the implications of McPhee's book, that keeping an Alaskan frontier is in fact a cultural safeguard, protecting certain valuable myths of independence and cooperation and personal enterprise that appear to be surviving there. Maybe noble lies can only thrive in open, clean places, and if they can survive, then maybe they can exert some regenerative power over the rest of American life.

# Ruskin as Guide

THE RELATION OF a traveler to his guidebook is a sensitive one; an unsuitable choice can blight your expensive and brief visit to a distant city as surely as finding yourself there with an incompatible lover, or a fussy eater, or someone whose feet hurt. Anyone who has trudged across miles of strange streets to find himself looking at a dull municipal mural or a museum that's shut has some intimation of the delicacy of this relation; not only must your guidebook have its facts straight, it must also understand what you have come there for.

For Venice, the Victorians had their reliable Baedekers and their abridged editions of Ruskin's *Stones of Venice,* from which they imbibed new ideas: for instance, that St. Mark's did not look, as Mark Twain had put the representative view, like a "vast and warty bug taking a meditative walk," but was beautiful instead. Ruskin is still a marvelous guide, stimulating if crotchety—a marvelous guide but an unsafe ruler, someone has said. But until now, seeing Venice with Ruskin meant lugging the heavy three volumes of *Stones* in your carry-on, or taking a Xerox of the appendix, "Venetian Index"; and you would find using it difficult because of the way everything has been moved and changed.

Ruskin brought to Venice not the dutiful receptiveness with which the authors of most modern guides smile, like the Last Duchess, on everything, but a historical thesis, a strong preference for Venetian Gothic, a passion for Tintoretto, and a dislike

of Titian, Renaissance architecture, and much else. His dislikes
are as invigorating as his passions: "it is impossible to conceive a
design more gross, more barbarous, more childish in conception,
more servile in plagiarism, more insipid in result, more con-
temptible under every point of rational regard," he tells you of
Palladio's San Giorgio Maggiore, which you had been thinking
looked quite nice. He forces you to justify your regard for Palla-
dian building or abandon it, but it is the dialectic that is energiz-
ing, and educates the eye. As Charlotte Brontë wrote of *Modern
Painters*, "I feel now as if I had been walking blindfolded—this
book seems to give me eyes," so do you need your eyes and wits
about you here, if only to argue with this opinionated companion.

In the *San Francisco Chronicle* (November 14, 1978), Alan
Temko, the architecture critic, praising an office-building complex planned for Levi Strauss, strikes out with truly Ruskinian in-
temperance at "preservationist spooks" and "the creepy Landmarks
Advisory Board, whose adoration of the past verges on necrophil-
ia" (the board had wanted some arches on a façade). In Manhattan
a high-rise develops a mansard roof; housing projects everywhere,
in sudden defiance of many tenets of the modern style, sport the
shed roofs and redwood siding of the northern California vernacular style. It is in the context, perhaps, of the growing division
between the mandarins of modern public architecture and buildings that people actually like that Ruskin begins to be truly intelligible, perhaps for the first time in the way he had intended. It
takes a modern city to help you see what Ruskin meant about
Venice then.

The interior of San Giorgio Maggiore "is like a large assembly
room," he says, and you have to admit it's true. He slyly concedes
that Longhena's great Baroque church, Santa Maria della Salute,
is graceful, explaining why ("the inequality of size in its cupolas,
and pretty grouping of the two campaniles behind them"), and
tells you interesting facts about Turner's painting of the steps. He
then comments on the hypocrisy of the buttresses, "for the cupola
is stated by Lazari to be of timber, and therefore needs none." As
modern people, largely because of Ruskinian principles that we

have assimilated from modern architecture, we join him in disapproving of sham. Little by little it begins to seem not only that whatever he says is of interest, but also that it is often, even usually, right—so persuasive is he, and so indulgent, too, of the truths of our nature: for instance, in the Doge's Palace, where he recommends that "the multitude of works by various masters which cover the walls of this palace is so great that the traveler is in general merely wearied and confused by them. He had better refuse all attention" except to a few of the important ones, to which he directs us, among them the great Tintoretto *Paradise,* three Veroneses he admired, and a Titian, *The Doge Grimani Kneeling Before Faith,* notable "as one of the most striking examples of Titian's want of feeling and coarseness of conception." (The really conscientious traveler can top up with one of the better and more thorough modern guidebooks, like Hugh Honour's *Companion Guide to Venice* in the Fodor series.)

Like other enthusiasts, Ruskin assumes a certain irreverent familiarity with his subject and feels free to stigmatize faults in buildings and painters he loves: for instance, of Tintoretto's *Adoration of the Shepherds* in the Scuola di San Rocco: "it is most curious that no part of the work seems to have been taken any pleasure in by the painter; it is all by his hand, but it looks as if he had been bent only on getting over the ground." This somehow animates one's idea of Tintoretto, drooping in ennui, hungover perhaps, painting in the background, and in turn gives the monumental accomplishment of the Scuola paintings some human scale. Thus does Ruskin animate all of Venice—its buildings, painters, the history of the place, the principles of its architecture. He explains, with diagrams, the orders of Venetian arches and how they developed, and Gothic capitals. He takes the viewer over the capitals of the Doge's Palace one by one, and requires him to look at the least distinguished Venetian palazzo, as well as its greatest buildings, with the care he himself took. Having your visual consciousness raised by Ruskin can even be risky, as when he writes about Tintoretto's Saint Sebastian, which he admired because the arrows impale the saint so gruesomely. "In the common martyrdom of Saint Sebastian they are stuck into him here and there like pins, as if they had been shot from a great distance and had come faltering down, . . . and rather bleeding the saint to death than mortally wounding him." This does, you will find, permanently qualify your regard for other pinstuck Saint Sebastians.

Arnold Whittick's *Ruskin's Venice* is an updated and augmented edition of the "Venetian Index," improved with considerable knowledge and editorial tact, correcting errors in Ruskin, who had a weak head for dates and for Italian names, and adding material from Ruskin's other works where the "Venetian Index" is cryptic; for example, when Ruskin passes over the great Tintoretto *Crucifixion* in the Scuola as being beyond analysis and above praise, Whittick provides Ruskin's own long analysis and praise from the second volume of *Modern Painters*. He also adds helpful or interesting information about events since Ruskin's day, takes note of things that have been moved, tells you about closing hours, and provides a map and many photographs as well as Ruskin's own drawings.

Whittick is an architectural historian, and his remarks on restorations in Venice are particularly interesting. He is enabled by recent work to tell us things that Ruskin would perhaps have liked to have known—for instance, that some of Tintoretto's skies have changed from mid-blue to reddish brown. One might complain that Whittick could have included even more material from *St. Mark's Rest, Mornings in Florence*, and others of Ruskin's works, and need not have abridged Ruskin's account of St. Mark's. He could perhaps have noted where Ruskin was later to change his mind, as he did about Titian, whose paintings at the time of *Stones* Ruskin found "as feeble as they are monstrous." No doubt Whittick was dictated to by considerations of length, and as it is, this is no pocket guide.

Only one serious complaint can be made: a reader unfamiliar with Ruskin's general point of view about art and architecture might find some of his commentary bewilderingly eccentric, and could profit by a general prefatory discussion of Ruskin's ideas and influence. Ruskin believed that there was a general relation of architecture to national character, and his purpose was to show that the architecture of twelfth-century Venice was superior to later Venetian architecture because it reflected the moral qualities of a "thoughtful Nation and a Pure Nation living up to its conscience." Buildings are hard evidence, and the fall of Venice from purity and thoughtfulness is, in his view, apparent in her decline from Byzantine Gothic into the Renaissance style; and of course he intended an analogy with the ugly building of Victorian England.

Better known is Ruskin's view that Gothic architecture was in general superior to other styles because it allowed freedom of expression to the workman. His ideas about the creative potential of each workman greatly influenced the arts-and-crafts movement, which in its turn influenced modern architecture but now seems to characterize the writings of an architectural counter-establishment, expressed in underground little books like *Handmade Houses: A Guide to the Woodbutcher's Art** and courses on how to build your own hut. His ideas on the relation of building to public morality were taken up, in quite elaborate disguises, chiefly that of functionalism to begin with, but are even more evident now in the rhetoric of a new architecture that wants doors to "celebrate the entrance experience," and so on.

Modern architecture is both the heir and the reaction to nineteenth-century ideas about building. Nikolaus Pevsner begins *Pioneers of Modern Design* by quoting a famous statement of Ruskin's that "ornamentation is the principal part of architecture," a statement that Pevsner takes as not peculiar to Ruskin but typical of the general attitude of his time. From the modern point of view, the Victorians liked their buildings as they liked their parlors, overdecorated. But in Ruskin's case, the remark about ornament has cost him, perhaps only until now, a serious audience for his architectural criticism. It seems a hard fate for Ruskin, whose life was so tormented anyway, that posterity would judge his ideas by standards even more puritanical than those dictated by

*By Art Boericke and Barry Shapiro (Scrimshaw Press, 1973).

his own evangelical conscience; for it is surely lingering puritanism that explains the modern disapproval of decoration, of mere added ornament, explains our idea that a love of ornament is rather childish or primitive, born in Ruskin's case (it has been suggested) of sexual frustration or even of an ocular defect.

Besides a foolish love of ornament, Ruskin's understanding of space has also been derided. Because he seldom discusses it, people have said he didn't understand it, or even that he was unable to perceive three-dimensional space, an idea that any of his brilliant architectural drawings ought to dispel. Or they have thought, despite the strangely fascinating chapters in *Stones of Venice* on walls, cornices, capitals, and other structural details, that he had no understanding of structural matters at all.

John Unrau's modestly contentious and convincing study of what Ruskin did really say about looking at buildings (*Looking at Architecture with Ruskin*), his aesthetic principles quite apart from his ethical ones, suggests that Ruskin's techniques of analysis were more shrewd and more theoretical than he has been given credit for. Unrau attacks these interpretations of Ruskin's ideas by demonstrating abundant references in Ruskin's writings to space and mass, and by showing that Ruskin uses the term "ornament" in a broader sense than is usually realized. It is we, not Ruskin, who are limited by our preoccupation with the metaphorical significance of "façade." Not only did he have a quite contemporary view of function, disapproving of superfluous ornament, as in his strictures against the useless buttresses of the Salute, he also devised sound principles of analysis which modern architectural critics could use.

It is true that Ruskin believed that ornament, in a very broad sense, distinguishes architecture from mere building, just as Le Corbusier believed it, in Ruskin's sense. Unrau says Ruskin means by ornament any major subdivision of a structure, depending on the distance from which it is to be viewed. At a distance the broad designs of buttresses or towers in the landscape are ornamental, and their propriety is to be judged in that context. Up close, the details of a frieze are ornamental. Ornament is never something extra added to a building to beautify it, though Ruskin has been thought to believe that is exactly what it is. Instead, he is clear on insisting on subordination of detail to the visual whole. The criterion for judgment is always appropriateness; finely finished details would be weak and useless on upper stories where they cannot be seen. Unrau stresses how much of Ruskin's considerable power of ridicule was directed at the architecture of his own day, which was loaded with mechanical, derivative, machine-made, "unfelt" ornament, a judgment with which posterity has tended to agree while unfairly blaming Ruskin, as an enthusiast of the Gothic, for its inspiration.

Another contribution of Ruskin's is to attempt to bring color into the discussion of architecture, which is conventionally treated, now as in the nineteenth century, as if it occurred in black and white and at an unchanging time of day. His attempts to formulate aesthetic theories concerning color were original if not definitive. He found when he "entered on it [that] there were no existing data in the notebooks of painters from which any first principles could be deduced," and Unrau points out that despite a century of experiment, visual psychologists still cannot explain why some arrangements of color are more pleasing than others. Nonetheless, Ruskin does advance some principles, the most startling of which, we might think, is that color should be "visibly independent of form," as it is in the Doge's Palace, where "wall surface is chequered with marble blocks of pale rose, the chequers being in no wise harmonized, or fitted to the forms of the windows; but looking as if the surface had been completed first, and the windows cut out of it."

It is well known that for nearly every opinion Ruskin expresses, it is possible to find in his works a contradictory view; and it is a common pitfall in studying Ruskin, as a way of getting over his inconsistencies, to relate whatever he said to his state of mind at the time, a procedure that results in most interesting studies of Ruskin himself but fails, usually, to elucidate the fundamentals of his ideas with the clarity with which Unrau has done here. By strictly limiting his focus, Unrau is enabled to conclude that Ruskin had several really very original contributions to make to the study of architecture: "his constant watchfulness for the modifying effect that small details can have on the eye's grasp of the overall composition would, if emulated, do much to increase the sophistication of contemporary analysis." And his understanding of the role of light, shadow, and color in modifying our perception of form should enter into a modern architectural criticism which largely ignores these elements and instead treats mass and surface as if they were abiding instead of different from one minute to the next. Finally, not the least of his accomplishments, Ruskin was a brilliant architectural draftsman.

Robert Hewison's survey of Ruskin's life and ideas, *John Ruskin: The Argument of the Eye*, succeeds gracefully in treating Ruskin's ideas and life both, and managing the contradictions, by holding (to summarize his view) that Ruskin's ideas seem to lack ordinary coherence because we approach them in the wrong way. Ruskin was not a logical thinker, and his habit of mind can be more easily understood in terms of a distinction elaborated by the visual psychologist Rudolf Arnheim between the scientific and the aesthetic observer, of which Ruskin was, obviously, the latter. The aesthetic observer does not systematize on the basis of constant qualities abstracted from perceived objects but is instead involved in their changing relation to a visual context. Ruskin was a looker of this kind, and then proceeded in a Hegelian manner to define things as a series of polarities, whose oppositions and contradictions would lead him closer and closer to Truth.

Viewing Ruskin in this way, his critics are at least relieved of a tendency to feel embarrassed at his changes of mind, though why changes of mind in seers and sages are found so distressing is a great question. Hewison's is a readable, unaffected book, very helpfully explicating the cultural and social influences on Ruskin's thought, in particular, at first, Wordsworth and evangelical religion, but also minor works on mineralogy and geology and romantic travel literature like Samuel Prout's *Picturesque Sketches* and H. B. de Saussure's *Voyages dans les Alpes*. He presents a clear discussion of his thought in the context of his biography; whatever the reasons, intellectual or emotional, Ruskin continued to read, grow, and change his mind throughout his life. As late as 1877, in Venice, he was studying Carpaccio. Hewison avoids what he, like many English critics, feels to be excessive psychologizing: "it does not seem to help very much to say that 'Ruskin associated Gothic architecture with sexual potency, and came to admire Gothic largely because it represented this quality,' " a judgment with which most of us would agree. "It is as works of mind, comprehending all the cultural and social influences at work as well as the psychological stresses, that Ruskin's writings must be treated," and so he has done.

Quentin Bell's 1963 short critical biography *(Ruskin)*, recently reissued, has the same intention and is a helpful introductory or summary presentation of Ruskin's life and work. The new edition differs very little from the original, a fact the jacket copy does not indicate. The new bibliography contains some recent references, and the *op. cit.*'s have been changed to *ibid.*'s. Like Hewison, Bell is tactful and judicious. It would be interesting to know to what extent Ruskin's influence has been modified by our knowledge of his sexual situation (impotency and nympholepsy), a variation of the old critical question about whether a bad man can write a good book. Certainly this aspect of his biography has drawn from posterity a debate more vigorous than has, say, the alleged character flaws of Milton, engaging indignant defenders of his virility, angry descendants of Effie Ruskin Millais, even partisans of Rose La Touche; and Mr. Bell is not unaffected by a sense of battle, as the terms of his discussion suggest: "Without an understanding [of Ruskin's sex life] we cannot assess the really serious charges that have been brought against him by Admiral James. No one will be so foolish as to blame him for being impotent, but he may more justly be accused of making his wife unnecessarily unhappy."

# The Loss of Patriotic Faith:
# C. D. B. Bryan's *Friendly Fire*

## I

IT APPEARS THAT the most heroic tale for the Bicentennial, the one with the greatest power to animate feelings of national pride, is of the struggle of the American against his government. Costumed Redcoats, fascists, communists, and other traditional enemies cannot generate in us the same dread and indignation with which many of us have come to regard our leaders and guardians, from whom we had expected better if only because they had the advantages of an American upbringing. Disillusion is a powerful emotion, which explains, in part, the force of this account of the disenchantment of a pair of decent Middle Americans, whose experience must awaken in each reader, in his own way, his own sense of loss.

Peg and Gene Mullen, farmers from La Porte City, Iowa, began by suspecting that the army had concealed some of the details of their son's death in Vietnam. In the end they came to ask themselves "what was the point of five generations of a family working the same land if they had become as enemies to that nation upon which their land rested," and their nation was in turn revealed as an enemy to them? This is only the first of many questions raised by this interesting work, which is concerned, finally, with more than just whether the army misled grieving American parents from a wish to conceal its own errors, or simply through the ineptness and bureaucratic insensitivity which the author sees as characteristic of war; or whether the judgment of the parents was distorted beyond reason by their sorrow. From the interaction of the reporter, C. D. B. Bryan, the Mullens, and the military, there emerges a significant and subtle reflection on the moral conditions of the society that produced, and variously tolerated or rejected, the war in Vietnam.

Michael Mullen was drafted out of graduate school, not wanting to go but not questioning his duty, sent to Vietnam with Charlie Company, and killed by American artillery fire. His parents were first led to believe his death resulted from Viet Cong infiltration of South Vietnamese artillery installations, the first of many misunderstandings. The Mullens could perhaps have borne their grief more easily if they had been able to resolve the many inconsistencies and imprecisions in the official explanations they received. Instead they became convinced that things were being deliberately concealed.

They understood the bureaucratic incompetency, but it was infuriating. The army could not keep Michael's rank, the nature of his wounds, or even his personal effects straight. Sympathetic letters ostensibly from two different officers were really sent by some staff clerk using the same slightly awry date stamp. The army docked Michael's paycheck by nine days, penalizing him for getting killed before he had served long enough to earn back his advance leave.

But grieving parents were not supposed to notice things like this. In its concern to market the war, the army kept a staff, like the PR department of an expensive mortuary, to come with the village priest to give the Mullens the news, to assist them with funeral arrangements, to attend the funeral wearing uniforms. Did they want a military funeral? A flag on the casket? And, in particular, the Mullens were asked for the name of one of Michael's friends in Vietnam, to escort his body home.

The escort business was a charade, too. In their grief, the Mullens were tenacious and combative. When Michael's body came back with any old escort, they bitterly persisted in their objections: "We were told that to have a deceased soldier's body returned accompanied by a special escort chosen by the next of kin was . . . a right accorded the families of *all* war victims."

The army tried to tell them it would take too long: "Tell that lady in La Porte City that she can have her escort in—take it or leave it—ten to fifteen more days." Peg's response was typically trenchant: "You can tell that sonuvabitch in the Pentagon that I'll wait fifteen years for my son to come back! My son's dead! We could put off having him come back in a casket forever!" When the Mullens continued to insist, they were threatened with reprisal against the escort, who, they were told, would probably be returned to combat even if he had a safe job now.

When Michael's body did arrive home, the wound bore little relation to accounts of his death, and the Mullens' anxieties were further aroused. They began to write and to receive letters from his comrades. And it wasn't long before they realized that deaths like Michael's, which was called by the army "misadventure" from "friendly fire," were non-battle casualties and therefore not being reported to the American people. There were other categories, too, by which the deaths in Vietnam could be reported in such a way as to make Americans think they were fewer in number than they were.

The Mullens resolved to spend Michael's gratuity pay in some way to bring this situation to the attention of other Iowans. They took a half-page ad in a Sunday *Des Moines Register*, showing, simply, 714 crosses for the 714 Iowans who had died in Vietnam. Encouraged by an uproar of questioning and concern, they were drawn more deeply into a campaign of obsessive letter-writing, phoning, visits, and public appearances. From the beginning their concern was to educate other Iowans—Middle Americans of whom, as Bryan says, they continued to think of themselves as representative, even when they appeared to be most alienated from the attitudes of their community.

As Midwestern, middle-aged farmers who had given a son for their country, they had an image untainted by radicalism in any form, and, perhaps unlike long-haired peaceniks, they did get answers to their letters, people in Washington returned their calls—and they also got what they would not have believed possible in a land whose goodness and integrity they had taken for granted: lies from American generals who looked them straight in the eye, insults and physical abuse in the course of peaceful protest, verbal abuse from their own senator (Jack Miller; Harold Hughes appears to have been responsive and concerned). They became enemies in the eyes of their country.

At one point Peg Mullen says to a Pentagon official, "Colonel, we can read. We're not just stupid farmers out here." It was this realization, however belated, that had panicked an administration that had counted on the support of "the heart of America." Now the Mullens, who thought of themselves as representative Americans, were placed on "lists," put under surveillance, and probably wiretapped along with the dangerous radicals and intellectuals. It was never clear who was meant to be left as the constituency.

How can one explain the reluctance of people in the Midwest to recognize what was happening in Vietnam? In part it may have been simple lack of information. Midwesterners who go to live elsewhere learn fast enough—and many express the feeling that there was much they did not hear at home, especially from the Midwestern press. People who live in urban centers forget, or perhaps cannot imagine, the regional variations in the treatment of current events in this country, even though local differences are taken for granted as natural, even charming, in much smaller nations like England. Add to this that Midwesterners are often deeply skeptical, not credulous, and it seems likely that many people didn't believe much of the news that came from untrustworthy Eastern places like Washington.

Nonetheless, many of them do seem to have difficulty with the distinction between protest and complaint. Stoicism is an admired virtue. A man should stand up for what he believes, but his beliefs should not seem to be self-serving. A man should oppose social injustice and face controversial situations, but in fact, in this homogeneous society, he seldom encounters any. La Porte City, for instance, was almost entirely Protestant and Republican (though the Mullens were Democrats and Catholics), and there was only one non-Caucasian, an Indian woman.

Mere complainers are deeply resented. Senator Jack Miller replied to one of the Mullens' antiwar letters by saying, "With few exceptions, the persons bearing the real burden of this war . . . have been the least complaining. . . . I regret that you are one of the exceptions," words that seem simply inhuman, but which must have echoed the sentiments of, say, the waitress at Mom's Cafe, who disapproved of Peg and Gene: "Other people have lost their sons, and they don't protest."

That they did not raise their children to protest is, now, one of the bitterest things the Mullens have to bear. "It's not that we didn't want Mikey to go, it's that we—we *let* him go!" And, "we raised Mikey in the belief that an individual, a man, *obeyed*. That you didn't question, and this was so wrong! So wrong. Mikey never went against an order. And this, this is our anguish! That we ever did such a thing to our child."

Bryan seems to deprecate Peg Mullen's emotional courage in recognizing this. "The one time during those five days I spent with the Mullens that Peg ever cried was when she spoke of having reared Michael to accept unquestioningly the authority of the United States Government. By magnifying the military's guilt, she could minimize this, the source of her own." But the military was partly to blame, and in accepting any measure of guilt, Peg Mullen showed herself brave enough to do what many parents have not done, that is, to accept the extent to which parents were in fact involved in the question of the drafting of their sons.

It is true that many American parents simply let their sons serve in the military, maybe out of principle, or out of ignorance, but some acting in the naïve but traditional belief that a few years in the army would shape up an otherwise intractable, troublesome, or immature kid, of whom, in the protesting, dope-ridden sixties, there were more than the usual number. In a curious, circular way, the resistance thus fed the war.

But geographical factors must also have played a part. Liberal parents on the coasts and sympathetic draft boards countenanced a greater variety of choices than Peg and Gene Mullen may have heard of—Canada, COs, jail. They may not have realized, in the very different moral climate of their town, the relative absence of stigma attached to these choices elsewhere. Before the end of the war something like half the draftees in Alameda County in California were refusing induction, something that was probably unimaginable in Iowa, even at the end. How can those mothers let their sons go, people would say in California, not realizing that those mothers did not have the company of thousands of others at every march and rally, and the possibility of a sympathetic judge in court. The regional inequity in the conduct of the draft will surely be a source of continuing bitterness in this society, for how can parents who lost their sons ever really forgive those who did not send theirs?

## II

C. D. B. Bryan wrote the Mullens' story because, concerned about Vietnam, he felt

there had to be some way to articulate the people's discontent, their estrangement from their government, their increasing paranoia and distrust. And what better way was there than to . . . [go] to Iowa? Iowans are among the most open, honest, friendly, trusting people in the country. If they seemed unsophisticated, then they were unsophisticated in the best possible sense: they believed in personal honor, that a man's word had meaning and that he was responsible for his acts. If the government of the United States had lost the loyalty and support of an Iowa farm family, then it indicated, to me at least, that the government was in very grave trouble indeed.

Eventually, Bryan was astonished at the intensity of the Mullens' indignation, and by the "seemingly inexhaustible volume of sources their outrage fed upon. Local school board elections, telephone company stock manipulations, draft inequities, Nixon's Vietnamization policies, farm subsidy programs, the voting records of incumbent congressmen and senators, the machinations of the military-industrial complex." Though Bryan was bemused by their original, romantic conception of America, he was also convinced that "the Mullens' surviving son and daughters would never possess so naïve a confidence in this nation's purpose or its leaders."

Bryan seems to be suggesting that in questioning the workings of these institutions, just as they questioned the workings of the military, the Mullens have failed to accept, or to grasp, that "manipulations," "inequities," "machinations," and the like are words that appropriately describe the modern world. Bryan seems to patronize them for resenting what he, on the other hand, appears to accept, though no doubt does not approve of.

I first read *Friendly Fire* in three parts in *The New Yorker*, the first two parts with sorrow for the death of Michael, sympathy for his gallant parents, troubled by the meaning of these events for our country, perhaps even at knowing how evil had come to innocent Iowa farms like the ones near where I grew up. Everyone must have found a great deal to identify with in Bryan's careful and compassionate account.

But I read the third part very uneasily. It was as if the Sinister Force had come in and finished Bryan's book for him in the night. Qualified, now, was the generous, sympathetic tone. A note of condescension had crept into his voice when he came to explain to the Mullens the "truth" of what he had discovered about Michael's death.

He tells them,

I don't believe the incident was deliberately covered up. I don't believe that there was ever a conspiracy. . . . The reason why you were never sent the results of the investigation was that the report was classified "For Official Use Only," a very minor security classification, but one which would nevertheless prevent it from being released to civilians without a "Need-to-Know." . . . the reason why the report was not sent was to spare you more anguish.

How did he know? It is not that he has himself investigated the military report; it is that he has visited Michael's battalion commander, a Lieutenant Colonel Schwarzkopf, and finds himself satisfied with the likable colonel's version of the events leading to Michael's death.

Despite some minor questions and inaccuracies, Bryan's conclusions will probably be the reader's conclusions, too. Why, then, should the reader find himself so dissatisfied? The problem may in part lie in the nature of New Journalistic accounts, in which truth is attested to, verified by third parties, taken from tapes, and so on, but dramatized like fiction. The reader experiences such accounts as both truth and fiction, that is, as adequate accounts of the real world, but also as having certain formal qualities we expect in art. If we complain that somehow coherence, integrity, unity have been violated in the work, the journalist can protest, like the student in a beginning creative-writing class, "But that's the way it really happened," and to a certain extent we have indeed contracted to believe him.

Perhaps, when, applying the criteria of both art and reality, you find tension or contradiction, you must just accept it as characteristic of this queer genre. Yet nothing in our experience of reality or of this book prepares us for, or can reconcile us to, the conclusion of the author that the officers were "fine men," and that Peg and Gene were, finally, tired fanatics whose obsession with their son's death was only their personal tragedy. One may object to these conclusions on the grounds of art—they seem capricious, unprepared—or one may accept them, and along with them the intransigence of facts in general, or one may simply feel, as I do, that the author betrays his work, like a painter who tires of his picture and, in abandoning his work too soon, leaves awkward blank patches.

For the reader, in this case, the effect is devastating. From the painstaking chronicle of official mendacity, mortal blunders, and moral evil, the shape of the circumstances of Michael's death emerges with a certain clarity: the certainty is that because of inadvertence, muddle, contingency, and waste, precise questions of guilt and accountability become impossible to ask or answer. The difficulty lies not in the fact that Bryan does accept the assurances of the military, but in the ease with which he does so, and in the suddenness with which he turns on the Mullens, who until now have been sympathetically presented.

This seems to transform him from a careful investigative journalist to something more like an unreliable narrator in a work of fiction, inviting scrutiny of his own motives and character. It is like what must have happened between Marlow and Kurtz out there in the heart of darkness, a realization of affinity, after which Marlow goes back and tells genteel lies about heroism to Kurtz's innocent fiancée. "I think it's important for you to know that both Schwarzkopf and Captain Tom Cameron, your son's company commander, were fine officers. Fine men," Bryan goes back and tells the Mullens. And it may be true; it probably is. Yet, in the context of this book, until now so strongly sympathetic to the Mullens, and for historical reasons, such as the army and government record for cover-ups, this conclusion needs more than simple assertion.

Bryan presents the Mullens with what he believes to be the truth about Michael's death. "I don't buy it," says Gene. "I don't buy Schwarzkopf, and I don't buy the military." For Bryan the Mullens become no longer prototypical Americans but fanatical, rigid in their hatred and bitterness. But the reader comes to wonder whether Bryan—trusting authority, easily lured by sincerity and surface plausibility, willing to accept "machinations" and "manipulations" as inevitable—is not himself a more representative American.

Here is one example of many: when Peg asks Bryan why the

soldiers who wrote to them were threatened with court-martials her question was probably Socratic, directed to the issue of the whole conduct of and justification for the war. But Bryan replies: "I tried to explain that if the boys had written, they would have directly disobeyed the order from American Division Headquarters stating that all communication with next of kin was to emanate from Division to ensure that parents were not given conflicting facts and accusations." This is the state of mind that bought "national security" as an excuse for everything. The exchange goes on:

> "We didn't get any facts!" Peg protested.
> "In other words," Gene said, "they only give out the facts they want the parents to know. To fit the story."
> "But there wasn't any story," I said.

And so on. They are talking at cross-purposes here, and Bryan's faith in the military makes him sure that the Mullens are simply irrational. (A few months later, the corruption of American Division was to be exposed by the Peers report.)

Probably Bryan's acceptance of military procedure is to be explained simply by his sense of reality. Himself an honorable man, he cannot resist another one, an officer and a gentleman who looks him straight in the eye. Just as people who have read *The Final Days* may have had their previous dislike of General Haig compromised by a realization that he had his problems, too, or by his moment of candor ("He's guilty as hell"), so was Bryan unable to resist Schwarzkopf's appalling sincerity—and even, perhaps, his more gracious social arrangements—his "home in Annandale, Virginia," his "wife, Brenda, a former TWA stewardess," his daughter "Cindy."

Never mind that he talks like the veteran of some sort of Defense Department encounter group: "I find the distortions, the twisting, the accusations [by the Mullens] to be a *dirty* business. It's highly upsetting to me and so I haven't been able to remain unemotional. . . ." About the artillery incident that caused

Michael's death, "like I said, I was furious! But don't get me wrong. . . . It wasn't because I blamed Kuprin directly as the man responsible, but it was as if my unit had done something terrible. . . . I was tremendously emotionally upset about that whole incident, and as I told the Mullens, nobody was more upset than I was."

Probably nobody was. We believe Schwarzkopf, just as Bryan does. But perhaps the word "tragedy" comes too easily to both of them. Schwarzkopf says,

> Michael's death was a terrible, terrible tragedy. A tragedy typical of a profane thing called war . . . I don't know how to express this, but try to think of it this way: Michael was killed due to an error . . . but I don't think it was an error of deliberate negligence. The error was made because of the unique set of circumstances surrounding this particular mission. All right, yes, it was an error committed by some individual and . . . I don't know the name of that individual. But . . .

And so on. These are modern sensibilities, men of the world. They accept "tragedy," ambiguity, human frailty. How unlike them is the concentrated passion of the Mullens. Theirs is the burden of hating; and the light of their moral indignation, like that of all fanatics and saints, is too glaring to bear in ordinary life.

It appears that experience of army life is a great qualifier of moral indignation. Schwarzkopf says, "Probably the most antiwar people I know are army officers," but the reader, remembering Westmoreland, Abrams, and other generals, knows better. Generals are interested in war, and even ordinary citizens who have been to war may be corrupted by it to the extent that they can then imagine it and take it for granted, like the man the Mullens knew who, when told that his brother was coming home from Vietnam early, said, "So what? I was there for two years and it didn't hurt me any," a remark that shows how it did hurt him. To the man of the world, the Mullens' rage is self-indulgence, a luxury of innocents.

Everyone agreed that Michael Mullen had been killed by friendly fire about three in the morning by guns shooting "defensive targets" at the request of an unknown lieutenant, and that an error was involved. Bryan tells the Mullens "the truth is neither in your favor nor their favor. It's somewhere in between," regarding the unresolved details, but in fact that is mainly the army's view of the situation, and it seems a fault that Bryan did not do more to resolve the details, for the reader if not for the Mullens. In a chronicle of concealments and evasions, the reporter still leaves us to wonder not only who called in the order for the firing, but also why the shots were delayed until three in the morning, which was so unusual that at least three of Michael's comrades wrote the Mullens about it. Or why another letter, signed by sixty of Michael's company, was intercepted by the army and never sent. Or why there were so many other instances of censorship.

If, as Bryan tells us, a record of every artillery shot was made, did he examine that record? Which officer received a reprimand and why? What about the report of the investigation, despite its minor security classification? Did the military prevent Bryan from seeing this? There are many questions of this kind; and, finally, one remembers that Schwarzkopf's version of events is based not merely on his memory but on an investigation carried out by the artillery officers involved.

Since these events (1970–72), we have had Watergate, the Church and Pike reports, and daily newspaper revelations to familiarize us with deceitfulness at every level of government. Even more than the Mullens could have then, the reader today will realize that the conclusions that Bryan has accepted rest upon the investigation of the responsible people by themselves; and the reader may question whether this *can* result in a fair inquiry (or, if it could, whether anything would be done). And if suspicion of self-investigations was not the reader's attitude, it would still be encouraged by the events that Bryan recites, but which he does not resolve. There were real people to be interviewed, real reports to be read. He concludes the book with a dramatization of what "really" happened, but it is only a very accomplished fiction, leaving the reader, already made skeptical by recent history, in the oddly solitary position of the Mullens, whose refusal to be reconciled to ambiguities mirrors the reader's own.

Just as the word "tragedy" is used rather lightly in this book to abridge complexity, so, too, is the word "truth" often loosely substituted for "right," in the sense of right and wrong, perhaps to avoid asking whether the Mullens or the military were "right." Yet to many Americans, now, this seems an easy question to answer. The people who most mind the discovery that their government was "wrong," of course, are the people who expected something and believed in it. The violated feelings of people like the Mullens probably cannot be argued or willed away. Perhaps their disaffection can be coaxed away, public confidence won back as one wins back the confidence of a wounded animal, feeding it little bits of truth, bit by bit, until it is sure that it isn't being fed poison. But it will take a long time—and who is to do it?

In the long run, Bryan finds the Mullens "naïve" to believe in an America out of "an innocent history primer, one capable of expressing a faith in a simpler America—an America which probably never even used to be." But that is too easy. It would be nice to think that nothing has been lost in America because there was nothing special there to begin with. But where does he imagine the Mullens got their idea of America? La Porte City, Iowa, is maybe an artifact, maybe a place left over from the past like one of those language pockets where people still speak Elizabethan English, and La Porte City may have been changed out of all recognition by recent events. But it is not an imaginary place. The values the Mullens learned there should not be dismissed as if they had never existed.

Mr. Bryan is certainly to be admired for giving us their story, but the heroes are the Mullens, who by refusing to surrender their grief and bitterness, or their sense of the discrepancy between the America they thought they had and the America they found upon closer inspection, or their struggle to retain the old America, take upon themselves and suffer the true burden of honorable patriotism.

# Rape

No OTHER SUBJECT, it seems, is regarded so differently by men and women as rape. Women deeply dread and resent it to an extent that men apparently cannot recognize; it is perhaps the ultimate and essential complaint that women have to make against men. Of course men may recognize that it is wrong to use physical force against another person, and that rape laws are not prosecuted fairly and so on, but at a certain point they are apt to say, "But what was she doing there at that hour anyway?" or "Luckily he didn't really hurt her," and serious discussion ceases.

Women sense—indeed, are carefully taught to feel—that the institution of rape is mysteriously protected by an armor of folklore, Bible tales, legal precedents, specious psychological theories. Most of all it seems protected by a rooted and implacable male belief that women want to be raped—which most women, conscientiously examining their motives, maintain they do not—or deserve to be raped, for violation of certain customs governing dress or behavior, a strange proposition to which women are more likely to accede.

While women can all imagine themselves as rape victims, most men know they are not rapists. So incidents that would be resented on personal grounds if happening to their "own" women do not have even the intrinsic interest for them of arguments on principle against military intervention in the political destiny of foreign nations, as in Vietnam, where the "rape" of that country was referred to in the peace movement and meant defoliation of crops. But unlike the interest in the political destiny of Vietnam, which greatly diminished when the danger to American males, via the draft, was eliminated, rape is an abiding concern to women.

Even if they don't think about it very much, most have incorporated into their lives routine precautions along lines prescribed by the general culture. From a woman's earliest days she is attended by injunctions about strangers, and warnings about dark streets, locks, escorts, and provocative behavior. She internalizes the lessons contained therein, that to break certain rules is to invite or deserve rape. Her fears, if not entirely conscious, are at least readily accessible, and are continually activated by a vast body of exemplary literature, both traditional and in the daily paper. To test this, ask yourself, if you are a woman, or ask any woman what she knows about Richard Speck, the Boston Strangler, and "that thing that happened over on ———— Street last week," and you will find that she has considerable rape literature by heart.

It seems important, in attempting to assess the value or seriousness of Susan Brownmiller's polemic on rape (*Against Our Will*), to understand that there are really two audiences for it, one that will know much of what she has to say already, and another that is ill-equipped by training or sympathy to understand it at all. This likely accounts for a certain unevenness of tone, veering from indignation to the composed deployment of statistics in the manner of a public debater. It is not surprising that women began in the past few years by addressing their complaints about rape to one another, not to men, and one infers that the subject is still thought to be of concern only to women. It remains to be seen what if any rhetorical strategies will prove to be of value in enlisting the concern of men.

That rape is aggressive, hostile, and intended to exact female submission, and that it is the extreme expression of underlying shared masculine attitudes, is, I think, most women's intuition of the subject, even women who have not been raped but who have tacitly accepted that this is how men are. Women who have in fact been raped (more than 255,000 each year) are certain of it after the indifference, disbelief, and brutality of police, doctors, judges, jurors, and their own families. That the actual rapists, making examples of a few women, in effect frighten and control all women seems obvious, even inarguable.

What is left to be explained, though neither Brownmiller nor Jean MacKellar, in another recent book on rape (*Rape: The Bait and the Trap*), can satisfactorily explain it, is what this primal drama of domination and punishment is about, exactly. Both books communicate an impression of an escalating conflict, with the increasing collective force of female anger and indignation about rape not only effecting some changes in judiciary and police procedures, * and even, perhaps, in popular attitudes, but also effecting an increase in anxiety about the subject, exemplified by the obligatory rape scenes in current movies and best sellers. Perhaps it is even female anger that is effecting an increase in rape itself, as if, whatever is at stake in this ancient hostility, it is now the rapist who has his back to the wall.

It is not too extreme to say that Brownmiller's book is exceedingly distressing, partly because it is exceedingly discouraging; it is a history of the failure of legal schemes and social sciences to improve society, at least society as viewed from a female perspective; it is the history of the failure of the social sciences even to address themselves to the peculiar mystery of male aggression toward those weaker than themselves. This failure seems in turn to demonstrate the powerlessness of human institutions before the force of patently untrue and sinister myths, whose ability to reflect, but also to determine, human behavior seems invincible.

---

*For instance, revisions of rape laws in several states, including recently California, and the October 1978 adoption by the Law Enforcement Assistance Administration (LEAA) of the Justice Department of a study whose recommendations are intended to be used by local authorities to improve methods of dealing with rape cases and identifying previous abuses. From this and other studies, excellent in their way, it seems clear that for the moment most proposed reforms will be merely conciliatory—directed at improving the way a rape victim is treated, but not particularly concerned with methods of prosecution of offenders or even of identifying recidivists.

The disobedient Eve, the compliant Leda, the lying wife of Potiphar are still the keys to popular assumptions about women.

But Brownmiller's book is also distressing in another way that wicked myths and scary stories are distressing, that is, because they are meant to be. Here in one handy volume is every admonitory rape story you were ever told, horrifying in the way that propaganda is horrifying and also titillating just in the way that publishers hope a book will be titillating. Brownmiller is trapped in the fallacy of imitative form, and by the duplicitous powers of literature itself to contain within it its own contradictions, so that the exemplary anecdotes from Red Riding Hood to Kitty Genovese to the Tralala scene in *Last Exit to Brooklyn* must appeal at some level to the instincts they illustrate and deprecate. The book may be criticized for an emotional tone that is apparently impossible to exclude from an effective work on a subject so inaccessible to rational analysis. Because rape is an important topic of a potentially sensational and prurient nature, it is too bad that the book is not a model of surpassing tact and delicacy, unassailable learning and scientific methodology. Instead it is probably the book that was needed on this subject at this time, and may in fact succeed where reticence has failed to legitimate the fundamental grievance of women against men.

Much of the book is devoted to an attempt to locate in history the reasons for rape, but inquiry here is fruitless because though history turns up evidence, it offers little explanation. One learns merely that rape has been with us from earliest times, that it is associated variously with military policy, with ideas of property and possession (to rape someone's wife was interpreted as the theft of something from him), with interracial struggles and complicated tribal and class polarities of all kinds (masters and slaves, cowboys and Indians), with intrasexual power struggles, as in the rape of young or weak men in prison by gangs of stronger ones, and within families, by male relatives of young girls or children.

None of these patterns is, except in one respect, wholly consistent with the others, but viewed together they induce a kind of dispirited resignation to natural law, from which are derived the supposed constants of human nature, maybe including rape. The respect in which violations of conquered women in Bangladesh and of Indian (or white) women in pioneer America, or of men in prison, are alike is that they all dramatize some authority conflict. In war between groups of males, women are incidental victims and prizes, but in the back of the car the dispute arises between a man and a woman on her own behalf. The point at issue seems to be "maistrye," as the Wife of Bath knew; and the deepest lessons of our culture have inculcated in both sexes the idea that he is going to prevail. This in turn ensures that he usually does, but the central question of why it is necessary to have male mastery remains unanswered, and perhaps unasked. Meantime, the lesson of history seems to elevate the right of the male to exact obedience and inflict punishment to the status of immutable law.

Anthropology seems to support this, too, despite Brownmiller's attempts to find a primitive tribe (the obligingly rape-free Arapesh) to prove otherwise. Rather inconsistently, she conjectures that the origin of monogamy lies in the female's primordial fear of rape and consequent willingness to attach herself to some male as his exclusive property. If this is so, it would be the only instance in which the female will has succeeded in dictating social arrangements. In any case, alternate and better hypotheses exist for the origin of the family, generally that it developed for the protection of the young. The insouciance of Brownmiller's generalizations invites cavil and risks discrediting her book, and with it her subject. Granting that a primitive tribe can be found to illustrate any social model whatever, one would like to know just what all the anthropological evidence about rape is. If rape is the primordial norm; if, as Lévi-Strauss says, women were the first currency; if male humans in a state of nature run mad raping, unlike chimpanzees, who we are told do not, is rape in fact aberrant? Perhaps it is only abhorrent.

It seems evident that whatever the facts of our nature, it is our culture that leads women in some degree to collaborate in their own rape, an aspect of the matter that men seem determined to claim absolves *them* from responsibility. Perhaps this is implicit in the assumptions about male power they are heir to. But every woman also inherits assumptions about female submission. In even the simplest fairy tale, the vaguely sexual content of the punishment needs no elaboration: every woman darkly knows what really happened to Red Riding Hood in the woods—and to Grandmother, too, for that matter. Most women do not go into the woods alone, but the main point is that the form of the prohibition as it is expressed in most stories is not "Do not go into the woods lest you be raped," but "Obey me by not going into the woods or you *will* be raped."

Thus the idea of sexual punishment for disobedience is learned very early, and is accepted. Who has done this to you, Desdemona? "Nobody; I myself; farewell," says Desdemona meekly as she dies. Everyone feels that Carmen, that prick-tease, is "getting what she deserves," poor Lucrece's suicide is felt to be both noble and tactful, maybe Anna Karenina's, too. So if a woman is raped, she feels, besides outrage, deep guilt and a need to find out what she has done "wrong" to account for it, even if her sin is only one of omission; for example, concerned citizens in Palo Alto were told a few days ago that "Sometimes women are raped because of carelessness."

To the extent that a woman can convince a jury that she was neither careless nor seductive, her attacker may be found guilty and she may be absolved from guilt, but more often in rape trials something is found in her behavior to "account" for her fate. The point is that whatever the circumstances of a rape, social attitudes and legal processes at the present time make the victim guilty of her own rape. Even the most innocent victim is likely to be told by her mother, "I told you never to walk home alone," and this is sometimes the attitude of an entire population, as in Bangladesh, where thousands of raped wives were repudiated by their husbands.

The unfortunate rape victim is in some ways worse off the more "feminine," the better socialized, she is, for she will have accepted normal social strictures: do not play rough, do not make noise or hit. Then she will be judged at the trial of her attacker on the extent to which she has struggled, hit, bitten (though she would not be expected to resist an armed robber). Not to struggle is to appear to want to be raped. In the courtroom men pretend not to understand the extent to which cultural inhibitions prevent women from resisting male force, even moral force, though in the parking lot they seem to understand it very well.

In the practical world, who are the rapists, who are the raped, what is to be done? It is here that Brownmiller's account is most interesting and most disturbing. Both Brownmiller and MacKellar agree on the statistical particulars: the rape victim is most likely a teen-aged black girl but she may be a woman of any age, and she will know her attacker to some extent in about half of the cases. The rapist is the same sort of person as other violent offenders: young, uneducated, unemployed, likely black or from another deprived subculture; the rapist is *not* the shy, hard-up loner living with his mother, victim of odd obsessions; a quarter of all rapes are done in gangs or pairs.

The sociology of rapists has some difficult political implications, as Brownmiller, to judge from the care with which she approaches it, is well aware. She traces the complicated history of American liberalism and Southern racism which has led to the present pass, in which people who have traditionally fought for human freedom seem committed to obstructing freedom for women. Historically, she reminds us, the old left, and the Communist Party in particular,

> understood rape as a political act of subjugation only when the victim was black and the offender was white. White-on-white rape was merely "criminal" and had no part in their Marxist canon. Black-on-black rape was ignored. And black-on-white rape, about which the rest of the country was phobic, was discussed in the oddly reversed world of the Jefferson School as if it never existed except as a spurious charge that "the state" employed to persecute black men.

Meantime, circumstances have changed; folk bigotry, like folk wisdom, turns out to contain a half-truth, or grain of prescience; and the black man has taken to raping. Now

> the incidence of actual rape combined with the looming spectre of the black man as rapist to which the black man in the name of his manhood now contributes, must be understood as a control mechanism against the freedom, mobility and aspirations of all women, white and black. The crossroads of racism and sexism had to be a violent meeting place. There is no use pretending it doesn't exist.

It is at this crossroads that the problem appears most complex and most insoluble. Not only rapists, but also people more suavely disguised as right-thinking, like the ACLU and others associated with the civil-rights movement, still feel that protection of black men's rights is more important than injustice to women, whether white or black. Black men and white women are in effect pitted against one another in such a way as to impede the progress of both groups, and in particular to conceal and perpetuate the specific victimization of black women. Various studies report that blacks do up to 90 percent of rapes, and their victims are 80 to 90 percent black women, who now must endure from men of their own race what they historically had to endure from whites. A black girl from the ages of ten to fifteen is twelve times more likely than others to be a victim of this crime.

In this situation, which will win in the long run, sexism or racism? Who are the natural antagonists? It seems likely, on the evidence, that sexism, being older, will prevail.

The MacKellar/Amir book, a short, practical manual about rape, something to be used perhaps by jurors or counselors, gives a picture of the crime and of the rapist which is essentially the same as Brownmiller's. But MacKellar's advice, when compared with Brownmiller's, is seen to be overlaid by a kind of naïve social optimism. What can women do? They can avoid hitchhiking; they can be better in bed: "if women were less inhibited with their men the sense of depravity that their prudishness inspires might be reduced," as if it were frustrated middle-class husbands who were out raping; authorities can search out those "many youngsters warped by a brutish home life [who] can still be recuperated for a reasonably good adult life if given therapy in time"; "Education. Education helps to reduce rape."

Maybe. But does any evidence exist to suggest that any of this would really help? Brownmiller has found none, but I suppose she would agree with MacKellar that for America's violent subcultures we must employ "the classical remedies of assimilating the people in these subcultures, economically and socially, in opportunities for education, jobs, and decent housing," and change the fundamental values of American society. "As long as aggressive, exploitive behavior remains the norm, it can be expected that individuals will make these errors and that the weaker members of society will be the victim."

Until aggressive, exploitive behavior is not the norm, a few practical measures are being suggested. The LEAA study, MacKellar, and Brownmiller are all in favor of prosecuting rape cases and of punishing rapists. Brownmiller feels the punishment should suit the crime, that it should be made similar to penalties for aggravated assault, which it resembles. MacKellar feels that the penalty should fit the criminal: "a nineteen-year-old unemployed black with a fourth-grade education and no father, whose uptight, superreligious mother has, after a quarrel, kicked him out of her home, should not be judged by the same standard nor receive the same kind of sentence as a white middle-aged used-car salesman, twice divorced, who rapes a girl he picks up at a newsstand during an out-of-town convention." She does not, by the way, say who should get the stiffer sentence, and I can think of arguments either way.

Both agree that corroboration requirements and courtroom questions about a victim's prior sexual history should be eliminated, and in this the government-sponsored study for the Law Enforcement Assistance Administration (Rape and Its Victims) also agrees. At present the established view holds that whether or not a raped girl is a virgin or is promiscuous is germane to the issue of whether a forced act of sexual intercourse has occurred in a given case. This reflects the ancient idea that by violating male standards of female chastity, a woman forfeits her right to say no.

The LEAA study found that prosecutors' offices in general were doing little to urge the revision of outdated legal codes, and that the legal system is in fact impeding reform. It observes (in a nice trenchant style that makes better reading than most government reports) that

> since rapists have no lobby, the major opposition to reform measures can be expected from public defenders, the defense bar in general, and groups, such as the American Civil Liberties Union, that are vigilant with respect to the rights of criminal defendants.

The conclusion one cannot help coming to is that whatever is to be done about rape will have to be done by women primarily. Brownmiller feels that law enforcement must include 50 percent women. She finds it significant that whereas male law-enforcement authorities report 15 or 20 percent of rape complaints to be "unfounded," among the ones they actually bother to write down, women investigators find only 2 percent of such reports to be unfounded, exactly the number of unfounded reports of other violent crimes. Apparently the goal of male-female law enforcement is not without its difficulties; women police officers in Washington, D.C., recently have complained that their male patrol-car partners are attempting to force them to have sexual intercourse. Since these women are armed with service revolvers, we may soon see an escalation of what appears to be the Oldest Conflict.

MacKellar and the LEAA report both favor some sort of rape sentencing by degree, as in murder, with rape by a stranger constituting first-degree rape, and third degree taking cognizance of situations in which the victim may be judged to have shared responsibility for initiating the situation that led to the rape—for instance, hitchhiking. This is a compromise that would be unacceptable to feminist groups who feel that a woman is no more responsible for a rape under those circumstances than a man would be thought to be who was assaulted in the same situation.

It is likely that the concept of penalty by degree, with its concession to history, will prevail here, but one sees the objection on principle. While men continue to believe that men have a right to assert their authority over women by sexual and other means, rape will continue, and this in turn suggests two more measures. One is control of pornography, which Brownmiller argues is the means by which the rape ethic is promulgated. In spite of objections about censorship and about the lack of evidence that pornography and violence are related, Brownmiller's argument here is a serious one. She also feels that women should learn self-defense, if only to give them increased self-confidence and awareness of their bodies. But it is easy to see that this is yet another way in which the female might be made to take responsibility for being raped. If a woman learns karate and is raped anyway, the question will become, why hadn't she learned it better?

Surely the definition of civilization is a state of things where the strong refrain from exercising their advantages over the weak. If men can be made to see that the abolition of sexual force is necessary in the long-term interest of making a civilization, then they may cooperate in implementing whatever measures turn out to be of any use. For the short term, one imagines, the general effect of female activism about rape will be to polarize men and women even more than nature has required. The cooperation of state authorities, if any, may ensue from their perception of rape, especially black-on-white rape, as a challenge to white male authority (as in the South). This in turn may produce an unlikely and ominous coalition of cops and feminists, and the generally severer prosecution and sentencing which we see as the current response to other forms of violent crime. But do we know that rapists will emerge from the prisons—themselves centers of homosexual rape—any less inclined to do it again?

# The Deaths at Jonestown, Part I

ANY SPECTACLE OF human credulity is painful. Now, three months after the terrible deaths in Guyana, nearly two-thirds of the bodies still lie unclaimed, unwanted, unburied, in some government depot under a Polynicean gloom of disapproval—in a mood, even, of unspoken anger that has stolen in upon the dismay and pity of the first days. Imagine parents who could kill their own children, people say now. We feel now that those people were fools, and fools could be us, and so we are anxious to know what happened, how it could happen. You can't know the moral of a story until you know the whole plot.

Things that seemed as plain at first as the documentary film from the hand-held camera of the murdered newsman, or as the helicopter photos of the festive-looking dead, now seem obscure, the questions mostly remain unanswered, the moral issues unresolved, and criminal matters proliferate. A continuing frenzy of investigation and denunciation is presumably more than mere acrimony, scapegoating, face-saving, or even skin-saving, though elements of all these are present. We really want to know. In Washington, Senator Dole has begun an investigation of cults, which is objected to by Jewish and Christian leaders, and by leaders of other cults. Former members of the People's Temple are denouncing Jim Jones, one another, government inaction—by California and federal authorities who had been warned of Temple conditions—and government corruption—by Guyanese officials who took bribes, and, in San Francisco, cover-ups by high officials who were compromised by their association with Jones. All these suspicions, accusations, appear to have foundation. Self-recrimination is notably absent all around.

Temperate press comment indicts abstractions: "society," "poverty," "ignorance," "alienation." Psychiatrists name "hunger for transcendence," or even *"la grande crise libidinale . . . le nouveau mal du siècle."* The rest of the country likes to think it's California that brings out these weird crimes, and the foreign press blames America itself, or capitalism. The many lawyers are plausibly blaming one another; and other convincing denunciations come from black leaders, who are blaming white people.

It seems clear that the white and black faithful so piously associated in the People's Temple were infected with two distinct strains of credulity not equally lethal, to judge from the bright white faces of the Temple upper echelon—prudent lieutenants splitting in good time before the event, away playing basketball or stealing out of the jungle with bags of gold. Most of the Temple elite were white. Most of the people who died were black.

In early February a meeting in San Francisco of the National Conference of Black Churchmen and the Southern Christian Leadership Conference took the persuasive view that "trusting blacks have been led down a path of deception to their own destruction by persons who stand outside the black experience," and that Guyana was "a tragedy perpetrated upon the black masses by unscrupulous and unprincipled white leadership," which is obviously true, as very often before. But in the interest of seeing that everyone comes in for a share of the blame, it could certainly be held that black leadership, in its zeal to cure whites of their racism, has done little to encourage black people to value education, and the powers of analysis and penetration that education supposedly confers; and that black ministers in particular sustain a traditional style of histrionic worship in which real and false prophets are no doubt more easily confused.

By "unscrupulous . . . white leadership," the ministers were probably speaking, more broadly than just of Jones, of all those white folks who were involved, and who appeared so solicitous of black welfare, so tolerant of fake cancer cures or any trick to lure people to the Temple for their own good. "Young women aides dressed in gray wigs, dark glasses to hide blue eyes, and skin dye faked crippling diseases," Javers and Kilduff report (in *The Suicide Cult*).

Anyhow, "unscrupulous" seems in one way too mild, in another too severe a word for Jim Jones, the crazy despot, tormented in his paranoia as his faithful, firm in their trust, were not. Jones is no mystery, only a kind of antinomian victim, playing the part of deranged demagogue with scrupulous attention to tradition. In the course of his deterioration he omitted no detail we have come, from our experience of Mr. Kurtz, Emperor Jones, Idi Amin, to expect: caprice, vanity, avarice, sexual excess, growing panic. His is a kind of huge version of the paternal exasperation we have seen in other fathers who kill their families. His torments become the reflex of his growing disgust for his followers, he moves from peevish autocracy to murderous rage. The people doing his bidding were sane. " 'You don't know how such a life tries a man like Kurtz,' cried Kurtz's last disciple," in the tones of a California lawyer.

After three months, to reread the three instant books published within days of the Guyana events is to be struck by how little has been added since then to our understanding of the duped and sad people who died there. Just as we knew Jones, we recognize the place itself in these accounts from its prefiguration in other books. People have always imagined Guyana: it is the heart of darkness. We know the landscape, the figurative meaning of the word "jungle." We have already read of the perversions, the sexual appetites of the mad leader, the tricks, in nineteenth-century Gothics like *The Monk* or *The Secrets of the Black Nunnery Revealed*. We might have read of the airstrip massacre in some Tarzan tale.

People tend to denigrate instant books as somehow morally despicable attempts to cash in on an occasion of pain and terror, but our desire for them, as much as the tradition to which they belong, legitimates them. They were got up frantically by reporters and staffs of newspapers, from witnesses and from feverish researches, and the parts don't entirely fit, but, being familiar with the genre and with all the metaphors, we can fill in the gaps ourselves. Even the form of these books—different chapters set up by different printers—mirrors the haste, the urgency, the immensity of human curiosity. What they sacrifice in accuracy they gain in the authentic animation of tone, and because they end, as the circumstances of their publication dictate, just after the climax, without responsibility for the denouement, they emerge with the shapely significance of fiction.

*The Suicide Cult* was written by Marshall Kilduff and an eyewitness, Ron Javers, reporters for the *San Francisco Chronicle*. *Guyana Massacre* is the *Washington Post*'s account, by Charles A. Krause, who was also in Guyana, and others. Each book has its special advantage, and the two are complementary. *Suicide Cult* is better on Jones and the history of the People's Temple because of a lot of prior research by Kilduff, who had been looking into the Temple for years and had published an exposé in *New West* in 1977 which precipitated Jones's departure for his Guyana colony. The *Washington Post* staff addresses some of the wider implications of the event in useful appendices of the affidavit of accusations made against the People's Temple by Deborah Layton Blakey in June 1978, correspondence between Leo Ryan and Mark Lane, and Justice Department material pertaining to the civil rights of cult members, which, it feels, are

. . . complicated by the difficulty, if not impossibility, of determining whether a member conforms his actions to the dictates of a sect leader because of a sincere religious belief that the leader speaks the will of God, or because the member is merely a victim of "brainwashing."

The third, and least interesting, book, *Hold Hands and Die!* by John Maguire and Mary Lee Dunn, draws upon the other two books, adds some discussion about cults and theories about cults, and includes some affecting letters written by People's Temple members to Jones. All three books have photographs, and each includes the same peculiar UPI photograph of a man, ostensibly the dead Jones, which does not show his face. Among them, the three books raise most of the significant questions that have since occupied discussion of the Guyana deaths.

Javers, wounded on the airstrip in Jonestown, is judicious and reporterly, but got sent home in a hospital plane without seeing the carnage itself. Charles Krause has rather more instinct for narrative, presenting himself in the role of a fictional protagonist whose initial mistakes and impetuous misjudgments will be tempered and corrected by events. He didn't want to go to Guyana in the first place. He is naïve. Even after the airstrip shootout he doesn't know if his is a big story: "Congressmen are a dime a dozen in Washington. They aren't often ambushed in the jungle, but they aren't Senators either." Before this, sitting around Georgetown with the Concerned Relatives—a group composed of reclaimed former members and relatives of members—he had concluded that they were the crazy ones, not entirely because he doesn't believe the nearly unbelievable allegations they were making about Jones. Krause has a lively sense of the cultural distance between himself (regular guy) and these "California crazies."

> Here was Grace Stoen proudly admitting that her husband, Tim, a practicing lawyer and graduate of Stanford Law School, had signed phony legal documents as an "act of faith" when he was a member of the People's Temple and a personal legal advisor to Jones. It was beyond my comprehension that a man with Stoen's credentials could have signed such documents.

Representing reason on this bad day for faith, Krause, we would like to think, speaks for a lot of people.

The Stoens, Tim and Grace, whose little son died with Jones, are among the more conspicuous of a large group of mostly white defectors and survivors who have played a part in events leading up to the deaths or afterward. Most noticeable are a number of "high-up aides" with starlet names—Grace, two Terri's, Debbie, Micki. (Javers quotes Jeannie Mills as explaining, "If you were really to be trusted, you had to be fucked by Jim.") Then there are a group of strong-looking youngish men mostly named Mike or Tim, and quite a few named Jones. Mike and Tim Carter, trusted lieutenants who survived, have for the moment faded into the shadows of grand-jury rooms, or perhaps into hiding. Terri Buford, once reported hanging around Swiss banks, has for some reason hired an attorney—Mark Lane. Stephan Jones has been interviewed in *Penthouse*.

The two rival People's Temple lawyers, Mark Lane and Charles Garry, were both in Jonestown on the death day, were miraculously spared, fled into the jungle, where they cooperated in their survival, and are now accusing each other of various things, as well as raising the really interesting question of whether, having known of conditions in Jonestown, either man should have revealed them. Each has been quoted as praising Jonestown (Garry said, "I have seen Paradise") and also as saying that they were aware of at least some of the conditions there. Maguire and Dunn noted that "Mark Lane said he knew before the massacre of the atrocities at Jonestown. Should he have told anyone? Would it have helped? Would it have compromised his 'responsibilities' to his client?" What is stupefying is that these questions are being asked seriously, not just here but widely, as if some legal reign of terror in this country really has got us to believe that a lawyer-client relationship is to be weighed against the lives of nearly a thousand people. To an ordinary person it might seem that Garry and Lane are guilty of a terrible crime for which they are not being prosecuted. But of course legislators, prosecutors, and judges are lawyers, too.

The number, prominence, and left-wing associations of the lawyers involved should astonish no one who watched Jones build himself up as the prospering radical leader of the "poor," the "black," the "oppressed," "the people"—an apparently perfect client for Lane and Garry, some of whose old Panther clients are now preachers, too. Tim Stoen has hired Patrick Hallinan. Stoen himself was former chief counsel for the Temple and also a former member of the staff of San Francisco District Attorney Joe Freitas, now himself under attack for having someone like that on his staff, and for covering up cover-ups Stoen may have been involved in where charges against the People's Temple had been made. Litigation, which is predicted to last until the next century, will keep lawyers eating off Temple matters at least that long, and the sole mention of morality comes from a famous Guyanese lawyer, Sir Lionel Luckhoo, who Garry announced would defend Larry Layton (still in Guyana, accused of the murder of Leo Ryan and others).

Maguire quotes Luckhoo as saying, "There's not enough money in the world to get me to handle this case. . . . I have to live with my conscience," a statement that stands out with quaint foreign force from the explanations common to the American lawyers, such as those of Garry, who admitted to interfering with the progress of the Stoens' suit for custody of their child because of Jones's threats of suicide—"Over one child he was going to destroy a movement"—not to mention the legal maneuvers Stoen admits to performing for Jones.

Since Guyana, San Francisco newspapers have been accusing another cult, Synanon (whose leader is under arrest, accused of complicity in a murder attempt on a lawyer), of manipulating the press with threats of endless suits by their huge corps of member-lawyers, the threat of destruction by litigation, a technique used by Jones, and by the Moonies, too. People may come tapping not only in the night but in the morning, with summonses, and you will rue it if you dare challenge these vindictive and relentless men who seem not to mind what cause they serve, but who are bent on defending the curious immunity from ordinary moral accountability lawyers seem to have achieved. Society should surely examine this, since the legal profession will not.

On the radio today two cowboy songs: the first cowboy is "going to California, where the people all live so fine," and in the next song, "there ain't no California, where the water tastes like wine."

Krause refers to "the international stereotype of California as the home of American mysticism," and the songs attest the common use of California as a metaphor for any unreal expectation of any kind. Americans themselves are too apt to believe that whatever happens in California has no bearing on the rest of the country. Californians almost believe this themselves; the events in Guyana sent them into fits of soul-searching and self-congratulation: Why does it happen here? Because we are so tolerant of "alternative lifestyles." It's inevitable, the reasoning goes, that in the general climate of tolerance, a few nuts will flourish. Probably true, and a calculated risk. But of course, in the determination to evade the tyranny of custom, the comforts of custom are lost, too. The Yale psychiatrist Robert Jay Lifton has suggested (*The New York Times Magazine*, January 7, 1979, p. 27) that the rootless, Protean style of the sixties is exactly what gives rise to the constricted behavior of cultists. California, hospitable to religious communal experiments since the nineteenth century, and traditionally uncritical of rootlessness, certainly has more than its share of alluring disciplines.

But it is a mistake to think that Jonestown is wholly a California phenomenon. In fact, few of the people who followed Jones to Guyana were Californians, except as recent migrants. They were products, like Jones himself, of other regions, and of other aspects of American culture—the poverty culture, the black culture, fundamentalism, and Protestantism. A century ago, Matthew Arnold found Americans in general to be people for whom, regarding religions, "it seems enough . . . that this or that doctrine has its Rabbi, who talks big to him, has a staunch body of disciples, and, above all, has plenty of rifles."

Only one element of the People's Temple, the white elite, seems all too characteristic of the California sixties, where young people, stoned on ideologies, anti-intellectual and sanctimonious, are strangely protected by their limited vocabularies of received phrases from any ability to question their own righteousness. You can't think thoughts you don't have words for. Former Temple member Laurie Ephron, being interviewed on the New

York Pacifica station after the deaths, when asked how a mind could conceive an idea so diabolical as Jones's plan of having parents kill their children first (as a way of procuring their own acquiescence to death), could only say, "You brought up some very heavy psychological points, and I don't know if I can relate to them fully. I don't know if anybody can relate to them fully. . . ." Deborah Layton's affidavit uses familiar political rhetoric: "I had grown up in affluent circumstances in the permissive atmosphere of Berkeley, California. By joining the People's Temple, I hoped to help others and in the process to bring structure and self-discipline to my own life." Self-described victim of affluence seeking self-discipline outside the self without perceiving the contradictions—but Californians were not the only ones who hoped to find an Other to do the work of bringing order to the Self.

Survivors or defectors, the ones who lived to tell the tale don't really seem to know what went wrong. They are united in their outrage at Jones, whom they now see as a monster who let them down, or went too far, or changed, although his ideas were "beautiful." What characterizes them as a group is the lack of self-inquiry. None (at least to judge from their published statements) appears to have examined his assumptions about politics, groups, religions, or leaders. One wonders how many of them will get involved in other cults, even if just anti-Jones cults like the one already established in Berkeley.

A partial exception is Jeannie Mills, formerly Deanna Mertle, who with her husband, Elmer, was one of the defectors who talked to Marshall Kilduff and Phil Tracy for their New West article, exposing the Jones thuggishness. She has now written Six Years with God, an account of her membership: "Everytime I tell someone about the six years we spent as members of the People's Temple, I am faced with an unanswerable question: 'If the church was so bad, why did you and your family stay in for so long?' This Book is my attempt to work out an answer." She doesn't, really, but the attempt is interesting, and the artless capitalization of the word "book" is a clue to an extremely credulous and literal state

of mind—such as few people write books in—which may be typical of a lot of People's Temple members, and other Americans
besides. Jeannie believes not only in God but in the Devil, too,
and in America. Jones had to assure them he wasn't a communist.
"I relaxed. As long as I knew that Jim wasn't trying to threaten the
democracy I loved, I would listen to whatever else he had to say."

Like many of the white as well as the black members, Jeannie
had come from a background of fundamentalism. She was a Sev-
enth-Day Adventist and had gone to religious schools, and started
with an extremely undeveloped critical faculty, to say the least:

> When he talked about the errors in the Bible, I agreed. I
> had looked up each of the texts he had quoted and, to my
> amazement, he was right. The Bible was not perfect. Not
> only had I found errors, but in one of the reference books he
> suggested I had found that the God of the Old Testament
> was a cruel tyrant. My mind was open to hear his message
> because my own beliefs had become very shaky.

When the Mills family finally leaves the church, having been
robbed and abused repeatedly, it is because they can't bring themselves to turn over yet another piece of property. They had already
given up nearly all they had. And they didn't like the idea of Guyana. But, like other members, they had accepted the brutality,
beatings, humiliation, sexual exploitation, and fraud to which
they had been subjected or seen others subjected. In an affidavit
prepared to protect themselves against the effects of the false
confessions they had signed under their real name of Mertle, the
new Mills come up with the only explanation they can think of
for their own behavior: "Pastor Jones operates through fear and
through tiredness."

Jones dealt with what People's Temple members were afraid of
already: being poor, the bomb, sex, race. One detail that recurs
in the accounts of all who try to explain the attraction of the Temple in the first place is the absence of racism, the sight of harmo-

nious black-white relations. It rings queerly. No doubt altruism and idealism are, somewhere, vital forces, and the goodness of this concept is in itself enough to weld allegiance and command sacrifice.

Nevertheless, it is hard to believe there wasn't more to it. Anyone who remembers how fast the peace movement collapsed after the draft was abolished will have had his belief in the animating power of idealism diminished somewhat. It's clear what there was in the idea of racial equality for the black members of the People's Temple, but what about the white ones? It appears that the whites who were most attracted to the idea of nonracism were those whites who under other circumstances might be most fearful of blacks, status-deprived, threatened economically by them, living in neighborhoods undergoing integration, or, in the case of younger whites, tense about integration in ways unknown to older whites.

Jeannie Mills gives a clue to this component of racial anxiety. At the first meeting she attended, "throughout the room, black and white people were seated together. . . . There seemed to be no racism in this atmosphere of peace and love and I began to relax." That is, *she* is helped out of her fear of blacks. Like the religious fear of sin, the fear of racial violence was one the intuitive Jones used most calculatingly. His bodyguards, for instance, were mostly blacks, because he thought people found blacks more intimidating.

Despite serious and well-documented accusations of fraud, beatings, extortion, kidnapping, and even murder in *New West* in 1977, nothing was done to expose or interfere with Jones, who had the endorsement of the local liberal establishment, including the mayor, the district attorney, prominent black leaders like Willie Brown, and many others. The local press, perhaps intimidated by threats of legal reprisal or perhaps because the professed goals of the Temple were ones it approved of, did not follow up either. The *New West* story had in fact been written for and rejected by the *San Francisco Chronicle.* Among those pressuring *New West* against running its piece was the local director of the ACLU. Jones, after all, had mounted a campaign to defend the rights of the press.

The destiny of nine hundred people was thereby affected by the self-interest and indifference of politicians and the press to the fate of menaced people—a fate that was weighed against their enthusiasm for what they considered to be the higher morality. As harrowing as the details are which Mills gives of the life within the Temple, her account of their attempts to bring things to the attention of responsible officials is almost more harrowing. They send Ralph Nader a letter. Two weeks later People's Temple lieutenant Mike Prokes calls in the middle of the night to say, "We know you sent it. Don't you know that Ralph has pledged his undying support to our group?" Another time they tell a friend, who tells Dennis Banks, the American Indian leader; it gets back to Jones, and they are threatened again. A relative writes an angry letter to the *Bay Guardian* protesting the paper's favorable coverage of Jones—and gets a call from the People's Temple lawyer: "If you ever do this again, we'll see you in court."

After their revelations in *New West*, the Millses expected to be murdered. Instead they would read, day after day, statements to the effect that "Mayor George Moscone said yesterday his office will not conduct any investigation into allegations that have been made about the Reverend Jim Jones. . . ." The influential columnist Herb Caen wrote that "whereas the People's Temple is 80 percent black, 90 percent of those making the wild charges are white." District Attorney Joseph Freitas was ready to announce that his office had uncovered no evidence of criminal activity and that the matter was "inactive."

The Millses say that someone in the DA's office told them that "since parents didn't complain, Jones could beat as many children as he wanted to; that if old people were foolish enough to turn over their life savings to him, it was legitimate." No doubt this is true. But it also seems likely that no one bothered to take the matter further because the People's Temple members were black (that is, Holy Rollers, with a history of Witch Doctors); and women (hysterics); and poor (and therefore ought to be into communal experiments whether they knew it or not). And the absence of widespread concern for the often rather pathetic-looking white members of other cults, in the face of charges by their concerned relatives which often resemble those made against the People's Temple, suggests a more general disdain, even hostility, toward people who relinquish responsibility for themselves. If there is a native strain of American populism that makes us mistrust a leader, it also makes us mistrust those who trust leaders. But this hardly excuses the indifference of public officials to the plight of these victims.

Eyewitnesses like Krause are still not sure that a number of the people in Jonestown were not happy, or happy enough, and wished to stay. Why? We know that something like brainwashing exists. By all accounts, the practices of the People's Temple conform to the best methods—"fear and tiredness," discipline, confession, and so on. Matters of free will and the implications of brainwashing are not frankly dealt with by our laws or in our thinking, and we have already seen some large inconsistencies. Brainwashing was rejected as an excuse in the case of Patricia Hearst and in cases where parents have sued to get their Moonie children back, but the notion was clung to, at least at first, in the case of the 913 suicides, presumably because it is easier to believe them the victims of a mad Svengali than to accept that they were making any sort of a comment on our society or on life itself.

Should the government have prevented or supervised the Guyana colony? The *Washington Post* volume concludes that "the State Department official who responded, 'We're not babysitters,' probably had it right." The position of the U.S. government has been that "any intervention in the practices of a religious sect must be based on a showing of 'societal harm,' and the degree of 'societal harm' must be balanced against the interest of the sect in practicing its religion." High-minded sounding, if a little hard to accept from a government that has shown few scruples about surveillance and manipulation when it suits.

But do children have an interest in practicing the religion of their parents? At the least, the principle of legal intervention by society to protect children where the religious beliefs of their parents endanger their health is well established, for instance in the matter of Jehovah's Witnesses and blood transfusions. Estimates of the number of people in cults in America range from three to twenty million, depending on your definition of a cult. A quarter of the people who died at Jonestown were under sixteen, and according to recent charges by Senator Alan Cranston, some of them may have been foster children.

Whatever the beliefs of their parents or foster parents, and whatever the interest of society in maintaining a cult member's right to his cult, surely these considerations do not apply to minor children; and surely the failure to prevent their deaths is not entirely to be laid at the door of Jones himself, or their parents. For the rest, perhaps the only last courtesy we can pay them is to assume that they had a measure of human volition and, however they had been persuaded to it, agreed, or wished, to die. Can there be power, really, without consent? The rest of us just don't like to think that society, life itself, can be as bad as they seem to have thought or that it is as easy, when all your friends are doing it, to step up and take your poison.

Or is that what happened? Numerous questions remain about which we are still curious. One of them is precisely how the people died, and another is, who actually shot Jones. And how much money was there, finally—estimates run up to twenty million dollars. And how many people finally survived? Krause was told by one defector that "if the Jonestown basketball team had not been in Georgetown for a game Friday night, we would all be dead. The basketball team was made up of sharpshooters, the ones trained to kill." Jeannie Mills feels "certain that Jones did not plan to die with his followers. A man who is planning to die doesn't give two trusted aides a suitcase filled with money and his own letter of introduction into another country [i.e., the Soviet embassy] unless he plans to leave with them." And "the coincidence that most of his sons were in Georgetown during the massacre and that so many of his staff people survived is convincing evidence to me that Jim Jones had planned to begin his monster-ministry some place else."

The sharpshooters and other survivors, including, apparently, three of Jones's sons, have come back here. One cannot help wondering what kind of people they are now, or were to begin with, and to what extent a terrible thing like Jonestown must compromise and corrupt the spirit of its survivors. At least one leading lieutenant, Mike Prokes, has shot himself. The villainy of the treatment of uneducated blacks by educated whites there would seem to exceed all they might have suffered from the neglect or cruelty of the larger society, and exceeds it in hypocrisy as well. Society claims to know something about healing victims, but what do we know to do for people with great cruelties on their souls?

# The Deaths at Jonestown, Part II

Oscar Wilde's remark about the death of Little Nell, that you have to be strong to read about it without laughing, suggests the qualities of character required to read the new books about Jonestown. The tone of so much accumulated pathos is finally blackly comic. Gone is the excited dismay that lent to the first books published about the events in Guyana an authenticity these more detailed and verified accounts seem to lack. After many retellings, the events of the suicide day take on a ritual, theatrical quality, like episodes in folk drama, with characters added, like Noah, for light relief.

James Reston, Jr., (in *Our Father Who Art in Hell*), transcribes tapes of Jonestown "white nights" on which Jones sounds like Lenny Bruce; Shiva Naipaul gives us a Graham Greene jungle of bickering journalists and third-world intrigue (*Journey to Nowhere*); Mark Lane describes sneaking away from the dying people with Charles Garry, Garry lugging into the jungle a heavy briefcase which proves to contain his hair dryer. For his hair, "ordinarily worn in what appeared to be a normal style, was not what it seemed. He was almost completely bald, with his hair growing just from the fringes, and at such enormous length that when twirled about his head, patted down, sprayed and dried it gave a different impression" (*The Strongest Poison*).

Nothing is what it seemed, everything gives a different impression. These books conflict, confuse, settle little, and do nothing to answer the great question of how Jonestown could happen. There are no certitudes, only clumsy ironies. Escaping, Stanley Clayton runs deeper into the heart of the jungle and is attacked by ants. Odell Rhodes survived the final hours because he had survived the American streets: "Once in Detroit when I thought this cop was going to blow me away I felt like that . . . just calm, calm and clear." Debbie Layton, whom Reston considers the heroine of Jonestown, remarks primly that she considers herself a victim in part of her education at Berkeley High, a school "lost to social experimentation and permissiveness," and plans to send any children of her own to private schools. So much for the lessons of the ill-fated social experiment Jonestown.

The first books published after the suicide in November 1978 left unanswered questions of how the people had died, who had shot Jones and what he had been planning, how much money the Temple had, who the survivors were and what would become of them, and, of course, what all this meant. The new books present conflicting answers, and say little on the more delicate questions of money and the survivors—the counsel of prudence, perhaps, in view of the fate of Al and Jeannie Mills, former People's Temple members who defected, wrote one of the earlier books, and have since been murdered by persons unknown.

On some points accounts agree: Jones was shot by someone other than himself. One report mentions the conclusion of the Guyanese investigator that he was finished off by Annie Moore, the last of his lieutenants to remain alive. Accounts agree that a number of the victims had been injected with cyanide or compelled to drink it, but there is a difference of opinion on the implications of this, from outright murder to CIA plot to mere logistical necessity in the course of implementing a collective resolution to die. Eyewitnesses Rhodes and Clayton (whose stories Reston considers suspect) suggest coercion and volition both.

The most important issues are raised by Kenneth Wooden (*The Children of Jonestown*) in his somewhat sensationalized but disturbing account of the negligence, dishonesty, and racist paternalism of American lawyers and public officials, who tolerated grotesque abuses of the rights of children, mostly black children, in order not to annoy the politically influential Jones, or with the idea of doing good, and who have since covered up their misdeeds and omissions. He also shows that a great many people, including every member of Congress, had been warned—by Jones himself—of the possiblity of a collective suicide.

Strictly speaking, the 276 children who died in Jonestown were all murdered, since a child cannot legally consent to suicide, any more than to sexual intercourse, until a certain age. More than forty-five children had been in effect kidnapped, placed with people not their parents as a result of questionable court actions in California, with the People's Temple collecting funds for their keep, and at least thirty-six were taken to Guyana illegally, some dragged onto Pan Am planes with hands tied.

Wooden's little case histories abridge volumes of tragedy: Julie Ann Runnels, whose great-aunt kept trying to rescue her, had to be held down, finally, and given the poison five times. A boy, Shawn Valgen Baker, had wanted to be a poet. Howard and Beverly Oliver, not members of the Temple, went to work one morning, leaving their teenage sons asleep in bed; when they got home the boys had been taken to Guyana. The frantic parents went to Guyana, but they were not allowed to see the boys, who later were murdered. "In almost every instance of guardian placement, relatives of the child expressed interest and concern for his or her sudden withdrawal from the family," but pleas, complaints, and legal actions were ignored by California and federal officials and obstructed by Temple lawyers.

In Guyana, officials who noted that "there were many more children at Jonestown than was normal for the few families and parents there" queried the State Department and received Kafkaesque replies:

DEPT. OFFICER CONTACTED CALIFORNIA STATE DEPT. OF BENE-
FITS PAYMENTS, COUNSEL FOR CHILD SUPPORT AND SUPPORT
ENFORCEMENT DIVISION FOR RESPONSE TO EMBASSY'S QUES-

TION . . . STATE OFFICIAL STATED THAT COUNTY OFFICIALS
HAVE PRIMARY RESPONSIBILITY IN CUSTODY MATTERS. STATE
OFFICIAL UNABLE TO ASSIST WITHOUT NAMES OF CHILDREN AND
CALIFORNIA PLACE OF RESIDENCE.

But the children were illegally captive in Jonestown. To their powerless relatives, unable to get help or attention from an implacable
bureaucracy, Wooden's suggested remedy must seem naïve:

> Without question, the Ethics Committee of the American
> Bar Association should conduct a professional hearing into
> the various roles and activities of all People's Temple attor-
> neys, including Mark Lane, Charles Garry, and Tim Stoen.
> If our government and the legal profession cannot identify
> and rectify the causes and means of the injustices done to the
> children of Jonestown, I call for an inquiry to be instigated
> by the Secretariat of Amnesty International.

The idea of the legal profession's even identifying ethical problems, let along policing itself, is remote, and for the government
unlikely; but it might indeed be a matter for the attention of Amnesty International. The plight of the 276 Jonestown children
was taken less seriously than that of popular media victims—
than, say, the children of Atlanta, or the American hostages in
Iran, who, meeting with difficulties in the line of work they volunteered for, were returned unharmed and now want a thousand
dollars a day apiece in compensation. Who can compensate the
children?

Wooden points out that there is no mechanism for protecting
children in other cults, and, indeed, that attempts to inquire into
their situations are often opposed by established religions, like the
Catholic church, as well as by the cults themselves. Cult children, Wooden says, "have starved to death in New York, Indi-
anapolis, and Yakima, Washington. Babies born into cults, their
births unregistered, are reported to have died of unnatural causes
and to have been buried in secrecy, like pets." In the Jonestown

case, issues of conspiracy raised by Mark Lane, whatever his credibility, and by James Reston, Jr., who after considerable difficulty gained access to tapes and material denied by the government to other reporters, provide incidental corroboration of many of Wooden's general charges of cover-up and duplicity.

Odell Rhodes, a drug-addicted petty criminal, Vietnam veteran, and general loser, emerges from Ethan Feinsod's lively account *(Awake in a Nightmare—Jonestown)* as a colorful, rather engaging character for whom, as for others of the poor black followers of Jones, Jonestown represented work and dignity. "I loved Jonestown. People might not understand that but it's true—I loved it." The involvement of people like Rhodes with the Temple is understandable, and that of the child victims lamentably clear in hindsight. Min S. Yee and Thomas N. Layton's rather gallant attempt to understand how Jonestown could have happened to the affluent and educated Layton family illustrates the poverty of psychological and sociological generalizations, the inability of the very vocabulary of psychology to reduce the complicated interaction of a family and an era to certitudes and themes *(In My Father's House)*.

Perhaps only a fiction about the Laytons would serve—or perhaps this is the fiction they have saved themselves with. Yee does a good job of presenting the "story" with all its fine novelistic ironies. When the father, a Quaker, was to become head of chemical-warfare research at the Dugway proving grounds, the FBI security checks so frightened the maternal grandmother, a Jewish refugee from Nazi Germany, that she committed suicide. The mother distressed the father by stepping on ants because "in Germany I learned to hate weak things. I can't help myself." She became a devotee of Jones, and later died in Jonestown of cancer, a few weeks before the suicide.

But these are just touches, and in the long run the Laytons do not seem much crazier or stranger than many other families— brother Tom and sister Annalisa were dutiful achievers, Debbie and Larry were druggy and rebellious. It was Debbie who escaped from Jonestown and succeeded where others had failed to draw attention to conditions there; Larry is at this writing (1981) on trial in San Francisco for conspiracy in the murder of Congressman Leo Ryan (who emerges from the collective accounts as a responsible and even heroic legislator).\* By all accounts, Larry Layton did not actually kill anyone but did attempt to kill two defecting People's Temple members, charges of which he was acquitted (strangely) in Guyana. He is the only scapegoat available.

At the end of Yee's account, the Laytons bicker in recriminating little afterwords. "It's getting to the point where the writing of this book is having a greater effect on our lives than People's Temple ever did," remarks Annalisa. She and Tom think Dad is now a broken old man, but Debbie points out that he dates women and is having a pretty good time. She thinks Tom and Annalisa, if they had rebelled against Dad earlier, would be better off now. Tom thinks Debbie is sort of dumb and "sees things in simplistic terms of black and white." She "has moved from the revolutionary third-world rhetoric of the temple into a business-world appreciation of Ronald Reagan." Dad, who emerges as the villain, believes that the hatred his children seem to him to express in the book "is really hatred toward parents who were trying to block, stop, or hold back the tide of the collapse of our traditional morality," by which he seems to mean mostly premarital sex. He insinuates himself into a starring role by feeling "that Larry and I are the real prisoners of Guyana." Larry Layton himself says little more than "I was a fool to leave California, but then I was a fool long before that."

The Laytons seek connections—Vietnam, breast-feeding, morality, Jonestown. Most people felt at the time that there was a connection between the People's Temple and something. The question remains what. James Reston, Jr., and Shiva Naipaul, in thoughtful books, come to opposite conclusions, and the difference of opinion is revealing. For Reston it was a matter "not just of America in the post-Vietnam period, but of human nature itself. Questions of loyalty and obedience, of belief and resistance,

---

\*The trial has since ended in a hung jury.

of totalitarianism and survival, of ends and means, of charisma, of the power of the word and religious abuse abounded," as no doubt they always do. More helpfully, what the People's Temple addressed, he feels, was the lack in the America of the seventies of a central social mission, a failure to sustain the idealism of the sixties.

This rather characteristically American self-reproach compares to Naipaul's belief that Jonestown had less to do with human nature than with America itself. He impugns not so much failed activism—though part of his discussion deplores our neglect of prisoners and blacks—as activism itself, the protestant, ameliorist optimism so characteristic of this nation, manifested by a number of ridiculous isms, like wholism or feminism (which he strangely sees as attracting the hairy: "shaggy feminists," "feminists, . . . hairy arms punching the air"). Hot tubs and Rolfing are bad, but the worst evils are Protestantism and its self-indulgent adjunct, environmentalism, both "anti-human." One of his examples of extreme American foolishness is taken from a moderate-sounding television preacher, Herbert Armstrong, of the Worldwide Church of God:

> "Poverty, ignorance *banished!* Smiles on human faces— faces that radiate! Wild animals tame! Air pollution, water pollution, soil pollution *gone!* Crystal pure water to drink; clean, crisp, pure air to breathe . . ."

It's a view of the world we most of us, in one way or another, donate money toward. But beware of where charity can lead you. "How different is the message of the extreme environmentalists? How different was the message of Jim Jones?" Our native credulousness worries him a lot. Finally, there's not much difference between Jim Jones and Jesus: "To escape the ravages of a sick and hopeless world, you embrace Christ, the divine dictator, who will come to rule with a rod of iron and who will tolerate no dissent. In the case of the People's Temple, you embrace Jones, a semi-divine dictator, who rules with a rod of iron and tolerates no dissent."

Naipaul is no comparative-religionist and not much of an observer of America; for all the wit with which he renders conversations with our sillier faddists or with Huey Newton, he doesn't get his finger on the pulse. He believes Buckminster Fuller to have been a significant apostle of the sixties, and fails, like many other foreign observers, to grasp the significance of Vietnam, or the truth in Rex Weiner and Deanne Stillman's idea, in *Woodstock Census*,* that the counterculture of that period "was based on traditional, not radical values, so it is no wonder [it] was so rapidly absorbed into the American mainstream," an idea he mentions only to deride. He believes that Jonestown was "ecotopia" and that the People's Temple followers were "the seekers of structure, the *I Ching* decoders, the Tarot interpreters, the higher-consciousness addicts, the catharsis freaks, the degenerated socialists, those who thirsted for universal justice and wanted utopia 'real bad.' " But that is not who the followers were. And is thirsting for universal justice really in the same category as the interpretation of Tarot cards?

No doubt he's right about many of our native forms of foolishness, but wrong to connect these to Jonestown. This would not much matter if his explanation for our "new world tragedy" were not taken seriously. The old world, to judge from encomiums in British newspapers, sees it as: "a brilliant achievement . . . brutally, even gloatingly honest, it picks at the scabs of a cruelly abraded world and jeers at its panaceas . . ." (*The Sunday Times*, London). Robert Coles was provoked by Naipaul's book to remark in the *Washington Post* that America is by no means the worst place in a world

full of horror, religious and racial bigotry in Britain, terrorism all over Europe, the vicious Gulag, the internecine

*Viking, 1979.

strife that millions of Africans and Asians still have to endure—including, Naipaul surely knows, the callous, murderous caste system of India, a brand of religious faith that
makes the most extreme Protestant fundamentalism seem
like a species of Unitarianism.

Naipaul writes from the perspective of Oxford, where, he says,
the sixties were barely noticed, and there is something corrective
in his mistrust, which makes one examine and on balance wish to
defend our no doubt goofy American hopefulness. It's almost
enough to put you, crazily, on Jim Jones's side. Apart from the
terrible abuses, Jones's utopianism was like that which has in
other places and times drawn many to it. The idea of Jonestown
is not one that his surviving followers are willing to repudiate. One
continues to feel that the monstrous Jones, because really de-
mented, was less culpable than sane collaborators who failed for
reasons of their own to control or defy or expose him. The allegiance of his followers and the question of Jones's sincerity remain mysterious.

# The Trial of Patty Hearst

THE REALLY GOOD TRIALS, for reasons that Aristotle could explain, have the power and appeal of folk drama. An evil deed has been committed off stage; now the chorus is assembled in a box to one side, the personified forces of destiny and the Furies speak. If the trial is a criminal one, the satisfying ending seems to be when someone guilty is led off to prison, and if the trial is a political one, then the popular ending is freedom and vindication.

Some of the malice and confusion among the vast audience of the Patricia Hearst trial was probably owing to its being a modern play—qualified, ironic, and absurd—and it was hard to know whether it was about crime, as billed, or about politics, as it seemed. Either way, the trial did not satisfy, and the audience was restless throughout; petulant bombers let off bombs, reporters jostled and sneered, red-eyed Swarthmore dropouts lined up twenty-four hours in advance in hopes of seeing Her; assorted people, ignoring the fact that publicity is thought to harm defendants in trials, mounted an angry demonstration protesting that the white bourgeois press was paying too much attention to Patty and not enough to their favorite trial, of the San Quentin Six. Most people I talked to here in San Francisco said that they didn't know much about trials, but they knew what they liked, and they hoped she'd really "get it."

Indeed, they probably could not have said why they felt that way. Seldom has the manifest content of the action (a "funky ten-thousand-dollar bank robbery," one witness called it) seemed more unrelated to the latent content, the grounds on which she was actually tried and convicted—an outcome that seems to have precipitated a national mood of self-congratulation.

Among those who wanted conviction were, first, everybody who hates the Hearsts—this includes a lot of the press and a lot of Californians; the large number of people who hate the rich in general and are glad to see that they can be brought to trial the same as you and me; all those who hate radicals, and, related to them, those who mistrust anybody who takes the Fifth; and a group whose number we might have thought had diminished since the sixties—those who mistrust the sexually "immoral," people who smoke dope, spoiled brats who try to "get their own way," and, in particular, undutiful children and rebellious women. How Patty got along with her parents and her fiancé, Steve, figured heavily in mail received against her by newspapers and government prosecutors. Finally, of course, we have all been taught to hate snitches. How cleverly the prosecution maneuvered the sympathies of these disparate elements into a symphony of public satisfaction.

Inside the courtroom the daily cast included the senior Hearsts, models of parental constancy; the fascinated sisters; F. Lee (called Flea in the San Francisco press) Bailey, a very smart man whose excellence as a lawyer was probably offset by local mistrust of smart imported lawyers; government prosecutor James Browning, a slow man who saw his main chance here; and the defendant, a five-foot-two-inch ninety-pound frightened young woman to whom all was happening just as her captors had promised it would. Under ordinary circumstances it is doubtful that any of these people would be in court at all, except perhaps in Judge Oliver Carter's court.

This was kind of a bum rap. "Patty Hearst or 'Joan Schmerdling' would have been tried for this robbery," Browning said, but in fact the government usually would not have rushed to prosecute probably the least culpable participant, one who had been kidnapped only seventy days before the crime and spent fifty-seven of those days locked in a closet. Even if we assume that she had by the time of the bank robbery joined her captors, that in itself is not uncommon, and precedent exists for the treatment of victims who accompany their captors in the commission of felonies. Duress is often assumed, and such people are not prosecuted. There is considerable unseemliness in prosecuting the victim and not even charging the kidnappers. But here the government seems to have special reasons for the unusually harsh treatment of Patty Hearst.

First, it was probably sensitive, and rightly, to charges of bowing to Hearst money and influence. "Joan Schmerdling" would have had a better chance. Federal and local authorities must have seen, also, that beyond indulging their own fondness for prosecuting radicals, a Hearst conviction might set her up to turn state's evidence in the penalty phase, something she was apparently not willing to do at the time of her capture, ostensibly because of fear, and possibly, of course, because of sympathy. It is also conceivable that the establishment Hearsts rejected an initial option to have Patty plead guilty and hope for mercy (the sensible course), not because they had been given to understand that no mercy was forthcoming, but from a naïve confidence that their victimized child would triumphantly bob up. In the event, of course, she sank with the Fifth Amendment tied around her neck like a stone.

It is also possible that the government, by maintaining to the last that this was a serious revolutionary movement it had to protect us from, sought to mitigate the damage done to the prestige of the FBI and law enforcement in general by the FBI's ineptness and by the singular atrocity of police behavior at the SLA shootout in Los Angeles. The American treatment of a situation that would have been met in, say, England by bringing up a chemical toilet and a box of sandwiches for the long wait, was a national disgrace abroad, however popular it may have been here. In its sudden and disproportionate violence, it seemed to reflect a peculiarly American taste in denouement.

In his summation, Browning reiterated the substance of the government contention that Hearst's story of having been coerced into joining the SLA was "incredible." "It's too big a pill to swallow, ladies and gentlemen. It just does not wash." To some it might seem more incredible that an abused and imprisoned victim could easily, without coercion, be taken in by the peculiarly incoherent ideology of the SLA, to say nothing of their cockroach-ridden life style. But the government usually seems to attribute to left-wing ideas an ineffable glamour which it supposes will make them irresistible to anyone but themselves.

By the defense the jury was asked to believe that the SLA treatment of Hearst was such that she felt forced to rob the bank to survive, and that thereafter—since there are seventeen months on the lam to account for—she went along with it in a state of demoralized acquiescence, convinced that the FBI was as likely as the SLA to kill her, and that her parents would not ever want to see her again; that her fear of law-enforcement agencies was very reasonably increased by viewing the SLA shootout on TV and hearing Attorney General Saxbe denounce her as a common criminal; and that she was afraid of being charged in the bank robbery.

On the stand Hearst appeared forthright but not forthcoming, an intelligent person who has for now exhausted her rather impressive range of adaptive responses. She could neither elaborate nor embroider, and sometimes simply could not answer to or account for her own actions. "I just don't know what happened to me, Mr. Browning," she had to say. A doctor who examined her at the time of her capture said that she is nevertheless dramatically improved since then, when she was literally stupefied and amnesiac. There is much she cannot, or cannot yet, explain.

The jury could not believe her. They had seen that grinning, power-saluting picture, heard her say she was "pissed off" at being captured (in a conversation with a girl friend, secretly recorded at the jail). The problem for Hearst was that the jury turned out to have no imagination. They could not imagine the kinds of life conditions people adapt to. They could not imagine that you might read the words of someone else into a tape recorder and not mean them, like poor Tokyo Rose, or could come to think you meant them. They could not imagine that they themselves, like most people, might clumsily assist, rather than resist, an assailant. They could not believe that there actually is such a thing as "coercive persuasion," or that revolution can seem attractive, or that the SLA were really assassins. In fact, people seem unable to imagine the existence of evil at all, unless it comes wearing evil costumes, as the Manson girls do. What people do understand, as Kant observed, is mere badness.

Therefore the trial became one about Hearst's badness. Listening to the kind of questions the prosecution asked, you got the feeling that here was Miss Teen-Age America on trial, for telling the nun to go to hell, for not being a virgin, for feeling ambivalent about getting married. Some schoolgirl lies were dredged up. Quantities of school reports and friends' opinions were introduced to show that she was independent and self-willed, that is, the type of girl who would join an SLA, instead of being ideally feminine and passive. Independence was spoken of as a moral defect; the prosecution even exerted itself to show that she was sarcastic, until the exasperated Bailey objected that his client was not on trial for sarcasm. Objection sustained. But "Did Miss Hearst ever use marijuana or other narcotics?" witnesses were asked by Browning. Objection: prosecution is trying to tell the jury about inadmissible prior offenses. Objection overruled. "Jury stunned by drug revelations," crowed the press, relieved that the day had produced at least one sensational detail. Nobody told the jury what percentage of American teen-agers smoke grass.

And, in fact, no one could really have told whether the jury was stunned or not. It appeared uncannily like a group of regular folks—necks no redder than most, faces impassive, unwrinkled polyester clothes. The government could only go on the assumption that inside them there existed the same prejudices that pervade the rest of society—against the young, the hip, the rebellious, the funky, and so on. Despite the jurors' sanctimonious protestations that it hurt them more than it did her, the government was right about them, and perhaps no one ought to have been surprised. The surprising and distressing thing was the ease with which the government also commanded the sympathies of the young, hip, rebellious, and funky in its prosecution of Hearst. It seems a rather sinister coalition.

Considerations of badness prevailed over convincing evidence of duress, at least where this initial crime was concerned. The gun of Cinque DeFreeze seems to have been pointed at her throughout the bank episode, and the government at first suppressed a photograph showing Camilla Hall's gun pointed at her, too. On the stand, Ulysses Hall, an old prison friend of DeFreeze, gave a convincing account of a discussion of the holdup, in which DeFreeze said that because he neither wanted to kill her nor dared to let her go, his plan was to "front her off" so she'd have to stay with them. He didn't quite trust her, he told Hall, for "though she say 'yes' this, 'yes' that, what would you say" in her situation?

In any case, the jury was instructed in effect to ignore her situation, though it was allowed to bear in mind what she did later. In theory one could view the robbery either as an effect of the kidnapping, or as an act—that is, a first cause capable of generating a further sequence of consequences, like the Mel's Sporting Goods Store incident; an act is one of free will. If the bank robbery is taken as an act, and the judge so took it, there can be no consideration of causes, and without consideration of causes there was in fact no question of her guilt, since she was plainly in that bank with a gun in her hand. Whether the conditions of her kidnapping constituted duress became beside the point, since cause and effect are not the same thing as guilt and innocence. The judge told the jury, in effect, to ignore the defense.

An imaginative jury might have borne it in mind, though. They saw the closet, they heard the testimony about the experiences of people to whom similar things had happened. (Though one prosecution psychiatrist said cheerfully that the closet wasn't so bad as Dachau.) There were things, however, that the jury was not allowed to see or know: for example, first, about the death threats and bombings that went on during the trial, though these seemed to bolster Hearst's contention that there are still others out there, of whom she is afraid. (The jury eventually did get wind of this via a prosecution blunder, but so poorly did it understand the implications that one juror expressed fear as they prepared to go home that Hearst's terrorist friends would go after them for convicting her.)

Second, the jury appears to have been heavily influenced against Hearst by hearing the so-called Tania tapes, in which she denounces her parents and affirms her love for Willie Wolfe and revolution. The judge admitted the tapes as evidence but would not admit expert testimony, based on analysis of speech patterns, that Hearst did not write the words spoken on those tapes. Dr. Margaret Singer, a University of California psychologist and well-known specialist in language analysis, was originally appointed by the court to examine Hearst and administer psychometric tests. After detailed study, Dr. Singer was prepared to testify that most of Tania's speeches had been written by Angela Atwood, and the last by Emily Harris. This type of analysis is regularly accepted in courts to decide cases of disputed authorship, and the judge received a brief so demonstrating, but declined to hear the evidence. Bailey had to contend continually against this kind of judicial caprice. Some observers felt that in this instance the elderly judge was simply unused to female expert witnesses.

The performances of the five psychiatrists gave rise to much merriment and derision, with Browning suggesting to the jury that the opposing opinions canceled each other, and observers predicting that here, at last, came the end of psychiatry in the courtroom. It was disturbing that the court made no distinctions in accepting the testimony of psychiatrists of widely varying professional qualifications. The court originally appointed Singer and Jolyon West, chairman of the department of psychiatry at UCLA, and two professors of psychiatry from USC and Stanford. They submitted reports, containing the coercive-persuasion diagnosis, to the court itself. Eventually the defense asked West to testify because of his extensive experience with Korean War prisoners, and added Martin Orne from the University of Pennsylvania and Robert Jay Lifton of Yale, each of whom had similar training. All of these people have distinguished national reputations, and are, one must suppose, incorruptible, unless it be by their enthusiasm for cases of this kind.

The prosecution psychiatrist Joel Fort, on the other hand, is, as one magazine put it, a free-lance courtroom witness, and is not certified in psychiatry. Up to the beginning of the trial he was equally prepared to testify for the defense. He describes himself as being into hot-line telephone therapy, was dismissed as director of a San Francisco clinic, and was described by a former California director of Public Health as someone who was "untrustworthy and not to be believed." A man who had worked under the other prosecution psychiatrist, Harry Kozol, head of the Bridgewater Institution for the Criminally Insane, testified in court that Kozol had expressed his dislike of the Hearsts before ever seeing Patricia Hearst, saying among other things that Mrs. Hearst is "a whore [who] tries to look like Zsa Zsa Gabor"—a remark Kozol denied making.

Perhaps the judge was right in instructing the jury that psychiatric evidence is "opinion"; perhaps not. But surely if there are to be such things as disinterested expert witnesses in court it must be admitted that there are such things as expertise and disinterestedness. Here the jury, apparently incapable of making professional distinctions, seemed actually to believe the chummy Fort, whose disinterestedness may be guessed at. His bill to the government will be around $12,500; Kozol's around $8,000. Jolyon West will charge some $1,000. (What Lifton and Orne are charging is unknown.) Fort is charging for the time it took to read a list of 274 books (some listed twice, though) in order to make himself an "expert" about brainwashing—books you might have expected an expert to have read already—and for time spent in "planning and strategy."

Anyway, the jury either didn't understand the psychiatric evidence or didn't believe it. Patricia Hearst was credited with free will and held to a standard of behavior more exacting than the standard the military has applied to its captured soldiers (although, when you think of it, the military conception of normal behavior can include looting and murder, and perhaps shouldn't be taken as the standard). But where is the line that society must draw in pursuing criminal justice? As Bailey said in his summation, "How far can you go to survive?"

In a sense, all criminals are people who have been put in closets; certainly all pleas of diminished responsibility involve saying: My mother, or society, or someone put me in the closet. This trial will probably do little toward a decision whether closets are to make any difference, but it may reinforce what one perceives as a general tendency in this country at present to return to the idea that the individual is responsible for his actions regardless of diminished capacity. Perhaps that is just as well; but duress is another matter, and duress was the moral heart of the case. The government was not interested in moral complexities; it wanted conviction. The judge piously instructed the jury that the government always wins when justice is done, whereas justice was the one thing no one seemed to want to bother with.

One never knows how to feel toward the victims of injustice. They become separated from us, marked by our sense of their peculiar destiny. It is hard to imagine how anything can go right for this poor heiress of ill-fortune now. In books people are ennobled by tribulation, but in the real world, fear and prison just make you dull and vicious. You can't help but wonder how any of the people whose lives have been blighted by these events can possibly transcend them.

Of course, a number of questions remain unanswered. Not until sentencing can we know the government's disposition toward mercy. It may be that a penalty bargain will be struck in return for state's evidence. In that case, the government would be further victimizing Hearst, placing her in a moral dilemma and possible physical jeopardy by urging that she testify against people who may have helped her. Some SLA associates—the Soliah sisters and others—are still at large. The legal status of people like the Jack Scotts, who are alleged to have been involved in harboring the fugitive Harrises and Hearst, is unclear. No one is sure whether others will be charged in the Carmichael bank robbery, where a woman was killed, and for which Steven Soliah is at present standing trial; this may depend on whether additional testimony can be extorted from Hearst.

Perhaps in an effort to head her off, Bill and Emily Harris are belatedly sounding like the People Next Door. From their account in *New Times** you would find it hard to believe that these thoughtful, diffident revolutionaries were ever members of the crazy gang that murdered the innocent Foster and kidnapped Hearst. Another inside report, in *Rolling Stone*,† seriously contradicts them, characterizing them as militant assassins, and both accounts are contradicted on some points by Hearst.

But the Harrises seem to have a surprising number of believers. Is it because there are two of them? Because they are married? Because they look so normal and Midwestern, and do not wear evil costumes, and do talk so volubly about truth and love? "I just felt like she turned against the friends she loved and trusted," sighed Emily over Patty's behavior at the trial. Patty is the Enemy of the People. Says the Harrises' lawyer, Leonard Weinglass, "She chose to go the route of wealth and power and deception. She wrongfully accused her friends and slandered her dead lover Cinque [sic], and vilified the political organization she chose to join." But luckily for him, Patty's credibility as a witness is damaged by her conviction, so she can't do the Harrises much harm, and, anyway, it was Patty holding the smoking gun at Mel's.

The Harrises do seem to lead charmed lives, or to have had, all along, a strong sense of self-preservation. William Harris has not been charged with the Hearst kidnapping; though she has testified that he was one of her abductors (in blackface), she is a convicted felon whom no one believes. The Harrises did not do the Foster murder, though, according to Hearst's testimony, neither did Remiro and Little, who have been convicted of it; if they were around for the Hibernia Bank robbery, they haven't been charged for that either. When they go on trial in Los Angeles, a

*March 5 and April 16, 1976.
†April 22, 1976.

lot of evidence—weapons, explosives, manifestoes—that was used against Hearst will not be admitted against them because it was seized illegally. (Bailey seems to have erred in the Hearst case by trusting prosecutor Browning's assurance that the evidence was obtained legally; Bailey therefore didn't make routine motions to have it excluded.) The first part of the Harrises' story in New Times was published just in time for the prosecution to learn from it that the stone figure in Hearst's purse had been given her by Willie Wolfe, information that clinched things for at least two of the sentimental jurors. "I think she really loved Willie Wolfe," confided one.

And, obviously, Bill and Emily were not around for the Los Angeles shootout. If they had succeeded in being arrested on the shoplifting charge at Mel's, they would have been separated even sooner from their more dangerously visible comrades. As it stood, it was the Harrises who fingered the neighborhood where the rest of the SLA were staying. Says Emily ingenuously, "The worst part of the thing at Mel's was that there was a parking ticket in the van that we completely forgot when we abandoned it after splitting from the store. That was how the police located the Eighty-fourth Street area, where SLA members were staying." "Yeah," says Bill, "police agencies didn't know that the SLA was in the LA area until Mel's. Knowing that makes all the other things seem unimportant and the psychological burden of that has been really incredible for me." As it is unlikely that they will receive the maximum penalty for the Los Angeles fracas, the psychological burden may be about the worst burden Bill and Emily will have to bear.

Probably people will lose interest in what happens to the Harrises. For them, for the Hearsts, for the others, innumerable ordeals are in store, but the audience has seen enough and goes home happy. Though at first the complicated plot was mystifying, all became intelligible by the end: the American system works. The rich cannot buy their way out of things. A stern lesson has been administered to terrorists. The victim is seen to have been asking for it all along. Flashy out-of-town lawyers and fast-talking shrinks have been beaten back by just plain folks. The government, like the big bad wolf, disguises its appetite for radicals beneath the lacy cap of egalitarianism, and in their pleasure at the fate of the rich snitch, the people rush to get into bed with Grandma.

# The Fate of Patty Hearst

THE RELEASE OF PATTY HEARST and her subsequent marriage may not serve this interesting book well; people may be finished with the whole business, may not want to read a very long day-by-day account of the trial, or any more about that time in the closet, or about F. Lee Bailey. Now that Hearst is out, the ugly implications of the legal behavior, like the ugly implications of public sentiment at the time, can conveniently be forgotten until some future occasion for public vindictiveness and private opportunism. The principal interest of Shana Alexander's account (*Anyone's Daughter*) lies in its detailed presentation of these aspects, but it touches as well on other matters that close followers of the case will have wondered about: Why did the Hearsts hire Bailey, a flamboyant lawyer associated in the public mind more with flashy criminals than with dignified victims? Why did the government decide to prosecute a young kidnap victim? What was the SLA really like?

Shana Alexander daily attended the trial and talked to many involved people—the Hearst family, the legal staffs of both sides, the many psychiatrists and other expert witnesses. Each character is described vividly—perhaps a bit too vividly: "Anthony Shepard, the young caramel-colored man on the witness stand, wears a coppery Afro, a Fu Manchu mustache, a short-sleeved shirt that displays his muscles, and a tough-guy swagger. He was the clerk at Mel's, and he is studying to be a cop."

What emerges is a kind of soap-opera drama of rivalrous lawyers and doctors, and Alexander herself, presented as one of the characters, attempting to account for her strong emotional involvement. Alexander does this in terms of her own problems as the mother of a daughter whom she could imagine acting in some ways as Hearst had done, and as a citizen of the America that produced this odd case. She presents her own reactions and reflections in detail, and some valuable conclusions.

In the most interesting section of the book, "Closing Reflections," she talks to psychiatrists Joel Fort and Jolyon West (who had testified for the prosecution and defense respectively), prosecuting attorney David Bancroft, defense attorney Albert Johnson, Charles Garry from the sidelines, and members of the jury. The weird divergence of views, the projections of personal hangups, is startling. From the left, Garry believes that Hearst was "a cold, calculating bitch," who "got in with a gang of thieves and she became just like them." "Spooky psychiatrist" Joel Fort believes that "Patty was eager for sex because she was a sexually active girl and had been so at an early age." Alexander herself comes to believe that "Patty *had* been brainwashed. She had undergone a pseudo-conversion, brought about through coercive persuasion, which resulted in role identification that after her capture did not sustain." This was the essence of the defense case, which most trial-watchers thought ill-judged.

Some interesting light is shed on the jury, whose seeming witlessness is to an extent explained by Alexander's revelations about the way they were treated—incarcerated more cruelly, perhaps, than Hearst herself, for whom, as the occasion of their misery, they can hardly have helped conceiving animosity: "They lived for sixty-six days without radios, television, newspapers, or magazines in single rooms equipped with alarms that rang if the door was opened after ten o'clock at night. Until the knock came at six or six-thirty the next morning, each one was entirely alone. . . . A juror could either eat alone in his room or go to a restaurant with the group. But since all sixteen had to eat together, it was difficult to avoid people one didn't like. The two drinks one was allowed before dinner were insufficient to relieve the tensions of the day. . . . Golf, jogging, and most other customary recreations were impossible because each juror would have required his own marshal."

And much more.

The whole book is an elaborate answer to the question it raises: why did this case come to trial at all? Alexander's analysis is valuable: "Who makes this determination that 'the American public demands vengeance'? . . . There are only persons and pressure groups and professional interests that—for reasons of self-interest—presume to speak in the public's name. These people can be lawyers, politicians, psychiatrists, family members, or press. In the Hearst case they all spoke. . . . An 'American public' demanding vengeance, or, indeed, demanding anything else simply does not exist."

If this trial was a "travesty," how can future travesties be avoided? Alexander feels that one way would be to bar pretrial publicity by doctors and attorneys, as is done in England. Some remarks made to her by Jolyon West stand out as the burden of the whole account: "Before the trial I had faith in the fairness of our judicial system. I had a deep-seated belief that the truth will come out and that fair-minded people, if they're faced with the truth will know it when they hear it. . . . This trial was the most disillusioning thing that ever happened to me. I mean the behavior of the government."

He concludes that "when you change the number-one value from fair play to winning, you go beyond duty." Despite its breezy presentation, this detailed portrait of a legal system devoid of values is really horrifying.

# *Old Glory*:
# Life on the Mississippi

EXPLORERS, LIKE METAPHYSICIANS, have always liked a river, straight route to the heart of things. Englishmen in particular have their tradition of great river explorations—it follows that it would be an Englishman who explores the Mississippi and gets at the heart of the American middle, unexplored darkness deep in the flyover. What doesn't follow is what has happened, that Jonathan Raban's book has proved to have interest, beyond the usual appeal of a well-written travel book, for other Americans. Following Raban, like an art dealer discovering the new market in primitives, America turns a speculative eye on downstate Illinois.

In one sort of travel book, by Stanley or Amundsen, you get to know the traveler and see how he comes through danger and unsympathetic diet, improved or broken by his ordeal. In books of the guidebook sort, you are concerned only with the place and mostly unaware of the noticing presence of the reporter, who forbears to remind you that he is staying in the dreary motel he tells you to avoid. Raban says he intended his book to be of the former type, about himself and his reaction to a place that had intrigued, perhaps obsessed, him since his childhood reading of Mark Twain, visited at a moment of adult spiritual crisis.

As a spiritual odyssey, *Old Glory* doesn't quite convince. Raban is too good-mannered to inflict his particular problems on us; perhaps he is too reticent to mention them. And the terms of his personal situation are so emblematic of the modern condition, so-called, that he becomes Everyman instead, afloat on a metaphoric river: "I had gone stale and dry. I felt that I'd run out of whatever peculiar reserves of moral capital are needed for city life. I couldn't write. For days on end I woke at five, confused and panicky, as the tranquilizers that I'd taken lost their grip." And as Everyman he enacts everyone's dream of a life where for a time "everything would be left to chance. There'd be no advance reservations, no letters of introduction . . . as much like a piece of human driftwood" as could be managed.

Disguised as harmless flotsam, Raban is exactly right for making sense of a land where, as Mark Twain said, river people will load up the gullible with picturesque and admirable lies and put off the sophisticated with dull and ineffectual facts. People are eager instead, it seems, to tell Raban the truth; he's the confidence man or mysterious stranger so fascinating to American writers and everybody else, the European invested by his accent, his ineptness with local utensils, and his slightly suspect intentions, with a glamour Americans just submit to, just like that.

The basin of the Mississippi is less well chronicled, at least in modern times, than the Yukon. Of the great many American writers to have come from the Midwest, only Twain wrote much about it; the others, having left with velocity, like champagne corks, couldn't be got back in again. T. S. Eliot was raised in St. Louis, but J. Alfred Prufrock lived in London. Even Twain, revisiting his childhood haunts along the Mississippi, had protected himself with the manners of an outsider, and had learned to speak French and German and (like nearly all the others) been living in Europe or the East. What Raban discovers is as strangely cheering as what Twain rediscovered.

Raban puts in around Labor Day from Minneapolis–St. Paul in a sixteen-foot open aluminum boat with a fifteen-horsepower motor, with the plan to go to New Orleans, more than a thousand miles downriver. Along the way he talks to people, mostly in the bars and other boats, and pauses in motels or hotels or with people who invite him to stay, according to his whim and chance.

Then he writes down what he sees and what the people say. He more or less lets them speak for themselves.

Raban is a wonderful writer, with great powers of description, and above all the ability to interpret with elegant tact and lightness in the sort of tone one might use to criticize someone else's child without giving offense. He captures, or else invests his companions with, so much pungent plain speaking that it belies his own criticism of the American language and "its fatal preference for theories, principles, and concepts over mere material objects and their intractable thingness." It is ultimately the thingness of the life along the Mississippi that Raban shows us—and that his readers, apparently, find so surprising.

It is on their thingness, too, that his informants constantly insist, in the teeth of coastal dwellers who doubt it. "You come from England? . . . That's what I thought. We got an English lady living here in town. She come over from England when she married Everett Asquith. He's got a paint store up on Main." "A *hotel?* You can stay at our place. Francie loves to have guests." "That Ed, God, he's such a dreamer. Ever since I've been in Muscatine he's been saying that crazy stuff about the Rio Grande. Every fall he talks about going down there. He ain't never going to get south of Hershey Avenue." "I had a son. He drowned in the river. . . . It takes its toll."

He meets some people who are embittered, alienated in their isolation from national concerns: "I don't vote for no one. If Jesus Christ himself was running for president, he wouldn't get my vote. Them politicians, they're a bunch of outlaws." Everything on TV is junk made by Madison Avenue. "Who do they think we are? I'll tell you: to them this is Flyover Land." He shows Raban his fancy rifle. "Eventually," says Raban, "I got the hairlines on target and saw what I was supposed to see: Washington politicians, Madison Avenue jerks, college presidents and beautiful people. One by one they staggered to their knees like struck deer."

But most people aren't alienated. It's them, they feel, who are *there,* and it's the others who are outside. What they don't like is that the outside doesn't understand this. "Why is it that every time they show a bumpkin on a comedy show he's supposed to come from Iowa?" In town after town, Raban's Midwesterners express basic satisfaction with their place, and a mistrust of elsewhere. He asks a group of eighth-grade kids in Savanna, Iowa, where they would go when they grew up. "I pressed them to daydream and offered them the freedom to be anything from a New York dentist to a movie star in Cannes." No, thanks. The kids intend to move no more than a mile or two away from Savanna, and they hate the idea of the city. "It's so noisy." "Everything gets stole." Raban grasps the Midwesterner's "sense of slight and belittlement, this precarious pride," everywhere, and the secret vanity, the belief that it is the region of balance and common sense. "We're the calm, thoughtful center . . . if you take us out of the United States, you drain all the basic common sense out of the country. I *know* what goes on in New York, and Los Angeles. I can make judgments about them because here I'm at a remove."

But of course they don't really know what goes on in Los Angeles, and Raban understands this, too. Urban social problems can only be imagined. They've only *heard* that everything gets stolen. Some people in a bar laugh at Raban because he's lent his boat to some blacks from Chicago. "All them Chicago niggers, I reckon they'll be saving up carfare for England," one man says. His wife objects. "That ain't right, Harry. Them black people, I think they're more honest than us. You don't know no blacks. You never talked to a black person in your whole goddamn life." "Shit," admits Harry. Another person chimes in, wonderingly, "I don't know what it is about them, but you never see a Negro coming back with no fish." The blacks did return the boat and they did catch some fish.

None of the schoolchildren had finished *Huckleberry Finn* because they couldn't understand the black dialect. Noticing that this part of the country was a "vast white ghetto," Raban asks why and a man in Dubuque just shrugs: "I don't know why that is. I guess they just don't like the climate around here. I don't blame 'em . . . the winters here, they'd freeze the ass off you . . . but it's a wonderful climate for hogs." A woman finds it funny that Jews, as she's heard, think carp a delicacy, whereas she herself wouldn't touch it. Her husband points out that Jews wouldn't eat pork, which she thinks a delicacy, and that it's all relative. She's never thought of that. But she's willing to think of it. The bigotry here seems naïve, open-minded, conventional, born of unfamiliarity with the problems other Americans have riots and hangings over. The responses are not so much reactionary as fixed, on values widely shared.

In a recent book about the Jonestown tragedy, Shiva Naipaul, another foreign observer of American society, concludes after a visit to California that American problems are connected to, among other things, the cynicism and bad faith of our treatment of the urban underclasses. From California he is unable to imagine, just as many other Americans are unable to understand (evidenced by the hectoring tone of media civil-rights reformers), that there is a vast part of America where the people can't imagine blacks or other ethnic groups—they can't even imagine cities. But if they can't summon more than an abstract sympathy for problems they can't imagine, they appear, on Raban's evidence, not to have closed their minds either.

Raban sometimes feels lonely. From the perspective of Minnesota, "London was a city just a little east of Boston." To the Midwesterners, Boston seems just a little west of London—both far, unfamiliar, inimical. The people are concerned with life where they are. When Jimmy Carter stepped off the riverboat at Guttenberg, Iowa, he was heard to remark, "Hey, is this Iowa?" Now "Hey, is this Iowa?" is a huge local joke. "People had rejected 'America' as an ungovernable abstraction," but the democratic process was alive and well in the politics of the local community. The woman who was running for mayor of Guttenberg had hated her two years in California. "I'd say I came from Iowa. *Iowa?* They didn't know if it was a city or a state." She worried most about the decline of liberal-arts education. "So many kids now are going into trade schools and technical schools, the whole vocational thing, and . . . unless we can get them back into liberal arts programs, they're going to lose their understanding of the whole democratic process. . . . We're raising a generation that isn't educated enough to know what it means to be a citizen." *Liberal arts?* It's a bet that educators in California have never even heard the term.

Raban goes on downstream with the current, noting the beauty, the desolation, the past, old glory of the once busy river towns. The Midwest doesn't photograph—the camera makes the people fatter than they are, the beautiful black earth seems flat and bleak. Raban brings the rich architecture to life as if no one had looked at it before, and perhaps no one has—the "glorious flights of unbridled nineteenth-century ambition"—Clerical, secular, Moorish, Steamboat Corinthian, Queen Anne, Gothic, Victorian, you name it. Muscatine, Iowa, watching television, "saw more than it wanted of Los Angeles and Manhattan. It felt that the imbalance was unjust. The floating mansions on its bluff . . . were really just as worthy of the loving gaze of the film camera as Rockefeller Center."

They don't hold this against Raban, representative of the outside world; instead they are anxious for his approval, want to know what he thinks of their place; they have the friendliness that foreigners so often deride in Americans. I felt, myself, a keen, American, hostesslike anxiety as Raban approached the place I grew up in, and keen disappointment when he didn't like it at all—found it full of "ageing jocks, with their acrimonious divorces, their giant power boats and their glowering paranoia." These would be the same guys I went to Calvin Coolidge Junior High School with, I guess. I was interested to learn that paranoia is a civic, not just a personal characteristic.

Calvin Coolidge, a regional hero. Raban speculates that the resurgence of born-again Christianity in America is really a nostalgic wish to return to a specific period of history, "a time when worldly ambition and spiritual virtue existed in harmony." Even now, the TV antennae and cars do little to disturb the essence of, say, Andalusia, a "bare conjunction of shack, forest, river and cultivated ground." This region strikes Raban as it struck Twain, as one whose days of greatest glory are over. These for Twain had vanished with the Civil War, and he hearkened back for testimony to the witness of still earlier travelers—Marryat and Mrs. Trollope. Raban hearkens back to Twain. There are no more recent accounts of this voyage, which is perhaps why people are so surprised to discover that America has a calm center, itself hearkening back and confirming itself, restoring its buildings, researching its history, defending its eccentricities against the frontier mentality of the West, the sissy affectations of the East, a rich storehouse of cultural certitudes trying to ignore the shifting values and faddish self-doubts of coastal America.

On downstream. Nauvoo, Illinois, where the Mormons were massacred; Hannibal, Missouri. The North merges imperceptibly at first into the South. Blacks appear, and catfish, and Civil War stories. People begin to say "you-all," grits appear on the menus. Raban meets a girl in St. Louis and tarries there awhile. His severest judgments are reserved for St. Louis, a place that, having had the sense to tear down its high-rise public housing, has been thought of by others as a model of urban intelligence. Raban thinks St. Louis "gaunt," crime-ridden, ugly, and dying; and installing fake gas lamps, cobbled streets, wine bars, gift shops and novelty restaurants, a stadium, a convention center, and a hideous arch that aims to be to St. Louis what the Eiffel Tower is to Paris—an aspiration that sends Raban and tourists from California into stitches—won't help. He can't see the point of a city rehabilitating itself on well-heeled transients who only attract crime and prostitution, while the real citizens live in the suburbs.

Missouri, Arkansas, Tennessee. He follows an election in Memphis and goes to a revival meeting. He meets riverboat pilots right out of *Life on the Mississippi*. In Vicksburg he meets people who talk Boston Irish, Manhattan, Harvard Business School—the accents of the New South. There is much talk of the New South. "There's a line I keep on hearing from fellows who've come from the North," a man in Mississippi tells him. "They say 'Look, I don't know whether you're thinking of seceding again, but hell, if you *are*, we're going to join you this time.' " One of the principal occupations for blacks in Natchez is acting in films, playing the parts of "field niggers" and "house niggers," and "when there's no movie work going," says a local, "they sit in the ditches playing banjos and singing old darky songs for the tourists. Then the NAACP comes in and tells them they're degrading themselves. So they wait till the NAACP guys get out of town."

In December he arrives in Louisiana. In Houma, Louisiana, a jittery addict pulls a knife on him. "Here in Louisiana, Christ . . . people here, they go out of their way to run a dog down. It's a goddamn sport," someone tells him. His last stop is Morgan City, Louisiana, where there "ain't nothing." That's the heart of darkness—Morgan City, Louisiana.

Mr. Raban is not one to shirk the consequences of his successes. On the jacket of his very good book about Arabia, he is photographed clutching a hookah. Now he's Book-of-the-Month Club. And he's been on CBS, gamely re-enacting scenes of his river voyage, with voice-over passages from the book: Raban stares glumly at weather reports on the motel TV, Raban revisits a couple of nice folks on their cabin cruiser. With becoming embarrassment, he sports a duplicate of the funny hat he lost. The media are full of wonder. He praises the bird life along the Mississippi; the camera finds birds. Mr. Raban, says the narrator, has visited places with names like Red Wing! Wabasha! Prairie du Chien! Bettendorf!

Another day finds NBC's weatherman in Indian headdress announcing with astonishment that he's in Davenport, Iowa! Later on we find Tom Brokaw interviewing Harry Reasoner—the two taking note with satisfaction that like them the important anchorpeople have mostly all been Midwesterners. Probably, they speculate, because Midwesterners are so sensible and nice. There are *two* different ballads on the cowboy music station with the refrain, "Miss-iss-ipp-i." It's like a Twain story, all right—the mysterious European stranger comes and sells to the locals something that's been theirs all along. The Midwest has been ours all along, after all, but for those who haven't known this, Raban's book makes a continuously interesting pitch.

# Books Discussed

## I. Self-Deceptions

### Kingston, Laird, and Momaday

THE NAMES by N. Scott Momaday (Harper & Row, 1977)

THE WOMAN WARRIOR: Memoirs of a Girlhood Among Ghosts by Maxine Hong Kingston (Alfred A. Knopf, 1976)

ENCOUNTER WITH AN ANGRY GOD by Carobeth Laird (Malki Museum Press, California, 1975)

### The I as Male: Charlotte Brontë

CHARLOTTE BRONTË: The Self Conceived by Helene Moglen (Norton, 1978)

### The I as Female: Elizabeth Hardwick

SLEEPLESS NIGHTS by Elizabeth Hardwick (Random House, 1979)

### The Traveling Self: Edward Hoagland

THE EDWARD HOAGLAND READER edited and with an introduction by Geoffrey Wolff (Random House, cloth; Vintage, paper; 1979)

AFRICAN CALLIOPE: A Journey to the Sudan by Edward Hoagland (Random House, 1979)

### Hollywood Make-Believe: Brooke Hayward

HAYWIRE by Brooke Hayward (Alfred A. Knopf, 1977)

### Experience as Melodrama: George Sand

MY LIFE by George Sand, translated and adapted by Dan Hofstadter (Harper & Row, 1980)

GEORGE SAND IN HER OWN WORDS translated and edited by Joseph Barry, introduction by Ellen Moers (Anchor Books, paper, 1979)

THE GEORGE SAND–GUSTAVE FLAUBERT LETTERS translated by A. L. McKenzie (Academy Chicago, cloth and paper, 1979)

THE DOUBLE LIFE OF GEORGE SAND, WOMAN AND WRITER by Renee Winegarten (Basic Books, 1978)

## Flaubert Dashes Off a Letter

THE LETTERS OF GUSTAVE FLAUBERT 1830–1857 selected, edited, and translated by Francis Steegmuller (The Belknap Press of Harvard University Press, 1980)

## Colette in Pieces

LETTERS FROM COLETTE selected and translated by Robert Phelps (Farrar, Straus & Giroux, 1980)

## Alice and Henry James

ALICE JAMES: A Biography by Jean Strouse (Houghton Mifflin Company, 1980)

THE DEATH AND LETTERS OF ALICE JAMES edited by Ruth Bernard Yeazell (The University of California Press, 1980)

HENRY JAMES LETTERS; Volume III: 1883–1895 edited by Leon Edel (The Belknap Press of Harvard University Press, 1980)

## The Diaries of Rose La Touche

JOHN RUSKIN AND ROSE LA TOUCHE: Her Unpublished Diaries of 1861 and 1867 introduced and edited by Van Akin Burd (Oxford University Press, 1979)

## More Letters From Ruskin

REFLECTIONS OF A FRIENDSHIP: John Ruskin's Letters to Pauline Trevelyan 1848–1866 edited by Virginia Surtees (Allen & Unwin, 1979)

SAVAGE RUSKIN by Patrick Conner (Macmillan, 1979)

# II. Fictions Stranger Than Fiction

## Norman Mailer

THE EXECUTIONER'S SONG by Norman Mailer (Little, Brown, 1979)

## Beryl Bainbridge

YOUNG ADOLF by Beryl Bainbridge (George Braziller, 1978)

## Terrorists as Moralists: Don DeLillo

PLAYERS by Don DeLillo (Alfred A. Knopf, 1977)

## Morrison, Jones, and McPherson

SONG OF SOLOMON by Toni Morrison (Alfred A. Knopf, 1978)
WHITE RAT by Gayl Jones (Random House, 1977)
ELBOW ROOM by James Alan McPherson (Atlantic / Little, Brown, 1977)

## Doris Lessing

STORIES by Doris Lessing (Alfred A. Knopf, 1978)

## Didion, Harris, and Jong

HOW TO SAVE YOUR OWN LIFE by Erica Jong (Holt, Rinehart and Winston, 1978)
A BOOK OF COMMON PRAYER by Joan Didion (Simon and Schuster, 1977)
LOVER by Bertha Harris (Daughters, Inc., 1976)

## Saul Bellow as Reformer

THE DEAN'S DECEMBER by Saul Bellow (Harper & Row, 1982)

## The Righteous Artist: E. L. Doctorow

LOON LAKE by E. L. Doctorow (Random House, 1980)

## Possibly Parables: Donald Barthelme

GREAT DAYS by Donald Barthelme (Farrar, Straus & Giroux, 1979)

# III. The Real World

## Ah, Wilderness

THE LAST COWBOY by Jane Kramer (Harper & Row, 1980)
COMING INTO THE COUNTRY by John McPhee (Farrar, Straus & Giroux, 1977)

## Ruskin as Guide

RUSKIN'S VENICE edited by Arnold Whittick (Whitney Library of Design, 1976)

LOOKING AT ARCHITECTURE WITH RUSKIN by John Unrau (University of Toronto Press, 1978)

JOHN RUSKIN: *The Argument of the Eye* by Robert Hewison (Princeton University Press, 1976)

RUSKIN by Quentin Bell (George Braziller, 1978)

## C. D. B. Bryan's *Friendly Fire*

FRIENDLY FIRE by C. D. B. Bryan (G. P. Putnam's Sons, 1976)

## Rape

AGAINST OUR WILL: *Men, Women, and Rape* by Susan Brownmiller (Simon and Schuster, 1975)

RAPE: *The Bait and the Trap* by Jean MacKellar, with the collaboration of Dr. Menachem Amir (Crown, 1975)

RAPE AND ITS VICTIMS: A *Report for Citizens, Health Facilities, and Criminal Justice Agencies* by the Center for Women Policy Studies et al., funded by the Law Enforcement Assistance Administration, Washington, D.C.

## The Deaths at Jonestown, Part I

THE SUICIDE CULT: *The Inside Story of the People's Temple Sect and the Massacre in Guyana* by Marshall Kilduff and Ron Javers (Bantam, paper, 1978)

GUYANA MASSACRE: *The Eyewitness Account* by Charles A. Krause, with Lawrence M. Stern, Richard Harwood, and Frank Johnston (Berkley, paper, 1978)

HOLD HANDS AND DIE! *The Incredibly True Story of the People's Temple and the Reverend Jim Jones* by John Maguire and Mary Lee Dunn (Dale Books, 1979)

SIX YEARS WITH GOD: *Life Inside Reverend Jim Jones' People's Temple* by Jeannie Mills (A & W Publishers, 1979)

## The Deaths at Jonestown, Part II

OUR FATHER WHO ART IN HELL by James Reston, Jr. (Times Books, 1981)

THE CHILDREN OF JONESTOWN by Kenneth Wooden (McGraw-Hill, paper, 1980)

AWAKE IN A NIGHTMARE—JONESTOWN: *The Only Eyewitness Account* by Ethan Feinsod (Norton, 1981)

IN MY FATHER'S HOUSE: *The Story of the Layton Family and the Reverend Jim Jones* by Min S. Yee and Thomas N. Layton (Holt, Rinehart and Winston, 1981)

JOURNEY TO NOWHERE: *A New World Tragedy* by Shiva Naipaul (Simon and Schuster, 1981)

THE STRONGEST POISON by Mark Lane (Dutton, 1979)

## The Fate of Patty Hearst

ANYONE'S DAUGHTER by Shana Alexander (Viking, 1979)

## *Old Glory:* Life on the Mississippi

OLD GLORY: *An American Voyage* by Jonathan Raban (Simon and Schuster, 1981)

## A Note on the Type

The text of this book was set in Electra, a type face
designed by William Addison Dwiggins (1880–1956) for the
Mergenthaler Linotype Company and first made available in 1935.
Electra cannot be classified as either "modern" or "old
style." It is not based on any historical model,
and hence does not echo any particular period or style
of type design. It avoids the extreme contrast between
thick and thin elements that marks most modern faces, and
it is without eccentricities that catch the eye and
interfere with reading. In general, Electra is a simple,
readable type face that attempts to give a feeling
of fluidity, power, and speed.

Composed by The Clarinda Company,
Clarinda, Iowa
Printed and bound by the Haddon Craftsmen, Inc.,
Scranton, Pennsylvania

Designed by Sara Reynolds